EDITORIAL BODIES

STUDIES IN RHETORIC/COMMUNICATION
Thomas W. Benson, Series Editor

EDITORIAL BODIES

*Perfection and Rejection in
Ancient Rhetoric and Poetics*

MICHELE KENNERLY

THE UNIVERSITY OF SOUTH CAROLINA PRESS

© 2018 University of South Carolina

Published by the University of South Carolina Press
Columbia, South Carolina 29208

www.sc.edu/uscpress

Manufactured in the United States of America

27 26 25 24 23 22 21 20 19 18
10 9 8 7 6 5 4 3 2 1

The Library of Congress Cataloging-in-Publication
data can be found at http://catalog.loc.gov/.

ISBN 978-1-61117-909-5 (cloth)
ISBN 978-1-61117-910-1 (paperback)
ISBN 978-1-61117-911-8 (ebook)

This book was printed on recycled paper with
30 percent postconsumer waste content.

To S. M. and N. M., *le grá*

χαίρετε λεπταί ῥήσιες [Greetings, slender words]

Callimachus, *Epigrammata* 27

Contents

Series Editor's Preface

Michele Kennerly's *Editorial Bodies: Perfection and Rejection in Ancient Rhetorics and Poetics* explores textual evidences of a developing editorial consciousness working to perfect and prepare for publication texts in classical Athens, Alexandria, and Rome during the first century B.C.E. and the first century C.E. Embedded in debates about what sorts of words should be published and preserved was a metaphor of the body. Establishing a framework of key terms and debates in a broad survey of early works, Kennerly then turns to detailed explorations of Latin poets and orators—Cicero, Horace, Ovid, Quintilian, Tacitus, and Pliny the Younger.

Kennerly brings fresh and vivid new understandings of how developing editorial, including self-editorial, vocabularies and frameworks claimed both grammatical correctness and rhetorical effect as their domains. Kennerly is a scrupulously judicious reader of her sources ancient and modern, unfailingly generous and zestfully eloquent. *Editorial Bodies* is erudite and accessible, offering a model of historical and critical practice and a fresh, compelling rereading of early textual cultures.

Thomas W. Benson

Acknowledgments

I am delighted here to demythologize the figure of the solitary genius: I have not been solitary. Joking aside, sustaining an argument can never be the work of one person, whatever the stamina of her indwelling spirit. I have been exceedingly fortunate in my structures of support.

To my professors at the University of Pittsburgh and Austin College who sparked and stoked my fiery enthusiasm for ancient rhetoric—namely John Poulakos, John Lyne, Mae Smethurst, Mark Possanza, Helen Cullyer, Todd Penner, Bob Cape, and Jim Johnson—thank you for humoring years of fanciful etymologies and Ciceronian sentences (in length, anyway). Each of you made me a better thinker, reader, and critic.

And from former institutions to current ones, Penn State boasts a first-rate library, upon whose human and nonhuman resources I relied daily. I gratefully credit the efforts of many librarians and other library workers. In all manner of ways, my colleagues in the Department of Communication Arts and Sciences have helped me secure time for thinking and writing. I thank especially Denise Solomon, Dave Dzikowski, Ben Henderson, Margaret Michels, Lori Miraldi, Lori Bedell, Rachel Smith, Jon Nußbaum, Rosa Eberly, Steve Browne, Cory Geraths, Brad Serber, and Lauren Camacci. Thanks, too, to Dean Susan Welch and the College of Liberal Arts for a substantial subvention of this book.

I am superlatively grateful for the fellowship I have enjoyed through Penn State's Center for Humanities and Information. I invoke fellowship in the senses both of sociality founded on shared interests and of a financial endowment in the form of course releases. When this project was at a crucial and vulnerable stage in its development, I found genuine zeal for it from Eric Hayot, Bonnie Mak, Lea Pao, Sam Frederick, Anatoly Detwyler, and Laura Helton. Another intellectual community of which I am happy to be a part is the International Society for the History of Rhetoric. I acknowledge Mike Edwards and Casper de Jonge for their unstinting encouragement and graciousness.

At the University of South Carolina Press, Jim Denton was a faithful steward of this book, perhaps the only one he has ever acquired that had "editorial" in the title (tactical thinking on my part), and Linda Fogle saw ably to the details of its production. I would also like to thank Lynne Parker for her editorial assistance and Jerilyn Famighetti for her copyediting efforts. Thanks are due, too, to Richard Leo Enos and Kathleen Lamp for their helpful criticisms of the original manuscript, especially the encouragement to be bolder in some of my claims. I hope I have not exceeded their wildest exhortations.

For various kindnesses and the warmth of shared academic affections through the years of this book's composition, I recognize Topher Kurfess, Janet Atwill, Vessela Valiavitcharska, Richard Graff, Brandon Inabinet, Casey Boyle, Nita Krevans, and Damien Smith Pfister. My dear friend Carly Woods and I found ourselves laboring on our respective books at the same time and set up a system for mutual and loving accountability. During my final weeks writing the original manuscript, several graduate students and I read and wrote side by side in silence (mostly); they included Jeremy Cox, Caroline Koons (who also helped with the index), and Tiara Good. Also during that time, work sessions with Debra Hawhee were immensely productive, since there are few things more inspirational than writing across the table from her, a remarkably generous, generative scholar.

A Note on Translation

All translations are mine unless noted otherwise. Because the diminutive green and red books of the Loeb Classical Library will be easy for readers of this book to find, I have relied upon Loeb editions for the Greek and Latin. Ancient works for which I have departed from that practice are listed in the Works Cited. If I were starting this book now, I would not use the word "slave" to translate the ancient Greek and Latin terms usually rendered that way. Instead, I would use "enslaved person," which requires one to think about the violent imposition of slavery upon someone.

INTRODUCTION
Corpus *Care*

Delere licebit quod non edideris.
You will be able to blot out what you do not put out.

Horace, *Ars Poetica*, 389–390

Editing is the defining burden of publication, the arduous process of making written words public and deserving of a public. Though that claim could be supported by thousands of years of examples across several graphic forms, it finds ample substantiation in the earliest centuries of adjustment to the wax tablet and papyrus book-roll alone. That evidence need not include actual, material rough drafts of an orator's speeches, a poet's verses, or a philosopher's dialogues, discovered by chance by someone of a later century.* To seek and potentially find such drafts would tie one to transitional texts that had a small chain of reception, if any at all, and thus limited reach before being reused for other writing, repurposed for wrapping, or left to molder. In pursuit of when and how textual tidying and tidy texts take on a public aspect, this book locates recommendations about and reactions to prepublication processes within works that, without a doubt, have been heard and read by many. Within such works, an editorial language of refining and polishing calls attention to itself, to those writers unwilling or unable to shoulder the editorial onus, and to what may be lost when it is shirked.

Because ancient editorial vocabulary covers a lot of chronological ground and indexes a variety of textual activities, I begin by firmly establishing the terminological perimeters that pen this inquiry. My use of "editing" requires prompt explanation. The Latinate origins of the word, highly relevant when

---

*For an attempt to read discarded and discovered papyrus fragments for evidence of correction, see Gurd, "Revision in Greek Papyri."

working with writings in Latin, are a little at odds with its current usage. The Latin verb *edo, edere, edidi, editus*—from the prefix *ex* (out, away) + the verb *do* (give)—enjoys a variety of meanings, from giving birth, to uttering words, to presenting something for inspection, to displaying it publicly, to publishing it.* Ancient Romans did not use *edo*-words as process words for prepublic textual activities. Instead, they dragged away, cut out, pressed, smoothed, polished, hammered, filed, and shaved. Much manual and metaphorical work was undertaken on written words to move them toward textual publication. As with *edo,* so with the Greek verbs for publication, *ekdidōmi* (to give up, surrender, empty oneself of) and *diadidōmi* (to hand over or distribute), which tend to appear in the company of active composition narratives.†

In Greek and Latin, respectively, the same words refer to the emendation a writer undertakes before publication, *and* that undertaken by someone else appraising a work before its publication, *and* that undertaken by someone at a chronological remove attempting to rid a given textual tradition of errors and establish an authoritative edition.‡ This book focuses on the first two types of corrective work, but the third type is not irrelevant to my efforts. As H. L. M. Van der Valk has noted, "ancient critics, for the same or other reasons as modern critics, could take offence to a line and, therefore, they simply omitted it from their text."§ Such evaluations could be founded on grammatical endings that may have been permitted in the text's time of origin but not in the critic's time of reading. If a given critic thought highly of Cicero, for example, then he might have been more likely to cover up what he presumed to be embarrassing errors in a Ciceronian text. To the extent that this corrector wanted to protect Cicero's reputation, this corrector resembled Cicero's contemporary friends who had helped Cicero identify infelicities *before* publication. An adjustment for "correctness" undertaken at a remove, however, could ruin the euphony of a line, a sonic possibility open to Cicero because of more capacious grammatical options in his

---

*I prefer "editing" to "revising" because of the former's etymology: the kinds of activities I trace are prompted by the pressures of putting something out publicly in writing (*edo*).

†For a study of *ekdosis* in terms of textual circulation, see van Groningen, "ΕΚΔΟΣΙΣ."

‡Take, for example, the Greek *epanorthoō* (correct, revise) and the Latin *emendo* (emend, correct). The use of *epanorthoō* by the fifth–fourth-century B.C.E. sophist Alcidamas is particularly interesting, since he used the word twice within his detailed account of the process embarked upon by rhetors who insist on writing out their speeches before delivery: they "correct at leisure" and "correct again based on the advice of the untrained" (Alcidamas, *On Those Who Write*, §4). For an attempt to discern how ancient scholars went about making an authoritative edition, see Montanari, "From Book to Edition."

§Van der Valk, "On the Edition of Books in Antiquity," 9.

time or because he composed for the appreciation of ears.* On a much greater scale, such as that undertaken in Hellenistic Alexandria, editorial work at a distance established textual lines and lists that shaped the way later people read and understood writers who came before them, down to the smallest lexical detail.

The English word "editor," which the Oxford English Dictionary dates to the mid-seventeenth century, derives from the Latin noun *editor,* but *editor* did not in antiquity refer to a person whose function or occupation was to prepare written works for publication or to streamline textual strains that included multiple versions of one work.† There certainly were people who readied writing for release, but writers within the time period bracketed by this book called them scribes (often slaves), friends, and booksellers. In Latin, *editus* (published) describes a written object released or wrested from the control of its writer, and "it might appear in as many editions as there were booksellers," or friends with scribes, "who cared to copy it"—by hand, of course, with no one copy exactly the same as another.‡ Copying errors were unique to each copy. During the transmission of a text, what started as an error could become an orthodoxy, and vice versa.

For my purposes, then, editing captures a whole catalogue of preparations at any stage of composition that the writer makes—commonly with help from others—for the eventual public exhibition and circulation of written words.§ My overall contention is that editorial tendencies and terminologies become absorbed into habits of writing, which, for orators, at least, could come to be absorbed into habits of extemporaneous speaking. Accordingly, disentangling a composing "step" from an editing "step" is seldom easy or, I argue, necessary. The availability of editing—as a practice and as a language for indexing that practice, even if only suggestively and not literally—makes for the possibility of recursive composition, composition that repeatedly runs back and reflects

---

*I address this possibility explicitly in the Conclusion through the work of Aulus Gellius.

†Lewis and Short, *A Latin Dictionary,* s.v. *editor:* 1) that which brings forth or produces; 2) an exhibitor.

‡Phillips, "Atticus and the Publication of Cicero's Works," 228. For details about the circuits through which ancient Roman texts could travel, see Starr, "The Circulation of Literary Texts in the Roman World." For attention to the state of social circulation and publication (that is, release to those beyond one's close associates) in Cicero's time, see Murphy, "Cicero's First Readers." For an overview of "Bookshops in the Literary Culture of Rome," see White.

§At least some of the writers featured here explicitly dictated to highly trained scribal slaves and so did, perhaps, very little of the actual, physical writing. For a treatment of such issues in the Roman context, see McDonnell, "Writing, Copying, and Autograph Manuscripts in Ancient Rome."

upon itself. Many metaphors of editing call to mind material practices of editing. "Polish" is a good example, since it can reference an activity or a quality, and the quality itself suggests the activity.* Accordingly, Latin *lexica* categorize the verb "polish" (*polio, polire, polivi, politus*) as potentially literal or figurative.† More than other evaluative words, such as "beautiful," "polished" points to the process responsible for that property, which brings to mind compositional labor, especially the actual material rubbing out of the rough stuff. In a polished text, nothing is there—or not there—because of a lucky accident or unbidden genius.

Admittedly, editing, even my expansive take on it, might seem boring and its relationship to ancient poetics and rhetoric far from obvious. It holds, however, a significant if misunderstood position within influential scholarly histories of those arts. Andrew Ford, for instance, places the origins of criticism in what he calls the "textualization" of song.‡ According to his narrative, the more attention an ancient writer afforded to his composition (the only "her" in this context is Sappho), the less likely that writing was to be occasional or urgent or to serve some purpose outside itself. For Ford, ancient writing and editing enabled a precursor to formalism, the notion that the merit of an aesthetic object can be gauged from its form alone. Textualization, then, seems inherently antirhetorical, since it pulls texts in on themselves and away from questions of affective reach and persuasive efficacy. In his book on Roman poetics, Thomas Habinek reacts against the view that song was thoroughly textualized and that poets lost interest in their public function. But he goes too far, including only *cano* (sing), *canto* (sing, play), *loquor* (say, talk about), and *dico* (speak, tell) in his list of ancient modes of poetic communication that had potency and immediacy —that *did* something.§ He can find no way to write about *scribo* that does not reinscribe the formalist narrative. Though the views of Eric Havelock on orality

---

*As is evident here with *politus* (having been polished [verb]; polished [adj.]), the past participle form of a verb often becomes an adjective.

†The Greek verb is *katarrinaō* (file down, make thin; polished, elegant), which appears during the poetic battle in Aristophanes's *Frogs*, treated in chapter 1.

‡Ford, *The Origins of Criticism*, 155.

§Habinek, *The Roman World of Song*, 59. In her review of the book, Lowrie criticized Habinek for simplifying the relationships and tensions between orality and writing: "Surely writing needs to be folded into the discussion and seen not only in its capacity as a vehicle for performance. I would argue that the Romans understood writing to provide certain advantages against song (i.e., longevity) and to have its own standing, while agreeing with Habinek that it does not diminish song's importance and can lead to further song (248)." Habinek dedicated a chapter to writing poets in his earlier book *The Politics of Latin Literature*, 103–121, but there he dwells on the tension between oral performance (presence) and writing (absence).

and literacy are not universally admired in Rhetoric or Classics, Havelock was right to quip that the Muse "learned to write and read while still continuing to sing."*

Traditional, popular histories of rhetoric also perpetuate an objectifying evaluation of writing and editing. George Kennedy, for example, identifies "rewriting and revision" as "a regular part of composition" from rhetoric's very start.[†] Kennedy warns against overstating "the influence of writing in the history of rhetoric," however.[‡] He claims that the "'application of rhetoric to written composition,'" his definition of the Italian term *letteraturizzazione,* "is largely a phenomenon of periods in which opportunities for civic oratory were reduced, often with the loss of freedom of speech that characterized Greek democracies and the Roman republic."[§] For Kennedy, there is no more telling indicator of *letteraturizzazione* than textual polish and publication. Strangely, then, he credits writing for its role in rhetoric's technical development but classifies writing, rewriting, and the criticism of writing as subsidiary—secondary, he would say— forms of rhetoric. More than that, he views secondariness as gaining a perverse primacy in times of political degradation: it is only when rhetors cannot speak forcefully that they settle for writing beautifully. According to the decline and decadence thesis of rhetoric and poetics, which I counter throughout this book, when concentrated political power imperils freedom of public speech, oratory and poetry take temporary shelter in pretty and impotent forms. In such conditions, editorial polish has been read as a marker of the loss of public function and a sign of a hypersophistication devoid of practicality and utility.

Other scholarly accounts may be found, however. Writing about ancient Roman poets, Luke Roman harmonizes autonomy (formalism) and instrumentality (functionalism) by showing that certain poets gave their poems a sense of thingly independence precisely to empower their poems to do things when inevitably separated from their maker.** As Roman stresses, "the underlying idea is that art can be a more effective force in the world if it is organized in an integral manner, if it rigorously respects its own principles and values, and if its practitioners partake of the focus bred of specialization."[††] It is a point that applies to oratorical speech-texts, too. Jeffrey Walker pairs rhetoric and poetics to suggest, contra Kennedy, "that the process of 'literaturization,' far from being a symptom of 'rhetoric' in decadence or decline, is in fact a major cause of its

*Havelock, *The Muse Learns to Write,* 23.
[†]Kennedy, *A New History of Classical Rhetoric,* 27.
[‡]Kennedy, *A New History of Classical Rhetoric,* 28.
[§]Kennedy, *A New History of Classical Rhetoric,* 28.
**Roman, *Poetic Autonomy in Ancient Rome,* 1–25.
[††]Roman, *Poetic Autonomy in Ancient Rome,* 11.

emergence.''* Walker submits that rhetoric arises from poetry and that the civic genre of rhetoric most resilient to the vicissitudes of political change is epideictic, its most poetic genre (for example, permitting of departures from the usual standards of speech, partaking of the written type of *lexis*). Sean Gurd, too, brings poetry and oratory together, demonstrating the value both poets and orators from Plato to Pliny place on making a written work better by talking it through with others.† Clearly, counternarratives are accumulating, and they encourage a reevaluation of the place of writing and, by extension, editing in ancient poetics and rhetoric.

For my part, I argue that editing—essentially, preparing written words for strangers, sometimes very distant ones—and contestations about editing in prose and verse may fruitfully and faithfully be considered reactions to the pressures of participating in ever-growing textual cultures whose participants strove to put their writing and writings they have read to public purpose. Likewise, it is plausible and productive to understand a concern for finish and polish as something other than a textual turn necessitated by restrictions placed upon the public voice. In fact, polish can signify not a retreat but a deliberate and active political stance. The stance can be one of insistence that current conditions demand refined works of oratory and poetry and that the stakes are too high within a given political moment for unprocessed words. The stance can also be one of defiance against current conditions that may favor quick, energetic speech over that which is paused and pored over. The hexametrical poetry of Horace contains both stances, since he believed that Rome's power and glamour demanded suitable poetry and that lots of élite Romans were generating ugly, insignificant verses that could diminish Rome's reputation.

Though it moves through the classical Greek and Hellenistic periods, this book settles in the first centuries B.C.E. and C.E. Rome. Explanations for enlarging upon that period diffuse throughout its chapters, but a major reason is evidentiary: a lot of Roman works survive (comparatively speaking), and many of them reflect upon their own creation and situation. Because they commandeered the book-rolls of places brought under their management, continued to copy them, and added works of their own, Romans enjoyed a voluminous textual culture.‡ Furthermore, within poems, and letters, and dialogues, and treatises,

---

*Walker, *Rhetoric and Poetics in Antiquity*, 41, 18.

†Gurd, *Work in Progress*.

‡Several chapters in König, Oikonomopoulou, and Woolf's volume *Ancient Libraries* focus on Rome's earliest book-roll collections and the occasionally violent means of their acquisition (not unique to Romans); the challenges of assembling a private library; and the forms and functions of public libraries in Rome and across the empire. For explicit attention to Ephesus, see Eidson, "The Celsus Library."

book-rolls flutter and unfurl, joining wax tablets and other writing implements in marking Rome's writers as reflective about the thoroughgoing textuality of much of their communication, both with others in their own time and with those of future ages. Rome's writers are aware of the extensive archive of earlier works and eager to draw from and improve upon their predecessors.

Another reason for the Roman focus is that the increasing geographic and chronological stretch of Roman influence and dominance made orators and poets mindful of their own span and curious about the interdependence of Rome and its writers. In his defense of the Greek-Syrian poet Archias in 62 B.C.E., for instance, Cicero pitied the "slight [*exiguis*]" influence of Latin writing and exhorted the jury—and, later, readers of the textually published speech—that Roman "fame and glory" ought "to penetrate [*penetrare*]" the same places as its spears, issuing a call for aggressive cultural conquest to match the military one.* In Vergil's *Aeneid,* the shade of Aeneid's father, Anchises, pronounces that other peoples will excel in sculpture, forensic rhetoric, and astronomy but that the distinctive *ars* of the Romans will be "to establish the customs of peace, / to show moderation to the defeated, and to fight the arrogant to the end."† It may be notable that poetry, especially a foundation poem full of battle, is missing from the list of excellent arts attributed to non-Romans. A few decades later, Horace estimated that the Latin tongue still tripped in its effort to catch up to its arms.‡ Both Cicero and Horace promoted the promise of editorial polish as a solution to the general failure of Roman writing to spread and stick.§

Roman writers also cared about conquering the divided attentions of people of their own times and places, crediting their editorial labors with making them worth hearing or reading then and there. Ultimately, though, concerns about longevity and legacy animate the hand that wields the editorial tool: one has to write to be preserved and edit to endure and to be endured. When a culture is eager to establish its all-around preeminence, as Rome was in the first centuries B.C.E. and C.E., the endurance and endurableness of its writers are not marginal matters. As used within the title of this book, the referents of "perfection" range

---

*Cicero, *Pro Archia,* §23.

†Vergil, *Aeneid,* 6.850–853.

‡Horace, *Ars Poetica,* 289–290.

§Cicero, *Pro Archia,* §30; Horace, *Ars Poetica,* 285–294. Vergil does not remark upon editing within his extant poetry, but a later biographer, Donatus, reports that Vergil "licked his verses into shape," as a mother bear does her cubs (§22). Donatus also claims that Vergil, on his deathbed, ordered his friends-*cum*-literary executors "not to publish anything he had not already published" (§39). He had not yet finished or published the *Aeneid,* on which he had been working for eleven years. They did not honor that request, on the "authority of Augustus." See Donatus, *Life of Vergil,* 39–43; Krevans, "Bookburning and the Poetic Deathbed"; Ziogas, "The Poet as Prince."

from completion to flawlessness, as in the figment of the *orator perfectus* in Cicero and Quintilian. Those of "rejection" range from a strike-out of a written word, to social ridicule, to expulsion from a *polis* or *civitas*. The pursuit of polish may have been a given writer's preference, but in antiquity (and not only there) it was a matter of creative and critical sociality and of public priority, as well.

Toward a Multicultural Approach to Editing

That ancient Greece and Rome are often called "oral cultures" seems to pose a significant challenge to assembling a collection of texts explicitly engaging editing that is sizable enough to scrutinize for patterns of praise, insult, and argument. Somewhat obviously, texts attributed to members of those oral cultures attest to the coexistence of textual cultures. Or literate or literary cultures. And reading cultures. A rhetorician may make bold to subordinate those four cultures to rhetorical culture. Or perhaps rhetorical culture is itself a subculture of performance culture. Each of those cultures appears prominently in influential or recent books about the ancient world and the organizations and prioritizations of its verbal habits.* That range of cultures informs this book, but I use "textual culture" throughout. I take a textual culture to be a formation whose participants enjoy—make use of, experience, benefit from—the material form and memorializing potential of words written on objects that can circulate and be copied by others. In particular, I am interested in those participants who receive or retrieve a wide variety of written objects to read and who write their own. My decision to use "textual culture" is a matter of emphasis, not of either-or absolutism.† It does not mean that neither the writers featured in this book nor I in writing it never mention speaking. Far from it.

---

*See, e.g., "oral culture" in Ong, *Orality and Literacy;* "textual culture" in Irvine, *The Making of Textual Culture,* which begins in late antiquity, to be precise, and "textual world" in Stroup, *Catullus, Cicero, and a Society of Patrons,* 34; "reading culture" in Johnson, *Readers and Reading Culture in the High Roman Empire;* "literate culture" in Yunis, *Written Texts and the Rise of Literate Culture in Ancient Greece;* "literary culture" in Fantham, *Roman Literary Culture,* in Keith and Edmondson (eds.), *Roman Literary Cultures,* and the subtitle of Ford, *The Origins of Criticism;* "rhetorical culture" in Farrell, *Norms of Rhetorical Culture;* "performance culture" in Goldhill and Osborne (eds.), *Performance Culture and Athenian Democracy.* Murphy uses "the Roman culture of publication" ("Cicero's First Readers," 492), an approach with which my efforts are utterly in league.

†I strenuously avoid "literary culture" and "literature," since their twentieth-century baggage is heavy in ways that do not advance conversations about ancient book-rolls and their readers. I am also sensitive to Habinek's point that scholars of the ancient world do not need to use those terms when they have other, more befitting options (Habinek, "Singing, Speaking, Making, Writing").

Limiting the relationship between orality and literacy/textuality to an either-or arrangement or zero-sum power struggle limits the study of communication in antiquity. No doubt mindful of his own contribution to that stubborn dualism or agonism given the title of his earlier book *The Literate Revolution in Greece and Its Cultural Consequences,* Havelock later lamented that "the word *revolution,* though convenient and fashionable, is one that can mislead if it is used to suggest the clear-cut substitution of one means of communication by another."* Ancient people saw, heard, and produced a muddle of media. What Harvey Yunis wrote about fifth- and fourth-century Athens applies also to the Rome of later centuries: "mixing of the media occurred in various permutations: books were read in private and aloud to groups; speeches delivered in public were circulated in written form; plays, composed for public performance, were read privately by students of literature; written documents were integrated into oral performances and speeches."† Extant ancient texts hold partisan attitudes toward one mediated form or another rather than absolute measures of a culture's ratio of permissible or preferred spoken words to written ones. Dualisms are insufficient.

Even after acknowledging the cultural complex in which ancient writers were working, one may be left with the feeling that ancient writers remained strategically unforthcoming about their textual labors. Such thinking goes: poets want to seem the medium of Muses, orators of moments. Emblematically, Carolyn Marvin has argued that a "mark of literate competence is skill in disguising or erasing the contribution of one's own body to the process of textual production and practice."‡ The imperative to hide verbal labor has long enjoyed status as a requirement for securing trust. As early as Aristotle's *Rhetoric,* an admonition appeared that "one should try to escape notice, and not to seem to speak artificially [*peplasmenōs*] but naturally."§ Many later rhetoricians have repeated that view.** Hard work, and the role of and toll on the body, should lie hidden.

Orators, to focus on them, depended on perceived spontaneity during their oral delivery of a speech. The smell of the lamp—idiomatic for signals a speech gives off that it has been prepared so much beforehand that even the daylight

---

*Havelock, *The Muse Learns to Write,* 23, italics *sic.*
†Yunis, "Introduction," 5.
‡Marvin, "The Body of the Text," 129.
§Aristotle, *Rhetoric,* 1404b18–19.
**For a sense of how widespread the "hide art" advisement is, here is a partial list of its occurrences: *Rhetorica ad Herennium* 4.7.10; Cicero, *De Oratore,* 2.37.156, 2.41.177; Cicero, *Orator,* §38; Quintilian 1.11.3, 2.5.7, 4.1.8–9, among many other places; "Longinus," *Peri Hupsous,* 17.1–2, 22.1, 38.3.

hours were not enough—was an odor of desperation and, perhaps, of deceit.* Either way, it provoked audience suspicion. That *correctio* and *emendatio,* two terms naming moments when an orator offers a correction or emendation after saying something he deems not quite right, were recognized rhetorical figures suggests their usefulness as a form of pseudo-spontaneity for those who *had* prepared their words.[†] Even within speeches circulated in material form subsequent to oral delivery, orators would be reluctant to showcase their desktop paraphernalia—especially editing tools—since such texts were meant to be reminders of and not reconfigurations of previously delivered speeches people have already heard or heard about. An orator would not want to draw attention to any postdelivery, prepublication touch-ups his speech had received, however many alterations he might have made. Orators conversing with other orators or instructing the rising generation, however, did not shy away from frank discussions of textual tools and treatments with and through which an orator builds a potentially lasting reputation for eloquence. Several such works survive, among them: Cicero's *Orator,* Quintilian's *Institutio Oratoria,* Tacitus's *Dialogus de Oratoribus,* and Pliny the Younger's *Epistulae.*

A final assumption warrants somewhat lengthier attention. Even if one permits that orators talk about textual publication very directly on occasion, editing seems to belong to *grammatikē,* not to *rhētorikē.* In an allegory from the fifth century C.E., Grammatica carries "a knife [*scalprum*], with which she cuts out the blemishes on the tongues of children, and then with a certain black powder, a powder she thought to be made of ashes or cuttlefish, carried through reeds," that is, ink in pens, "she restores health." Among her tools is also "a file thoroughly polished [*limam ... expolitam*] with great skill, which, divided into eight golden parts joined in different ways, vibrated, and by light rubbing she gently cleansed gritty teeth, and defects of the tongue, and the filth contracted in the polity of Soloe," that is, solecisms.[‡] In her dress, equipment, manner, and mission, Grammatica resembles a doctor, and she corrects, cuts, and cures ailing speaking or writing bodies.

Editing written words involves, of course, substantially more than seeking and correcting embarrassing errors, such as "bad" grammar. Yet, even what is typically and simplistically translated as "correctness" ranked as an *aretē* (distinctive excellence) of verbal style in Aristotle's *Rhetoric;* indeed, he named it the

---

*For an overview of ancient attitudes toward lucubration, see Ker, "Nocturnal Writers in Imperial Rome."

†*Correctio* appears in *Rhetorica ad Herennium* 4.36; *emendatio* in Quintilian 9.2.17, 9.3.89. For an inquiry into how and why archaic poets played with modes of spontaneity, see Scodel, "Self-Correction, Spontaneity, and Orality in Archaic Poetry."

‡Capella, *De Nuptiis Philologiae et Mercurii,* §223–226.

archē (first principle) of style.* "Correctness" translates *to hellēnizein,* "Greek-ness," which appears as *hellēnismos* in later texts. Oppositional terms include *soloikismos* (solecism) and *barbarismos* (barbarism), both of which refer to strange-sounding vocalizations: the former is geographic, the latter onomato-poetic. Within this lexicon, it is remarkable that an artistic departure from the usual, that is, a thoughtful or playful violation of the normal, is called, approvingly, *xenos* (foreign).[†] The dividing line, then, between a solecism and a witticism comes down to audience or reader perceptions of a speaker's communicative intention and overall command of the language.[‡] Another irony: to some ears, speaking or writing a given dialect of Greek too perfectly was a dead giveaway that one did not come from the area in which that dialect was spoken. The dialect of Greek that came to be considered the most pure was Attic, *Attikismos.* Yet, according to tales not contemporary with him, Aristotle's eminently eloquent student Theophrastus of Eresus was identified immediately as a stranger by an old Athenian woman: he spoke in a manner "too Attic for Athens."[§]

The Roman analogue of *hellēnismos* is *Latinitas,* fault-free and correct Latin. Even a quick appraisal of how Roman rhetoricians and grammarians approached Latinness shows *Latinitas* to be a matter of shared and acute concern. The first surviving attention to pure and proper Latin in a rhetorical handbook appears in the *Rhetorica ad Herennium,* written in the first or second decade of the first century B.C.E.: orators should use words customary to the everyday. Here, as in later texts, departures from everyday conventions are called *vitia* (faults, defects, vices). The author refers readers interested in more depth and detail to his *ars grammatica,* which has not survived, but the reference itself reflects the overlap.** The august orators featured in Cicero's *De Oratore* want to pass over *Latinitas:* "for no one ever admired an orator because he spoke proper Latin: if he does otherwise, he is laughed at, and they think he is neither an orator nor a human."[††] Varro, a grammarian contemporary and occasionally friendly with Cicero, enumerated four "offices" of grammar: reading (*lectio*), explication (*narratio*), correction (*emendatio*), and judging (*iudicium*).[‡‡] *Emendatio* he defined as

---

*Aristotle, *Rhetoric,* 1407a19–20.

[†]Aristotle, *Rhetoric,* 1404b, 1405a.

[‡]That basis in judgment is hinted at in Aristotle's *Rhetoric* but is very clear in Quintilian, who tells orators how to differentiate mistakes from figures of speech at 1.5.5.

[§]Cicero, *Brutus,* §172; Quintilian 8.1.2. Theophrastus is the teacher of Demetrius, who features prominently in chapter 2.

**Rhetorica ad Herennium* 4.12.17.

[††]Cicero, *De Oratore,* 3.9.38–3.14.52.

[‡‡]Varro, *De Lingua Latina,* fr. 236 (in Funaioli, *Grammaticae Romae Fragmenta*). Varro addresses this work to Cicero. See Gurd, "Cicero and Editorial Revision," 71–72, for more on Cicero's relationship with Varro.

"the correction of errors in writing or speaking." At first, Quintilian seemed to cede "speaking correctly [*emendate*]" to grammar, but then he devoted an entire section of a book-roll to editorial emendation of the kind this book makes its subject.* *Emendatio* does not belong exclusively to grammar or to rhetoric.

The adverb *recte* (rightly, correctly) appears across Roman rhetorical, grammatical, and poetic texts from the first centuries B.C.E. and C.E.[†] Disagreements about what it looks and sounds like to write and to speak *recte* drove lively debates about standards of language use, how they are determined, how they are maintained, and by whom. The early first-century orators of Cicero's *De Oratore* believed élite Roman boys learned proper Latin from everyday and at-home conversation, *Latinitas* being an acquisition that is "natural, natal, and genuine."[‡] Some Romans of the midcentury, however, believed that Rome's increasing cultural pluralism necessitated that Latinness be codified and standardized into an official *ratio* (method): no longer would there be a customary way but instead the correct way.[§] An aristocratic if not xenophobic discernment of slipping standards of linguistic precision and perfection pushed this language reform. By the late first century C.E., Quintilian explains that he did not set out write an *ars grammatica*, but nonetheless he advises that *oratio* ought to contain nothing evocative of "the foreign or the outside [*peregrine et externa*]" and observes that "foreign [*peregrina*] words have come to us from nearly every nation, as have much of our population and many of our institutions."** An orator must dig deep to stay native, but not so deep that he taps archaic roots; those, too, are off-putting. The past is a foreign country.

An additional complexity is that *recte* can bear a sense of decorum, of something "rightly" said or written, which is a thoroughly situational, rhetorical designation. The tension between an inflexible standard of rightness and an adaptable one stretches throughout the succession of contestations over the so-called Attic style in Greek and in Latin and is the chief reason such debates are sometimes considered linguistic or grammatical and sometimes considered rhetorical.[††] Rightness belongs to both rhetoric and grammar. Capella's

*Quintilian 1.5.1 (three virtues of *oratio*: to speak correctly [*emendate*], clearly [*dilucida*], and elegantly [*ornata*]); 10.4.

[†]Consider, e.g., Cicero, *Brutus*, §285, and *Orator*, §157; Horace, *Sermones*, 1.4.13 and *Ars Poetica*, 25, 109; Ovid uses the antonym at *Tristia* 3.14.23; Quintilian 1.4.2, 10.1.44, 12.10.58, 12.10.69; Pliny, *Epistulae*, 9.26.

[‡]Cicero, *De Oratore*, 3.12.48; Bloomer, *Latinity and Literacy Society at Rome*, 2.

[§]I narrow in on a portion of this debate, that involving Cicero and Caesar, in chapter 3.

**Quintilian 8.1.2, 1.5.55. Quintilian castigates grammarians for continually creeping into rhetoric's realm at 2.1.4.

[††]Several scholars have treated that distinction as a false dualism; most recently, O'Sullivan, "'Rhetorical' vs 'Linguistic' Atticism: A False Dichotomy?" In an earlier essay,

aforementioned personification of Grammar, with her correction tools and zeal to use them, hails from the fifth century C.E., centuries removed from the writers who feature in this book, and Capella had a compositional interest in keeping the arts of the *trivium* distinct.* To say that editing written words for "rightness" in the first centuries B.C.E. and C.E. was "simply" a matter of grammar is to ignore the robustly rhetorical dimension of "rightness" and to misunderstand the complexity of grammar.

Bodies of Work

Physiological metaphors suffuse ancient writing about rhetoric, poetics, grammar, and texts, evidencing coincident concern with verbal parts, forms, and sizes. The corporeal is an enduring aspect of composing, criticizing, and publishing for which Romans are a through-line rather than an origin, but their texts feature corporeal language plentifully, and typically with polemic and public purpose.† In chapter 1 I focus wholly on its emergence in classical Athens, whose texts are of immense importance to Romans and their textual culture, but it is worth getting into some technical details here.

Many ancient words for units of speech take bodily form. The constituent parts of utterances, whether verse or prose, are corporeal, such as fingers (Latin *dactyli*, Greek *daktuloi*), feet (Latin *pedes*, Greek *podi*), and limbs (Latin *cola* and *membra*, Greek *kōla*).‡ The temporal relationship of those concepts to the rise of writing is by no means clear, but with the papyrus book-roll the template of the

---

Hendrickson refers to the "grammatical-rhetorical tendencies" of the debate, and that hyphenate seems a good classificatory compromise ("The *De Analogia* of Julius Caesar," 98).

*James Zetzel argues that Philology "herself" is geminate: "one often calls herself Lady Literature," while "the other is often Mistress Grammar the dominatrix" ("The Brides of Mercury," 46). Casper C. de Jonge's work (*Between Grammar and Rhetoric*) on the Augustan-age Greek critic Dionysius of Halicarnassus demonstrates the difficulty of separating grammar and rhetoric, since both composition and criticism happen in a space to which both lay claim. Jeffrey Walker writes of the "grammatization" of poetry, evidenced in Horace's *Ars Poetica*, which is full of "grammatical material, with its emphases on convention, correctness, and propriety" (*Rhetoric and Poetics in Antiquity*, 305).

†Bodies continue to inform our divisions, revisions, and criticisms of writing. A section title is a "heading"; to "recapitulate" is to run back through the headings, to summarize the main points. The core of a composition is its "body." Citations and extensions of claims appear in "footnotes." We "cut out the flab," add body to "bare bones," or "flesh out" what lacks full development, preparing our words for presentation to readers with presumed aesthetic preferences of concision, of weightiness, of form. Critically, writing is "thin" when it lacks substance, "turgid" when it lacks elegance. One can find those same terms—except citational "footnotes," which are an artifact of a later century—in ancient texts.

‡See, e.g., Aristotle, *Rhetoric*, 1408b–1409a; Cicero, *Orator*, §149–233.

human body became an organizing principle of composition and criticism, of synthesis and analysis. Take, for example, the Greek *kephalē* and the Latin *caput,* both meaning "head." Plato and Quintilian propose that a speech be constructed like a body (*sōma, corpus*), starting with a head.* Isocrates and Cicero call a major point of a speech a "heading" (*kephalaion, caput*).† Knocking the two heads together, Aristotle puns that attentive listeners would need no introductory orientation beyond an articulation of the "headings [*kephalaiōdōs*], so that the body has a head [*sōma kephalēn*]."‡

It was not only parts internal to a piece of writing that were corporeal. Individual papyrus book-rolls also were broken up and spoken of anatomically: luxury book-rolls came wrapped in a *membrana* (a protective "skin," like our book "jackets"; Greek *diphthera*) and had a front side called a *frons* (brow, forehead), cylinder-rolled edges known as *umbilici* (belly buttons; Greek *omphaloi*), and decorative roller knobs referred to as *cornua* (horns).§ Book-rolls were specialty items made on commission, though booksellers commonly posted excerpts from volumes to which they had access for copying or to which they wanted potential buyers to think they had. Allowing for potential exceptions, James Zetzel estimated that "it is hardly an oversimplification to say that if a book was not read and copied by someone who could afford to have a fancy copy made, it does not survive."** Luxury book-rolls were so hardy that writers who dispensed with rough-draft-appropriate materials—cheap, with a short shelf life—and jumped right to the extravagant stuff were deemed foolhardy.††

As Joseph Farrell emphasizes, "the ancient book, not unlike its modern counterpart with its 'spine', but more obviously so, was a collection of body parts."‡‡ *Corpus,* like its Greek counterpart *sōma,* can signify a number of bodies, in whole or in part, for example the body of a human or nonhuman animal, alive or dead; flesh or plumpness; the structure of a speech; the trunk of the body; a concrete object; an organized body of people; or a compendium of scientific, literary, or other writings.§§ Ancient writers occasionally let those various *corpora*

---

*Plato, *Phaedrus,* 264c; Quintilian 4.1.62.

†Isocrates, *On the Peace,* §142; Cicero, *Brutus,* §164.

‡Aristotle, *Rhetoric,* 1415b8–9. Plato uses *kephalaion* in *Phaedrus,* too, when Phaedrus is still pretending not to have a book-roll of Lysias and tells Socrates he will recite the "headings" he remembers (228d).

§Maehler, "books, Greek and Roman"; Farrell, "Horace's Body, Horace's Books," 184–185; Kenyon, *Books and Readers in Ancient Greece and Rome,* 58–59.

**Zetzel, *Latin Textual Criticism in Antiquity,* 237.

††Catullus, *Carmina,* 22.

‡‡Farrell, "Horace's Body, Horace's Books," 185.

§§*Oxford Latin Dictionary* s.v. *corpus,* definitions 1, 3, 5, 6b, 7, 11, 15, and 16. The last definition of *corpus* requires expansion, as it differs slightly from our own conception of

interlock, as bodies are wont to do. By means and mention of editorial tools, certain writers extended the figuration of their anatomical art: they composed a body and then cared for it as such. In recognition of their bodily basis, I call invocations or representations of editing "*corpus* care." *Corpus* care involves the metaphorical application of abrasive or destructive implements—files, pumice stones, chisels, razors—to words judged coarse or extraneous. Actual pumice or pumice dust was applied to fibrous papyrus to make it more suitable and soft for writing upon. My titular concept of "editorial bodies" gestures not only to the corporeal vocabulary of writing, editing, and book-rolls but also to the bodies of writers who took pains to edit and to the critical bodies that received and evaluated their work.

As Larue Van Hook demonstrated in his enduring 1905 dissertation, many metaphors travel through ancient rhetoric and criticism, including water, flowers, heat, and light. "The human body: its conditions, appearance, dress, care, etc.," the title of his section on the body, hints at the reason it is "one of the most fruitful."* The body makes for a vivid, variable, and accessible metaphor. Since the basic composition of a body is familiar and unvarying, bodies are easy to visualize, describe, and compare. As metaphors, bodies permit of easy layering and extending. Bodies have interiors and exteriors. Bodies can be deceptive, looking one way but being another. Bodies also require attention, preparation, and regulation if they are to avoid offending or if they are to get and stay in shape. Because "it is not always easy to draw the line between legitimate care . . . and artificial beauty culture," the borderline between appropriate and excessive treatments undergoes frequent negotiation: expressed subtly, argued vehemently, suggested wryly.† Bodies can be nude or piled with fineries, hairy or smooth, plain or painted. Bodies appear in forms other than verbal—in painting and sculpture, for instance—allowing for comparisons among arts and artists, which are common in ancient accounts of the historical development of rhetoric and in treatments of the types of speaking (*genera dicendi*).‡ Words such as "filed" and "polished" come from the working of metal and stone, often figured into

---

a "body" of work. We call an author's entire *oeuvre* her *corpus*, whereas, for most of classical antiquity, a *corpus* was the sum of all the book-rolls (singular and in Latin: *volumen*, *c(h)arta*, *liber*, or *libellus*) that made up one single work. Ovid's *Metamorphoses*, for example, is a *corpus* composed of fifteen book-rolls, and he refers to it that way himself in his *Tristia* (*ter quinque volumina*, three by five volumes, 3.14.19).

*Van Hook, *The Metaphorical Terminology of Greek Rhetoric and Literary Criticism*, 18. The body is also hailed by rhetorical *schēmata* and *figurae* and the *staseis* (stances).

†Wilner, "Roman Beauty Culture," 26.

‡See, e.g., Pollitt, *The Ancient View of Greek Art;* Kennerly, "The Mock Rock *Topos*."

human forms.* That bodies grow and develop, and into all manner of shapes and sizes, also recommends them to histories of rhetoric; Cicero, for example, refers to eloquence as "*nata et alta* [having been born and grown up]" in Athens.†

Bodies are also sexed and gendered, every nuance of their appearance and movement subject to measurement by instruments of judgment calibrated according to culture. For instance, immensely sensitive to the sway of such evaluations, Cicero made Piso's eyebrows a key part of his accusation against him.‡ Within the textual realm, the corporeal language of composing and editing reflects upon its own operation within cultures that mark particular traits and gestures with masculine or feminine characteristics. Orators and poets do not avoid the categorization of "bodily care" but do introduce two kinds: athletic and cosmetic, a typology that goes back at least as far as Plato's *Gorgias*. Within the sensual vocabulary of *corpus* care, the desirable, masculine effect is often paired with the undesirable, effeminate one: with regard to how one looks, one can be flushed with a healthy circulation or blushed with paints; with regard to how one smells, one can be redolent of mild athletic oils or dosed in flowery unguents; with regard to how one feels, one can be hard or soft; with regard to how one sounds, one can register as subtly rhythmic or sing-song; with regard to how one tastes, one can convey a hint of sweetness or be thoroughly saccharine. Common, too, is the addition of a scrawny, thin sort of masculine style that lacks power but boasts precision. Less frequently appearing in my discussions are treatments of the limit qualities of the boorish or barbaric, but Ovid's exile poetry draws upon the latter, as I show in chapter 5. With their care, word-workers need to avoid both repulsive inattention to and repulsive obsession with the sensual dimension of language and its power to influence. Influence ought to work more militarily than meretriciously, more through tactics than haptics. *Edo*, the Latin verb for making something public, cannot always shake connotations of "putting out," a concern about which Horace was explicit.§

The body is the medium of life. Those who enter public life, whether through verse or prose, find that physiological metaphors deployed as criticism presume a consistency if not an absolute congruity between how one speaks or writes and how one lives or looks: harsh speaking or writing suggest harsh living. As Erik Gunderson has observed of orators in particular, "the social place of the orator in the Roman world is secured as part of a thoroughgoing corporeal

*Van Hook, *The Metaphorical Terminology of Greek Rhetoric and Literary Criticism*, 37–39. "Filed" is *katarrhinēmenon* in Greek and *limatus* in Latin, and "polished" *glaphuros* in Greek and *politus* in Latin.

†Cicero, *Brutus*, §39.

‡See, e.g., Hughes, "Piso's Eyebrows."

§Horace, *Epistulae*, 1.20.

project."* Today's rhetoricians have staked vigorous claims for the significance of the body to rhetorical training and performance, and the body stretches beyond there, into every limb of rhetoric and foot of poetry and into every editorial metaphor and the body of work they purport to polish.†

Hic Liber

This book proceeds chronologically and by collecting several Greek orators and poets together in the early chapters before affording a given Roman orator or poet nearly sole attention in each later chapter. Its form performs one of its central arguments: texts accumulate over time, but the corporeal language with which writers distinguish their texts from what came before and also from what is newly written does not change very much. A key explanation for this terminological continuity seems simple: body-based critical language about speaking and writing appeared in the writings of those who came first, some of those writings were read and copied by those who came after, and some of those writings continued to be read and copied by those who came after them. The line starts in fifth-century B.C.E. Athens, extends to Hellenistic textual centers such as Alexandria, and terminates, for my purposes, in Rome. The line is, of course, not really a line, but the zigs and zags and the accidents and serendipities and the fashions and lulls that meant some part of a writer's *corpus* survived and another did not are difficult to trace. What is remarkable is that particular Athenian writers seem to have set the terms for what counts as worth pursuing for and preserving from an orator or a poet and themselves to have been continually served by those criteria. They created the critical conditions for their own canonicity.‡

It is in Athens, then, that I begin, arguing that the evaluative corporeal vocabulary of poetics, rhetoric, criticism, and texts developed there under democratic circumstances. Chapter 1, "The Polis(h) of Classical Athens," extends across poetics and rhetoric to demonstrate that *corpus* care heralded not a growing formalism devoid of practical value but rather a curiosity about what treated words can do and for whom. The wordplay in this chapter's title sports with the visual similarity—and that is all it is—between the Greek word *polis* and the English word polish. (Giambattista Vico once claimed that "from *politeia,* which in Greek means civil government, was derived the Latin *politus,* clean or neat," so I am in good company.)§ Within contests between fifth-century dramatists

---

*Gunderson, "Discovering the Body in Roman Oratory," 189.
†E.g., Hawhee, *Bodily Arts;* Holding, "The Rhetoric of the Open Fist."
‡I address the tricky concept of "canon" in the Conclusion.
§Vico, *The New Science,* 115.

and between fourth-century rhetors, the fact or quality of verbal preparations were an obvious agonistic element, suggesting a perception that matters of composition and revision were of public interest. Meanwhile, poetic and rhetorical works started to use body language with increasingly complex detail. The individual work that receives the most attention in this chapter is the *Panathenaicus* of Isocrates, in which he narrativizes its lengthy composition, thereby demonstrating the amount of labor, lively discussion, and deletion required to form a lengthy *logos* that can both court and support a pan-Hellenic reception.

Chapter 2, "Hellenistic Gloss," recognizes the acclaim the Hellenistic period rightly enjoys for editorial energies applied to the writings of others, most famously in the Library-Mouseion in Alexandria. Yet, my central contention is that the period's own word-workers continued to develop the kind of *corpus* care evidenced in earlier Athenian texts—and for public, *polis*-related purposes. The key figures are Demetrius of Phalerum, the philosopher and politician, and Callimachus of Cyrene, the bibliographer and poet, both of whom produced works known for their polish and learned compression. The chapter transitions to second-century B.C.E. Rome, offering a parallel pairing of an orator and a poet: Cato Maior and Lucilius, both of whom came to be known for their lack of refinement but who clearly engaged with textual culture within their own speeches and poems. The chapter closes with an analysis of the body language in the oldest surviving Roman handbook to cover all five parts of rhetoric, the unknown *auctor*'s *Rhetorica ad Herennium*. In the fourth book-roll, dedicated entirely to style, the *auctor* offers a corporeal classification of types of speech and extends the metaphor to describe speech that goes to unhealthy limits of thinness or thickness. Subsequent discussions of speaking, writing, and editing in Roman rhetoric build on those bodies.

The Roman part of the book thus holds mostly to Rome from the 90s B.C.E. to the 90s C.E. and focuses on writers writing in Latin and explicitly about editing as I have operationalized that concept. Greeks such as Dionysius of Halicarnassus and "Longinus" do appear, however. Though I originally considered representing an equal number of orators and poets, in the end the orators won out; my thinking was that it was more important to provide abundant evidence that even they who are often classified foremost as "public speakers" wrote and worried about editing.*

Chapter 3, "Tales and Tools of the Oratorical *Traditio* in Cicero," does not focus on what Cicero wrote about his own speech composition and publication

---

*Roman, *Poetic Autonomy in Ancient Rome,* alone includes Catullus, Propertius, Martial, and others.

processes in his letters, work that has been done thoroughly by others.* Instead, it keys in on midcentury contestations over the Attic way of speaking and what, precisely, it means for speech to be "filed." Young orators who fancied the verbal thinness of certain Attic orators jeopardized Cicero's standing and legacy by either criticizing or altogether ignoring his oratorical fullness. He responded with several rhetorical works, all of which attempted to teach those young orators the error of their preferences. The first, *Brutus,* surveys hundreds of years of oratory to demonstrate that not only writing but also editing are tools of an orator's trade and of the oratorical tradition and that they permit a handing down of speech-texts and reputations, both individual and national. The second, *De Optimo Genere Oratorum,* which seems never to have been released publicly, introduces a translation of Demosthenes and Aeschines, inimical orators, that Cicero undertook to showcase the range within "the" Attic style. The third, *Orator,* combines the productive and preservative capacities of writing, arguing that rhythm—that most oral, aural, social, and influential of qualities—is best achieved by writing and rewriting, whose inclusion into the early stages of the rhetorical process enable an orator to give a speech that both sounds good and reads well. Across those works, Cicero pits the entire oratorical, rhetorical tradition, both Greek and Roman, against the new Atticists.

The next chapter, "Filing and Defiling Horace," counters the common claim that Horace's fixation on editing resulted from his verses being less free than those of his satiric predecessors of the previous century. While Horace's political position and positioning are not without complexity, his attempts to enforce the rectitude of writers testify to recurrent tensions between decorous restraint and the obnoxious freedom to let it all hang out, completely unmanaged and unrestrained by ethics or aesthetics. Considering his hexametrical poetry, I claim that Horace's enthusiasm for the editorial file (*lima*) was not only a poetic stance but also a civic one. The file is an emblem of careful writing—and not of fearful writing, as some critics currently read Horace—that points to his distaste for poetry produced quickly under public pressure or from a poet's desire for fanatical readers, regardless of their critical standards. Ultimately, bad poetry reflected poorly on Rome itself.

In Chapter 5, "Ovid's Exilic *Expolitio,*" I argue that Ovid exploited the terms and conventions of textual culture to embed—thoroughly and repeatedly—his sad tale and buoyant hopes within his poems from exile. *Expolitio* (thoroughly polishing, finishing off) recommends itself in particular as an Ovidian trope

*See, especially, Gurd, "Cicero on Editorial Revision," and Gurd, *Work in Progress,* 49–76.

because on one hand it straddles the domains of style and argumentation and on the other trains attention on how Ovid repeatedly deployed lamentations about his lack of thorough polish as an argument. I proceed through two of his exilic works, *Tristia* and *Epistulae Ex Ponto*, demonstrating that his reiteration of certain elements of his current compositional conditions punned and played on the language of appropriateness, a language belonging to poetic, rhetorical, and legal nomenclatures. In his epistolary output, he called upon fellow poets by name, recalling their past editorial sociality as a way of calling them to his side for this present need.

Chapter 6, "The Cares of Quintilian," ventures over all twelve book-rolls of the *Institutio Oratoria* to demonstrate that Quintilian's entire instructional method bears an editorial tinge. More particularly, the lifelong rhetorical process he presented privileges care. Quintilian's challenge was to offer a kind of care that enhanced the goodness of the *vir bonus* rather than called the good man's masculinity or ethical rectitude into question. Quintilian's solution was to emphasize both the abundance and the ease that rhetorical training establishes *and* the elimination of excess that may result from them. This principle informs the creation of the *Instutitio Oratoria* itself, since Quintilian read around extensively to find the best material, synthesize it, and compress it for the edification of readers.

Chapter 7, "Past, Present, and Future Perfect Eloquence," remains in the late first century c.e., first entering Tacitus's dialogue about the state of eloquence, a capacious category in which the interlocutors include both oratory and poetry, and the relationship between perfect eloquence and imperfect political circumstances. The chapter closes with Pliny's letters, which abound with opinions about how, why, and when a preeminent orator should edit a speech for broad publication. Tacitus and Pliny show how extensively nearly every poet and orator treated in this book shaped their thinking, their vocabulary, and their preferences about how eloquence may be perfected in various political conditions.

In the Conclusion, "Kissing Tiro; or, Appreciating Editing," I focus on Tiro, Cicero's cherished scribal slave turned freedman, to make a variety of closing points. A primary objective is to highlight the many others—many of their names lost beyond recovery—who provided services or savvy to ancient writers, from friends to booksellers. In contrast to Tiro's comparative celebrity, very little is known about enslaved and freed contributors to the editorial and publication processes of ancient writers, both when writers were alive and after their deaths. Furthermore, acts of continued copying and preservation enabled explicitly "classical" thinking, that is, the notion that certain past and "first-rate" writers were most worthy of knowing and emulating. That sort of editorial work kept old texts very much alive, since old texts sparked debates about forms and norms of correctness that could result in an old text being emended, even at the expense of aesthetic appeals undertaken purposefully at its point of origin. Because so many of the writers treated in the following chapters were and also went on to be big names, I deem it important to situate them in contexts abounding with the mostly unnamed others upon whom they and their legacies relied.

So as to remind readers frequently that this book enters a galaxy far, far away from Gutenberg's and different, too, from the world of the codex, I translate the Greek *biblos* and the Latin *liber* as "book-roll" rather than "book."* In terms of what we would call word count, an ancient book-roll was roughly equivalent to a chapter in a book of today.

*I am alluding, of course, to McLuhan, *The Gutenberg Galaxy.*

CHAPTER ONE

THE POLIS(H) OF CLASSICAL ATHENS

When a first-century B.C.E. critic expressed amazement at Sappho's *sōma*, he was admiring not *her* body but that of one of her poems.* That he did not need to specify his somatic referent suggests that body-based analysis was by then a familiar critical idiom. This chapter details the earliest development of that idiom. Its core concern, though, lies with how editorial language—what I am calling *corpus* care—formed and fared as Greeks accommodated themselves to writing technologies, the papyrus book-roll especially, in the fifth and fourth centuries. The public merit of writing-enabled polish became a focal point of play and polemic across poetic and rhetorical forms. In the rough and tumble of fast-moving and agonistic politics, in which both poets and rhetors operated, the usefulness of words worked over in writing was not self-evident. Emphasizing craft (*technē*), time (*chronos*), work (*ponos*), and what they produce, the incipient vocabulary of *corpus* care signified not a growing formalism devoid of practical value but rather a curiosity about what treated words can do—for oneself, for others, for the *polis*—that untreated words cannot.

These lines attributed to Sappho would be a remarkable point of emergence for writing-implicated body language were they not a product of the twentieth century: "may I write words more naked than flesh, stronger than bone, more resilient than sinew, sensitive than nerve."† Sappho's poems pulse and flush with bodily energies and colors. "Is it not amazing how she pursues the soul, the body, the hearing, the tongue, the sight, the skin, all as though they were estranged

---

*"Longinus," *Peri Hupsous*, 10.1–3; *sōma* at 10.1. I am persuaded by Casper C. de Jonge's view that "Longinus" may have been a first-century B.C.E. contemporary of Dionysius of Halicarnassus. See de Jonge, "Dionysius and Longinus on the Sublime," 294. Further work from de Jonge on this topic is forthcoming.

†At a very far remove from sixth-century B.C.E. Lesbos, Theresa Hak Kyung Cha created the prayer and attributed it to Sappho in the epigraph of her 1982 book, *Dictée*. For more on Sappho's scattered *corpus*, see duBois, *Sappho Is Burning*, 55–76, and Carson, *If Not, Winter.*

and escaping," gushes the aforementioned critic.* In no extant poem, though, does Sappho clearly render words flesh to coordinate their composition.

To find genuine evidence, one must move from Sappho's sixth-century Lesbos to fifth- and fourth-century Athens, where the somatic-graphic analogy appears in works by natives and visitors, verse and prose writers alike. It evinces a range of functions. To name a few to which I return later: Agathon's *sōmata* suggest that a writer and his writing resemble one another; Alcidamas's *sōmata* signify oral fluidity versus written stiffness; Plato's *sōma* speaks to the arrangement and analysis of writing; and Aristotle's *sōma* provides a model for sentence length and plot size.[†] Writers with occasionally divergent communal and intellectual commitments nonetheless came to terms with speech in a similarly material and specifically corporeal way. As I mentioned in the Introduction, the parts of words, sentences, and book-rolls also assumed a bodily form. Descriptions of composing, correcting, and criticizing bodies began to appear. Such vocabulary and visions recommended to critics metrics for textual bodies that were typically used to scrutinize fleshy bodies, among them size, weight, symmetry, balance, beauty, wholeness, and even parentage. Sometimes a writer and his writing were subjected to the same somatic terms. Behold the original "anatomy of criticism."[‡]

My claim that interest in textual polish emerged in fifth-century democratic Athens vexes the contention, popularized by Kennedy, that *letteraturizzazione* intensifies during periods of reduced political freedom. What did build throughout that century is textual culture. Textual culture matures through the sheer accumulation of texts, and anyone with access to a text or its cultural uptake can borrow from, allude to, compete with, or overtake it. The pursuit of polish—the smooth connection and compression of one's selection of the available means of persuasion or delectation—need not necessarily point to or portend political decay and decadence, when practiced by rhetors or poets. That point is important to make in the context of Athens precisely because neither its internal power arrangement nor its position of power within the geographical region held steady across the fifth and fourth centuries. There is no polish quotient that dips up and down along with it.

Rome, too, was far from stable in any of its postmonarchical but preimperial historical periods.[§] My findings in this chapter bear on the texts and contexts of

---

*"Longinus," *Peri Hupsous*, 10.3.

[†]Aristophanes, *Thesmophoriazusae*, 160–167; Alcidamas, *On Those Who Write*, §28; Plato, *Phaedrus*, 264c and 265e; Aristotle, *Rhetoric*, 1409a35–b1, and *Poetics*, 1451a3–4.

[‡]I borrow this phrase from Frye, *Anatomy of Criticism*, though he does not write about editing.

[§]See, e.g., Flower, *Roman Republics*.

the first centuries B.C.E. and C.E., since Romans of that time (and Greeks, too, though, again, they fall outside my purview) envisioned how Greek writers who were by then well regarded worked their words for publication, scouring venerable *exempla* for evidence and supplying their own suppositions. No one appearing in this chapter goes unmentioned by them. That Romans could read "ancient" Athenian works at all is a credit to Hellenistic textual organization, which I address in the subsequent chapter.

The Muse Learns to Edit

Detailed accounts of written composition from the middle decades of the fifth century, a period by which the take-up of the papyrus book-roll is assured, are not at all plentiful. From a few decades of distance compositionally, though narratively proximate, Plato's *logos*-lusty character Phaedrus reports that "the most powerful and proud in the *polis* are ashamed both to write speeches and to leave behind anything written, fearing for their reputation at a later time, so that they will not be called a sophist."* From the even greater distance of the second century C.E., Plutarch reports that Pericles, for example, left behind no writing except the decrees he proposed, and only a few of his memorable sayings are preserved.† During the middle decades of the fifth century, Herodotus of Halicarnassus and Thucydides of Athens were gathering materials for their sizable histories, both of which contain speeches. Although the proto-genre of history differs from oratory, even when it contains oratory, thinking about Herodotus's process yields questions not inapplicable to other, shorter written genres, such as a given *logos politikos* of Isocrates.

Each of the nine book-rolls that constitute Herodotus's *Histories* is named for a Muse, very likely the doing of a later organizer of the work and indicative of classification confusion about where Herodotus fit within what were then still-solidifying generic structures. Herodotus also bent syntax to his purposes, using the genitive case to begin his work with his own name. (It does not show in my English translation.) In that proem, Herodotus announces: "This is the display [*apodexis*] of the inquiry [*historia*] of Herodotus of Halicarnassus, so that things done by humans may not be lost in time [*tōi chronōi*], and that great

---

*Plato, *Phaedrus*, 257d. For evidence that modern claims for uniquely sophistic book-ishness are overstated, see Pfeiffer, *History of Classical Scholarship*, 17, though he regards as "true that their contribution to the development of the book was one general service the Sophists did for Greek civilization as a whole and for future scholarship in particular" (32). For a more modest appraisal, see Thomas, "Prose Performance Texts." Pfeiffer includes references in Aristophanes and Plato to places in Athens where book-rolls were available for sale (27–31).

†Plutarch, *Life of Pericles*, 8.5.

and wondrous deeds, some displayed [*apodechthenta*] by the Hellenes, some by the barbarians, not become uncelebrated and unheard, including, among others, what was the cause of their waging war on one another."* On show here, in the very first lines of this monumental work, are the demonstrative, preservative, and instructive capacities of written words. *Histories* displays the work undertaken by its writer and the feats of those he wrote about; it prevents both from being forgotten; and it aids in understanding causes and origins of major events.

Herodotus was collecting, compiling, and composing from the 450s to the 420s, a sizable stretch of time decades removed from the war upon which his work focuses, the Greco-Persian War, but contemporary with a new war, the Peloponnesian War. Herodotus's weighty work, then, deals with a past conflict whose details and entailments were being disputed in a present conflict, as he was writing.† His was a hot history. In her efforts to enfold Herodotus into his own cultural matrix, Rosalind Thomas has argued that a stubborn scholarly tendency to read Herodotus as an archaic storyteller "implicitly treats Herodotus as more old-fashioned than the period in which we all agree he is writing."‡ The oral-textual tension pulled tautly within most interpretations of Herodotus results in some strange assumptions about his methods. The challenge of assembling and editing a work as massive as Herodotus's *Histories* with the tools of the time is hard to fathom; indeed, we cannot be sure what tools he had at hand. Writing in the 1950s, Richard Lattimore focused on what Herodotus did *not* have: "what we would call good paper, good ink, good scissors, or a good eraser."§ For that reason, Lattimore supposed that "the whole History is, substantially at least, a first draft which was never revised, nor meant to be, because the first draft was always meant to be the final draft."** What Lattimore perceived to be narrative drifts and digressions suggested to him that Herodotus must have written "in a continuous forward sequence," just as one would orally narrate a story.†† Such supposed drifts "do not perhaps *prove* that systematic rewriting and revision were unknown to Greek literature until a relatively late period. They are, however, what we should expect to find in the work of gifted writers who rejected, or did not know of, that kind of revision."‡‡ Must Herodotus be either a rebellious genius or a naïf?

---

*Herodotus, *Histories*, 1.1.

†At 7.139.1–5, Herodotus courts counterargument when he calls Athenians the "saviors of Hellas" for their role in battling back the Persians.

‡Thomas, *Herodotus in Context*, 5.

§Lattimore, "The Composition of the *History* of Herodotus," 9.

**Lattimore, "The Composition of the *History* of Herodotus," 9.

††Lattimore, "The Composition of the *History* of Herodotus," 16.

‡‡Lattimore, "The Composition of the *History* of Herodotus," 16.

More recent scholarship on Herodotus has not lost sight of the technical and material challenges posed by the enormity of his unprecedented project, but it has questioned the appropriateness of applying modern standards of narrative linearity to ancient texts. As Homer did, Herodotus often employed a ring composition, whereby what may seem to us to be a wandering account circles back on itself. In the middle of one of his seeming meanderings, Herodotus discloses that seeking out "additions [*prosthēkas*]" has been his approach from the start.* That is how one conducts a work of *historia*. Searching and researching, his writing is accretive and inclusive by design.† Herodotus's errant moments are not necessarily unedited errata—or even errant, at all.

Lattimore "guess[ed]" that it was not until the first half of the fourth century that Greek developed a lexicon "for such stages and processes as successive drafts, revision, editing, etc."‡ I would argue for an earlier date. Editing's earliest public representation was not on a page but on a stage, *the* stage: the Theater of Dionysos, in the last quarter of the fifth century.§ That it should have appeared there is significant, given the thoroughly political nature of the theater as an institution and an experience. The comedies I treat were produced and performed for a portion of the *dēmos* during the Greater Dionysia, an annual city-wide theatrical contest. One's attendance was determined by one's active involvement in the polis as judged by one's deme, a political subdivision of Athens. Upon arrival, a citizen would take his seat among fellows from his deme, just as he would in other venues where formal politics were conducted (and in battle), and prepare for an entire day of performances.** Then he would come back for two more days. It is likely that resident noncitizens and visitors attended and possible that women did, too. Every element of the festival contributed to democratic life.†† As Oddone Longo cautions, to consider an Athenian drama an autonomous, timeless artistic object is to fundamentally misunderstand "the complex institutional and social conditions within which the processes of literary production in fact took place. These conditions predetermine the possible 'creative' area of the individual poet, and they offer a preliminary framework to the coordinates within which admissible poetic trajectories will be plotted."‡‡ Poets sometimes dramatized those very processes of literary

---

*Herodotus, *Histories*, 4.30.1.

†Thomas, "Introduction," xvii.

‡Lattimore, "The Composition of the *History* of Herodotus," 20, f.n. 18.

§For an argument that writing enabled the genres of comedy and tragedy, see Wise, *Dionysius Writes*.

**See Winkler and Zeitlin, "Introduction," 4.

††For details, see Goldhill, "The Great Dionysia and Civic Ideology."

‡‡Longo, "The Theater of the *Polis*," 15.

production, including editing, thereby describing or prescribing the poetic *and* democratic relevance of such activities.

Only patches remains of the earliest play in which editing occurs on a very public stage. The *Pytine* (*Wineflask*) of Cratinus won first place among the comedies produced for the Greater Dionysia in 423 B.C.E. In the play, it seems that Cratinus's wife, Kōmōdia (Comedy), accuses him of cheating on her with Methē (Drunkenness). One fragment contains a scene in which Kōmōdia suggests edits to Cratinus while he composes. Reading over his shoulder, she tells him, "You're talking nonsense! Write [*Graph'*] it in a single episode," and "rub out [*aposbesas*] *Hyberbolus* and write [*grapson*] *in the market of oil lamps*," since it will be funnier.* In Kōmōdia, the stereotypical critical wife has become the new critical reader. Throughout antiquity, Muses are depicted with book-rolls or called to or pictured at a poet's side, but this seems to be the only depiction of a personified art pushing for the alteration of a composition to enhance its chance of succeeding with an audience.† Sean Gurd calls it "a *radically* meta-poetic moment," since "by showing himself as comic poet changing a text, Cratinus reminds us that this scene of revision may itself have been revised as well, that in addition to what we read there may have been other versions, other words, and other jokes that he explored but ultimately changed or rejected."‡ Poets make active, editorial choices of inclusion and exclusion. Cratinus publicizes the collaborative early stages of poetic decision making, and with an expectation that the revelation will amuse. The humor plays on the stage in performance and on the page thereafter, perhaps especially there.

Finishing in third place in that contest of 423 was the *Clouds* of Aristophanes, in which an overdrawn Athenian seeks the rarefied knowledge of Socrates so that he might use it to trick his creditors. Aristophanes did not suffer the embarrassment quietly.§ Through the chorus leader of *Wasps*, produced in the following year, Aristophanes impugns spectators for not rewarding him for his savage attack on those who would harm the city, as Socrates ostensibly was doing.** Aristophanes also opted to revise *Clouds*. Only the (or a) revision has reached us, and we do not know whether Aristophanes circulated the revised

---

*Kassel and Austin, *Poetae Comici Graeci,* fragments 208 and 209.

†For a study of depictions of book-rolls from this period, see Immerwahr, "Book Rolls on Attic Vases." Immerwahr shows that the many surviving book-roll scenes show a Muse holding "the *biblos*".

‡Gurd, "Revision in Greek Literary Papyri," 160.

§The rivalry between Aristophanes and Cratinus went around and around. The *Wineflask* likely represents Cratinus's retort to Aristophanes's criticism of him in *Knights* (526–536), produced in 424.

**Aristophanes, *Wasps*, 1037–1047.

play during his lifetime or his literary executors let it loose. It is clear, though, that it is not the version originally staged because the chorus directly addresses the Athenians about their decision to award top prizes to lesser poets. Aristophanes deems the spectators clever and deserving of his service to the *polis*, but he questions their poor judgment about the original version, which resulted from his great labor and elaboration.*

About a decade after the production of *Clouds* and Cratinus's winning *Wineflask*, Aristophanes recognized that yet more humor could be pulled from descriptions of dramatists at work. In his *Thesmophoriazusae* (411 B.C.E.), Aristophanes showcased the activities of Agathon, one of Athens's well-known and award-winning poets, in a way that suggests editorial labor. If this scene constitutes an early, open probe into whether and what kind of editing is a *polis*-pertinent activity, and I think it does, then such questions may be considered of interest to the broad range of politically active Athenians who would have attended the performance. Does Agathon's method produce poetry that is *agathos?* By what (and whose) understanding of *agathos:* morally good, of good quality, or good-looking? The play also asks those who encounter it to wonder what public good those various types of goodness serve, if any.†

In the opening scene of *Thesmophoriazusae*, the tragedian Euripides and his father-in-law (called Mnesilochus) pursue Agathon, wanting the young tragedian to dress up as a woman and infiltrate the women's secret fertility celebration, the Thesmophoria. Euripides suspects the women of Athens will scheme to kill him for insulting them with his portrayals of their sex. Euripides prevails upon Agathon's slave to interrupt his master, who is versifying in the near-holy silence of his workshop. Years earlier, in *Acharnians*, produced in 426, Aristophanes's character Dikaiopolis had importuned Euripides's slave to interrupt Euripides in the middle of his elevated work. Euripides's slave describes his master's poetic method as "collecting verselets [*sullegōn epullia*, the diminutive of *epos*]," that is, piecing together lines he had written previously.‡ Wanting to speak for peace but (purportedly) possessing no way with words, Dikaiopolis asks Euripides for assistance in making himself look pathetic and beggarly when he makes his public petition. Euripides complains he has no *scholē* (leisure time) or spare props to offer, but Dikaiopolis persuades Euripides to part with a few

---

*Aristophanes, *Clouds*, 518–563; *ergon pleiston* at 524 and *epragmateuomēn* at 526.

†Aristophanes flits along the borders of accounts that see rhetoric as beginning only when Plato named it as such (e.g., Cole, *Origins of Rhetoric*). At the core of Aristophanes's interest in Athenian word culture (poetry, oratory, texts) lay a curiosity and concern for their supposed and actual benefit for the *polis*.

‡Aristophanes, *Acharnians*, 399.

items.* Given Dikaiopolis's mockery of the dramatic stage machinery and costuming Euripides favored, Aristophanes clearly had knowledge of the staging of Euripides's plays, and presumed his audience did, too. More striking is Dikaiopolis's snarky allusions to actual lines of Euripides. Besides suggesting that Aristophanes may have composed with the tragedian in various stages of unrolling all around him, this also suggests that his audience would have caught the allusions. That they could have recognized exact lines is possible, but more plausible is that they recognized the sound of Euripides.† Aristophanes capitalized upon their good ears.

The set-up of *Thesmophoriazusae* mirrors the set-up in *Acharnians*. Agathon, his slave reports, "bends new tiers of words [*kamptei de neas hapsidas epōn*]," "turns" them (*torneuei*), "gums" them together (*kollomelei*), and "smooths them out in wax" before "casting them into metal [*kērochutei kai goggullei kai choaneuei*]."‡ That active mish-mash may neither register as editorial nor seem to pertain to writing except through the stretch of metaphor. Because writing on papyrus was a relatively new technology, its lexicon was not disambiguated from that of the plastic arts; *graphō*, the master verb for writing, bears the mark of this ambiguity and can mean "scratch," "scrape," "represent," "draw," "paint," or "write." *Kamptō* denotes "bending" or "curving," while *torneuō* refers to turning an object on a lathe or chiseling it until smooth and shapely. By using the verb for gluing, *kollaō*, Aristophanes draws our attention to the messy materiality of the graphic process: writers would glue papyrus patches atop errors to hide them or to insert emendations on top of them, or they would simply cut out the offending section altogether. Bending and turning words could point to the synthesizing of scraps and segments in an effort to capture a smooth order one can seal together with some glue. That Agathon works in wax before metal seems a clear analogy to the method of sculptors: first model a figure in a cheap and pliable medium, and then move to one expensive and unforgiving. But the wax could refer to a wax tablet, which was less costly than papyrus and more appropriate for the early stages of putting one's thoughts in order or figuring out what they are in the first place. Comparing papyrus to metal became a commonplace of later editing-advocating writers.§

---

*Aristophanes, *Acharnians*, 407, 411.

†As Marshall stresses, "a playwright could and would not willingly disenfranchise himself by learned obscurities. For an audience (or sub-audience) knows when it is being excluded from understanding a point. . . . The playwright is going to try to encompass as much of his audience as he can." Marshall, "Literary Awareness in Euripides and His Audience," 95.

‡Aristophanes, *Thesmophoriazusae*, 52ff.

§For a longer study, see Kennerly, "The Mock Rock *Topos*."

Through that crafty description, Aristophanes represents Agathon's poetic process as driven by the "fabrication, elaboration, adaptation, and linking of 'materials,' and which is far from the idea of a creative work that flows mysteriously and obscurely from the mind of the genius," as Gian Franco Nieddu sees it.* Agathon is an artisan. The doubling capacity of Aristophanes's verbs permits him to play up the unsettled artistic identity of writers and to distinguish Agathon as a determined word-worker. Agathon's method, though, is a matter of principle: because poems necessarily resemble the nature of their poets, "it is bad form [*amouson;* literally, without the Muses] for a poet to look course and shaggy [*agreīon onta kai dasun*]."† When Mnesilochus plays along, pretending to find this assessment revelatory, Agathon credits an understanding of the relationship between the state of his body and that of his verses as the explanation for why he takes such good care of himself (*emauton etherapeusa*).‡ Agathon suits Euripides purposes precisely because of that care. "I am gray-haired and bearded," Euripides stresses, whereas "you appear pretty-faced, freshly scrubbed and shaved, lady-voiced, tender, and good-looking."§ When Agathon refuses to leave his poetic workshop, Euripides convinces his father-in-law to shave, asking Agathon if he can borrow one of those razors he is always carrying (*zurophoreīs*).**

While orators typically receive credit for emphasizing the continuity between a person's ways and his words, that attitude seems expressed here as a pun on Agathon's name.†† Euripides also recognizes Agathon for being well able to articulate much in a short form because he cuts and shapes his words (*suntemnein*).‡‡ Agathon's fondness for razors applies to several *sōmata:* his human body, his words, and his material texts. His editorial efforts are representative of his bodily preening, his bodily preening of his character. In Aristophanes's later play *Ekklesiazousai* (392 B.C.E.), several women of Athens conspire to take over the *ekklēsia,* the deliberative body of several thousand citizens that gathered on the Pnyx. To prepare for their infiltration, they discard their razors, one woman describing how she has become so hairy that she no longer resembles a woman.§§ Agathon's ubiquitous razors, on the other hand, suggest he *does* resemble a

---

*Nieddu, "A Poet at Work," 334, n. 11.

†Aristophanes, *Thesmophoriazusae,* 160, 167.

‡Aristophanes, *Thesmophoriazusae,* 171. Compare the poet Artemo, who composes too quickly and whose armpits stink of goat (Aristophanes, *Acharnians,* 851–853).

§Aristophanes, *Thesmophoriazusae,* 191–192.

**Aristophanes, *Thesmophoriazusae,* 217–218.

††See, for instance, Cicero, *Brutus,* §117, §132; Quintilian 11.1.30.

‡‡Aristophanes, *Thesmophoriazusae,* 177–178.

§§Aristophanes, *Ekklesiazousai,* 65–67.

woman, which is precisely why Euripides sought him out to mingle with the women celebrating the Thesmophoria.* Aristophanes describes Agathon's gender fluidity through the reactions of Mnesilochus when he first sees Agathon, who is dressed as a woman, since, in his view, a poet "must take on the habits [*tous tropous*] of his characters."† Mnesilochus calls Agathon a "womanish man [*gunnis*]" mired in "confusion."‡ In turn, Agathon's "confused" gender mixture confuses Mnesilochus: "Are you a man? Where's your penis? . . . Are you a woman? Then where are your breasts?"§ Gender troubled, Mnesilochus attempts to categorize Agathon on the basis of sex characteristics, but Agathon's various bodies resist such simplistic readings.

Only a few verse-long fragments of Agathon's plays survive, but they evince a fondness for closely shaven schemata. The third-century c.e. work *Poikilē Historia* (*Assorted History*), a sizable collection of customs and quotations gathered by Aelian and revised and published by his friends after his death, features an amusing anecdote about Agathon: "Agathon used a lot of antitheses in many of his works. When someone with the idea of correcting [*epanorthoumenous*] him wanted to remove [*periairein*] them from his plays, he said, 'My good friend, you have failed to notice that you are destroying the Agathon in Agathon?'"** Style that seems self-indulgent to his friends Agathon perceives to be self-constituting. Here again an ancient author aligns Agathon and his words, and Aelian provides a glimpse at the part of the editorial process whereby writers sought out—but did not always accept—the critical opinions of trusted friends.

Agathon appears again in Aristophanes's *Frogs* (405 b.c.e.), produced mere months after Euripides and Sophocles died. There, the patron god of the theater, Dionysus, recounts that he was "reading to himself [*anagignōskonti moi*]"—the reflexive pronoun alone does not confirm that he was reading silently—Euripides's *Andromeda* when he was overcome with longing.†† He pines for the recently departed poets, framing their absence in terms of the *polis*. When asked about Agathon, also recently deceased, he says, "a good poet [*agathos poiētēs*] and much missed by his friends."‡‡ The suggestion is that the loss is personal rather than political in scale. Punning again on Agathon's name, Aristophanes separates the

---

*See Duncan, *Performance and Identity in the Classical World*, 25, 57. I return to questions of gender and editing in later chapters.

†Aristophanes, *Thesmophoriazusae*, 149–150.

‡Aristophanes, *Thesmophoriazusae*, 136–147.

§Aristophanes, *Thesmophoriazusae*, 141–143.

**Aelian, *Poikilē Historia*, 14.9.

††Aristophanes, *Frogs*, 53.

‡‡Aristophanes, *Frogs*, 83.

good from the best.* Dionysus decides to descend into Hades, find Euripides, and pull him back to Athens. He arrives to squabbling. Stirring up the riffraff to support him, Euripides has laid claim to the Chair of Tragedy, a foremost honor in the Underworld and one that had been occupied by Aeschylus since his death, in 455. To settle their dispute, Hades announces a contest, and Euripides suggests seeing how his words measure up—literally—to those of Aeschylus. A scale will register the weight of words, and Dionysus will determine the winner.† The chorus describes the contest as pitting the "urbane and filed down [*asteion ... kai katerrhinēmenon*]" against an almost natural force that enlists roots, branches, and the wind itself.‡

The scale prepares the audience for the bodily emphasis of the adjectives by which Euripides and Aeschylus take the measure of their styles. The Euripides-Aeschylus debate produces the first sparks in a recurring clash between the dainty and the hefty throughout ancient poetics and rhetoric. Some think the contest contains incipient rhetorical theory, the earliest extant discussion about style.§ Euripides reckons that Athenians will prefer his light poetics to Aeschylus's heavy one, and the comedy itself has prepared spectators and readers to think Dionysus will choose Euripides. Euripides charges Aeschylus, his poetic forebear, with passing on to him an art (*tēn technēn*) so swollen with bombast (*oidoūsan hupo kompasmatōn*) and so word-heavy (*rhēmatōn epachthōn*) that he set to sucking it in (*ischnana*) and taking away its weight (*to baros apheīlon*) by means of small scraps of verse (*epulliois*) and walks all around the place (*peripatois*).** Euripides's aesthetic leanings have a kinesthetic dimension, too: his words move about to work off their weight. Is that an oblique reference to circulating drafts among others whose editorial feedback would help tighten the text even more? He also feeds poetry bright beets and liquid glibness strained from little book-rolls (*bibliōn*). Euripides and Aeschylus agree that the function of a poet is to give sound advice that improves people in the *polis,* but they disagree about which of them has done that better.††

When it becomes clear that individual lines of Euripides will never outweigh those of his competitor—Dionysus deems the word "*Peithō* [Persuasion]"

---

*Agathon and Aristophanes party together in Plato's *Symposium,* a night of drinking and speechifying that occurs after Agathon's tragedy wins top prize.

†Aristophanes, *Frogs,* 795–813.

‡Aristophanes, *Frogs,* 901–905.

§O'Sullivan, *Alcidamas, Aristophanes, and the Beginnings of Greek Stylistic Theory.* Yet he cautions those who would take Aristophanes's "size imagery" as the source of this critical language (15).

**Aristophanes, *Frogs,* 939–943.

††Aristophanes, *Frogs,* 1009–1110.

particularly airy—Aeschylus suggests that Euripides pile his whole family and all their "book-rolls [*biblia*]" onto the scale.* Later writers include Euripides among Greeks remarkable for their book-roll collections.† Euripides's fondness for the slim and trim in the end makes him the biggest loser: Dionysos opts to bring Aeschylus out of Hades and back up to Athens to assist the city once more. One can size up many of the assorted poetic judgments Aristophanes issues in *Frogs* as a burgeoning kind of public criticism marked by, among other things, a collective critical savvy and increased bookishness. Before the *agōn*, the chorus assured the poets that the audience would be able to follow every subtlety of their debate: having read the *biblion* (little book-roll)—though they have always been naturally quick on the uptake—Athenian theatergoers are now whetted and sophisticated.‡ Precisely what little book-roll it is that has contributed to their common critical know-how has long puzzled readers of *Frogs*, but it marks Athenians as informed enough about poetic arts to be intolerant of plays whose parts, even down to the word, are flimsy, thin, or insignificant.

The Craft of Rhetoric

It is not only into the work habits of poets that Aristophanes gave us a look. In *Knights*, which won first place the year before *Clouds* placed third, Paphlagonian (a thinly veiled portrayal of the rhetor Cleon) and the Sausage Seller discuss speechmaking. "Paphlagonian mocks the confidence of the Sausage Seller, imagining him muttering through the composition of the speech all night long, babbling it to himself as he walked around, exhibiting it to his friends and annoying them, and all the time thinking that made him a *rhētōr*."§ Apparently, it is as unpleasant to watch a sausage seller make a speech as it is to watch one make sausage. Though there is no mention of writing in that description, it contains several features that join editorial language in later accounts of written composition, such as working through the night, rehearsing excessively, and sharing one's *logos* with a limited number of people—the Sausage seller ostensibly tries out his speech on both strangers and friends—before publicizing it more widely.

Transitioning from Paphlagonian to actual orators of around that time—the 430s and 420s—does not yield much direct textual evidence about their compositional methods. The famous *epitaphios logos* attributed to Pericles by Thucydides in his *History of the Peloponnesian War* likely bears some resemblance to what Pericles said in the winter of 431/430, even if Thucydides himself did not

---

*Aristophanes, *Frogs*, 1390–1398, 1409.

†Athenaeus, *The Deipnosophists*, 1.4; see also Too, *The Idea of the Library in the Ancient World*, 216.

‡Aristophanes, *Frogs*, 1113–1118.

§Aristophanes, *Knights*, 348–350.

hear its delivery.* The oldest peek we have into Pericles's process comes a few decades after his death, and from Plato's Socrates. Narratively, it is some years after Pericles died of plague, and the deliberating men of Athens are struggling to decide which rhetor should deliver that year's fast-approaching funeral oration. Socrates tells Menexenus, increasingly anxious for whomever they should choose, that the task is not all that challenging, since an Athenian will be praising Athenians to Athenians, and rhetors have speeches like those already prepared.† Menexenus puts Socrates on the spot: if it is so easy, then Socrates should be able to give one without requiring time to work it out. Socrates agrees, since he heard a funeral oration only yesterday, which he shares, though he has not been authorized to make it public.

The person rehearsing it was Aspasia, a Milesian immigrant who was very dear to Pericles and who has been teaching rhetoric to Socrates, or so he says. Socrates recounts that she extemporized some parts and supplied other parts by gluing together (*sugkollōsa*) scraps left over from the funeral oration she composed for Pericles.‡ In his own life and thereafter, Pericles was recognized for the thundering nature of his delivery; Plato would have us believe that the electricity of invention, the zig of arrangement, and the blaze of style were all Aspasia's, and not just that but a lot of textual work and reworking, too. In this instance, she pastes together second-rate textual strips that had ended up on the cutting room floor when she edited her speech for Pericles. This exposure of Aspasia's method doubles as an impeachment of Pericles's rhetorical talent and work ethic: not only was he not gifted but also he was lazy. Hard work truly compensates for nature's deficiencies only when it is one's own work.

Remaining in Plato's time of florescence opens the evidence vista considerably. Plato grew up in an Athens whose collective ear was first tickled by the prose and promises of so-called sophists. Just before Plato was born, Gorgias of Leontini came to Athens in an ambassadorial capacity, representing his city of Leontini (in current-day Sicily); apparently, he dazzled Athenians with his verbal displays (*epideixeis*) and inability to be stumped by any question. Gorgias and other wandering wise guys made Athens part of their rounds and were typically hosted by élite Athenian families. Sophists have the distinction of being considered both flamboyantly orally-aurally attuned *and* textually adept.§ That distinction is paradoxical only if "sophists" is a group-adopted identity bent on uniformity (and it was not), and only if the oral and the textual are utterly

---

*Thucydides, *History of the Peloponnesian War*, 1.22.
†Plato, *Menexenus*, 235d, 236a.
‡Plato, *Menexenus*, 236b.
§See, e.g., J. Poulakos, "*Kairos* in Gorgias' Rhetorical Compositions."

distinct (and they are not). Focusing on the capacity of a textually published speech to sound oral or to read as textual, Rosalind Thomas observed that "Gorgias' epideixeis seem to be varied and extempore, not the labored and prepared pieces of Hippias."* In this time before Aristotle and his three civic genres of rhetoric, *epideixeis* referred broadly to any verbal display.

Alert to the logical inconsistency (*alogon*) at its nib, in *On Those Who Write Written Speeches or On Sophists*, the rhetor Alcidamas of Elaia wrote a counterstatement to what he saw as a worrisome *meletē tou graphein* (care for the written).[†] The very title of the work elides writers with sophists, but Alcidamas does not seem to have meant the likes of Gorgias. Indeed, Alcidamas may have been an enthusiast of Gorgias and a detractor of Isocrates, whose work I analyze in the next section. Whatever the allegiances of Alcidamas, he tries to circumscribe the proper function of writing. Likely releasing his text in the early fourth century, Alcidamas posits many crucial differences between one who speaks from the moment and one who speaks from a memory crammed with exhaustively edited writing. He asserts that rhetors who intensively write are more aptly called poets than sophists (*poiētas ē sophistas*), a classification that may rely on the guild-directed lampoons of comedic poets.[‡] Alcidamas observes that even those who lack instruction in words and their ways can produce something worth saying (and hearing and reading) if permitted to scratch away for a long time (*pollōi chronōi graphai*), correct at leisure (*kata scholēn epanorthōsai*), refer to various sources, compose some more, correct again (*epanorthōsasthai*) on the basis of the advice of trusted prereaders, and clean up (*anakathērai*) and write over (*metagraphai*) yet more after repeated inspection (*episkephamenon*).[§] Bookish types and tyrants, the latter of whom control the pace of debate, may have a surfeit of time during which to produce and preen words, but rhetors speak from positions of deficiency.[**]

Alcidamas's objection to the "polished precision [*akribeia*]" with which writers outfit their words for the assembly, courtroom, and even private conversation is its inability to bend in response to the shifting nature of communicative interaction.[††] Editing rhetors behave as if they are the only ones communicating. Their writing tools are almighty mouths with no ears. That lack can be more than an artistic or interpersonal problem if life hangs in the balance, as it often does in courtroom speeches about accused capital offenders or

---

*Thomas, "Prose Performance Texts," 178.
[†]Alcidamas, *On Those Who Write*, §29, §15, §26.
[‡]Alcidamas, *On Those Who Write*, §2.
[§]Alcidamas, *On Those Who Write*, §4.
[**]Alcidamas, *On Those Who Write*, §11.
[††]Alcidamas, *On Those Who Write*, §9.

assembly debates about war. Extemporaneous rhetors are always on call, ready to react at a moment's notice "whenever there is need to advise the mistaken, to console the unfortunate, to soothe the provoked, [or] to refute sudden allegations of blame."* Their kairotic communication speedily serves corrective and philanthropic functions vital to sustaining communal order and sociality.

For that reason, Alcidamas does not ease up on editing rhetors: "for whenever someone habituated to working words thoroughly little by little and to putting phrases together with exactitude and rhythm [*hotan gar tis ethisthêi kata mikron exergazesthai tous logous kai met' akribeias kai rhuthmou ta rhêmata suntithenai*]" must get his thoughts moving quickly, he bumbles, and not in a way that endears him to an audience suspicious of faultlessness but in a way that marks him as inept.† Further, no more vocally able than those with untrained, weak voices, he twitters out words that are neither lithe nor of any aid to others (*hugrōs, philanthrōpōs*).‡ The philanthropic dimension of extemporaneous speech animates it: *logoi* that emerge immediately resemble "true bodies [*alēthesin ... sōmasin*]" in their soulfulness (*empsochos*), liveliness (*zēi*), and ability to act (*tois pragmasin*), whereas written *logoi* on the whole lack that sinewy quality of activity-in-motion (*energeia*).§ In emphasizing the comparative fitness that keeping a good grip on *kairos* demands, Alcidamas employs several body-based athletic analogies in which the extemporaneous rhetor outperforms the editing rhetor in speed and agility.**

What about public texts fashioned for those distant from the sites where speakers usually extemporize? Alcidamas succumbs to writing's various seductions, boasting that with just a "squeak of work [*mikra ponēsantes*]" he can outdo editing rhetors in their own medium, explaining that not everyone has had a chance to hear him in person, adding that writing over time reflects growth in one's thinking and thus can be viewed as wholesomely diagnostic, and admitting his desire to leave behind "a memorial of myself [*mnēmeīa ... autōn*]."†† In the end, Alcidamas and the writer to whom he may have been most opposed, Isocrates, call their rhetorical projects by the exact same name.‡‡

---

*Alcidamas, *On Those Who Write*, §10.

†This description resembles Plutarch's second-century c.e. account of Alcibiades's speaking habits in *Moralia, Precepts about Statecraft*, 804a. See also Plutarch, *Lives, Alcidamas*, §196.

‡Alcidamas, *On Those Who Write*, §16; see also §26.

§Alcidamas, *On Those Who Write*, §28.

**Alcidamas, *On Those Who Write*, §7, §17.

††Alcidamas, *On Those Who Write*, §30, §32.

‡‡Isocrates, *Antidosis*, §7.

Similarly discomforted by writing's use for serious purposes, Socrates teases writers—of poems, speeches, and laws—who are fanatical about getting everything in its right place, "turning back and forth at length what they have gathered and written over time, both gluing over and taking away [*sunethēken hē egrapsen anō katō strephōn en chronōi, pros allēla kollōn te kai aphairōn*]," perhaps the earliest reference to cutting and pasting.* Plato pictures writers as shufflers of pieces who hope to hit upon a pleasing order by accident of messy rearrangement. Like Alcidamas, Plato also points to how much time (*en chronōi*) it takes to refine a *logos*. Earlier in the discussion in *Phaedrus*, the still Lysias-enraptured Phaedrus responds with incredulity when Socrates asks him to recite the discourse on *erōs* he has just heard that sophist deliver: does Socrates expect him to have memorized a *logos* that Lysias "had leisurely put together over much time [*en pollōi chronoi kata scholēn sunethēke*]"?† Just when Socrates prevails upon Phaedrus to draw up from memory any snippets not beyond recollection, Socrates notices sticking up beneath Phaedrus's garment the telltale sign of textual arousal: a stiff new copy of Lysias's speech.‡

In the final third of the dialogue, Socrates analyzes Lysias's *logos*, which Phaedrus had earlier read aloud. The problems Socrates identifies in its structure and style echo errors he had identified earlier with its sensibility: a fixation with control renders Lysias's *logos*, like the non-lover he champions within it, unfeeling and deadened. Structure-wise, Lysias reiterates the few points he sets forth several different ways, showing a reluctance to wander or explore.§ Style-wise, Socrates judges Lysias "to have thoroughly turned/chiseled [*apotetorneutai*]" his words in an effort to render them "clear and compact and precise [*saphē kai stroggula, kai akribōs*]." In vain, of course.** Plato's lexical choices here cast Lysias as an artisan of cold, hard objects. *Stroggula* refers to the result of wearing-down processes—like erosion—that polish rough, jagged edges over time periods of near geological length. This word can also be used to characterize rotund bodies that lack sharp angles. As I show in chapter 3, Lysias played a significant role in the Atticism debates of the mid-first century B.C.E. (and thereafter).

Moving Alcidamas's critique of spoken written words onto the medium of a book-roll, Socrates frames written words not as *akinētos* (unmoving) but as

---

*Plato, *Phaedrus*, 278e. It is reputed that Socrates wrote nothing. Plato-as-writer fascinated ancient writers, as I show in chapter 6, and continues to fascinate. See, e.g., Allen, *Why Plato Wrote*, and Long, *Socratic and Platonic Political Philosophy*.

†Plato, *Phaedrus*, 228a.

‡Plato, *Phaedrus*, 228d–e.

§Plato, *Phaedrus*, 235a.

**Plato, *Phaedrus*, 234e.

superkinetic.* Socrates reminds Phaedrus that "every word, once written down, is rolled around [*kulindeītai*] among both those who understand and those who have no interest in it."† That rolling around (*kulindō*) smacks of textuality, since readers unroll and re-roll texts. Written words may be fixed, but texts move, and their interpretations fluctuate from one reader to the next, even in the same reader from one sitting to the next. Therefore, "anyone supposing he has left behind any art in writing, and anyone supposing he has received something clear and firm-footed from writing [*saphes kai bebaion ek grammatōn*]," Socrates proclaims, "would be awfully naive [*euētheias*, also "guileless"]."‡ Whirling and whittling words in the pursuit of precision is foolish at best.

Whereas Alcidamas concerns himself with the immediate reaction of an all-eared audience to an editing rhetor—usually, eyes narrowed in suspicion—Socrates concentrates on the relationship that develops between writer and reader as a book-roll unfurls.§ Of most interest to Socrates, then, relationship guru that he seems to be in the *Phaedrus*, is how or even whether the relationship between unchanging texts and ever-changing readers can be managed rhetorically. The rhetorical management he recommends takes two forms that act in concert to "confer a certain life on a text."** The first is to endow what one writes with a somatic structure that communicates meaning through an order and proportion such as one expects of its bodily equivalent: "neither headless [*akephalon*] nor footless [*apoun*], but to have both a middle [*mesa*] and ends [*akra*], drawn together [*gegrammena*] appropriately [*prepont'*] in terms of one another and the whole."†† The second is to write and record in a spirit of play (*paidia*).‡‡ A writer who scribbles away in a playful spirit does not dread inevitable misunderstandings, because he refrains from committing to papyrus anything serious (*spoudaīos*) or resulting from much exertion.§§ Because a book-roll "knows not to whom to speak [*legein*] or not," whenever it is "read off-key or unjustly abused, it always needs its father to come to the rescue; for it lacks the ability to defend or to rescue itself."*** Lysias's little *biblos*, for example, has rolled away from its father and is now outside the city walls and without pro-

---

*Alcidamas, *On Those Who Write*, §28.
†Plato, *Phaedrus*, 275e.
‡Plato, *Phaedrus*, 275c; see also 277d.
§Alcidamas, *On Those Who Write*, §12.
**Ford, *The Origins of Criticism*, 233.
††Plato, *Phaedrus*, 264c.
‡‡Plato, *Phaedrus*, 276c–e, 277e, 278a–b.
§§Plato, *Phaedrus*, 276c–e, 277e.
***Plato, *Phaedrus*, 275e. This father-child analogy of a writer to his book-roll emerges poignantly in Ovid's writings from exile, as I show in chapter 5.

tection from Socratic snark. If a published text is a child out on its own, then its writer-father should equip it with stranger-danger defenses, making it either dazzlingly clear or dizzyingly complicated; the first fends off unwelcome misunderstandings, the second unwelcome (that is, lazy) readers. Since, for Socrates, absolute written clarity is unattainable and utter complexity would yield a distorted textual body of which no one could make head or tails, a violation of his *logos*-as-*sōma* criterion, they are not viable options; thus, play.

The Philoponic Rhetoric of Isocrates

At the end of the *Phaedrus,* Socrates heralds the philosophical promise of Isocrates.* If one is meant to understand by that appraisal that Isocrates resembled Socrates in his opinions on communication, then Plato himself must have been playing: Isocrates wrote a lot and utterly failed to live up to the *paidia* principle. A philoponic rhetoric underlies nearly all of his extant work. Through this attitude of labor-love (*philia* + *ponos*), he disclosed the care and time he had bestowed upon a *logos,* from its conception, to its composition, through its revision, to its publication. He showed not only his thoughts but also the thinking of his thoughts: all manner of qualifications, elaborations, and reiterations testify to how much he had thought, overthought, and rethought while he prepared a public-bound text, and he made the disclosure of that process part of the publication. He spoke not only for the *polis* but also for the polish that made his *logoi politikoi* shine, and by implicating one with the best interests of the others. To put it in a rhyming form, which befits the figure-loving Isocrates: political discourse without polish is all bluster whereas polished discourse without political import is all luster. They need each other, Isocrates proposed, to be at their best. Isocrates labored, and he undertook his labor in high seriousness.

His *polis*-polish link has two orientations in time. In his time, it provided the benefit of advisory words born of extensive reflection and revision.† Isocrates laboriously produced thoughtful and actionable meditations on broad and significant cultural matters, asserting the superiority of his polished political discourse over the bang of inexperienced youngsters and the flash of the new sophists. In the long term, his tributes to Athens and to certain esteemed members of the greater Hellenic political community functioned as an enduring record of the kind of verbal artistry and civic virtue his *polis* inspired and honored. In particular, Isocrates valued the ambassadorial function of book-rolls, but they could do political good over great distances only if worded with great care.

---

*Plato, *Phaedrus,* 278e–279b.

†How much praise Isocrates received in his own time is unclear and made no clearer either way by the teasing of his contemporaries.

Later rhetorical critics routinely named his *Panegyricus* the archetype of exceedingly long and painstaking composition.* In the narrative of that work, Isocrates gives his readers permission to laugh and look down on him if he "speaks" in a way incongruous with all the time he has spent not only "rubbing away at [*diatriphthentos*]" his *logos* but also living.† Published in 380 (though begun a decade earlier), the *Panegyricus* takes its name from a pan-Hellenic festival; there were several across the Greek world, and Isocrates's text refers to the celebration in Athens. A decade (or two) into the fourth century, Sparta retained its position of power, and there was no shortage of squabbling among the lesser *poleis.* As a solution to the fragmentation and conflict, Isocrates called for the formation of a pan-Hellenic union—co-led by Sparta and Athens, just as in the Persian Wars of the early fifth century—whose aggressive energies would be focused on the ostensibly resurgent Persian threat. Isocrates's attempt to turn division at home into a unified front abroad was unsuccessful.

In 357, Philip II, ruler of the northern Greek *polis* of Macedon, began to absorb territory. He laid claim to Amphibolis and Pydna, *poleis* that Athens had occupied decades before but that repeatedly refused allegiance to Athens; one refusal had resulted in Thucydides's exile from Athens. In 347, prompted by Philip's continued campaigns, a delegation that included Demosthenes and Aeschines brought terms of peace to Philip in an effort to stunt Macedon's further growth, an effort to which I return later. Athens and Macedon entered into a precarious peace, which some prominent Athenians thought would not hold for long. Over ten years, Demosthenes delivered a series of speeches known as the Philippics, urging Athenians to regard Philip as an enemy and to ready for war. Isocrates took a different tack.

Isocrates's *To Philip*, dated to 346, assumes an epistolary form, which does not mean we should read it as "private" correspondence. In addition, whether the letter reached Philip is unknown. In the letter, Isocrates fits his vision of pan-Hellenic unity to power's new shape: he exhorts Philip to use *peithō* (persuasion) to unify the Hellenes and *bia* (force) to subdue the Persians.‡ If it seems odd that Isocrates should employ such a strategy as a means of managing Philip's ambition, it seemed downright traitorous to Isocrates's friends. Or so Isocrates tells Philip, who no doubt would have found Isocrates's recommendation curiously un-Athenian. Isocrates describes how those close to him reacted

---

*At least ten years: Dionysius of Halicarnassus, *De Compositione,* §25; Longinus, *Peri Hupsous,* §4.2; Quintilian 10.4; Plutarch, *Moralia* 350e–351a.

†Isocrates, *Panegyricus,* §14.

‡Isocrates, *To Philip,* §16, §30–31.

when he told them his plan to address Philip directly, and protreptically at that.* Contrary to habit, they spared no criticism. They accused him of losing his senses in his old age (Isocrates was ninety): how could Isocrates be so silly as to presume he has the ear of Philip, who has no shortage of advisers he can trust, if he seeks advice at all? Isocrates tells Philip he responded to his new critics first with shock and then with clever rejoinders and a promise that he would circulate the speech only within their small group until they were pleased with it. When he presented his written *logos* a few days later, his friends reversed their judgment, apologized for doubting him, and urged him to send it to Philip at once. Isocrates offers that short story about editorial practices within his coterie to demonstrate the endorsement he has received to speak as representative of Athenian interests, of Greek interests.

In the subsequent few sections, Isocrates prepares Philip to receive the *logos,* advising patience above all: keep going, even if something "strikes you as incredible, or impossible, or inappropriate [*mē piston ē mē dunaton ē mē prepon*]."† Isocrates concedes that written *logoi* on the whole lack the reputation for seriousness and timeliness that spoken ones have; moreover, certain that someone will be reading it aloud to Philip, he worries that the reader will drone on tonelessly, as if enumerating an inventory. Isocrates declares himself incapable of producing the rhythm and complexity so distinctive of his earlier works; all Philip will find here are "simple facts [*tas praxeis haplōs*]."‡ Isocrates's disclosures of ridicule from his friends, of doubt that his text can hold Philip's attention, of no flourishes or funny business, are attempts to earn trust.

Thought to have been published in 339, *Panathenaicus* affords a prolonged look at Isocrates's aging editorial body, as well as at the corps of present and past pupils he gathers around him to hear his words and give him advice. Its intensive editorial interlude makes this *logos* one of a kind in Attic rhetorical culture.§ Its length and internal narrative about its own composition evidence a keen sensitivity to the demands of publication, especially of cross-cultural texts. *Panathenaicus* seethes with agonisms that Isocrates attempts to lift into if not cooperation then at least understanding: conflict cropping up within Athens between himself and those who critically shred his *logoi* in the Lyceum; aggression coming from the north that Isocrates is trying to redirect east toward Persia; and tension arising between Isocrates and his students about what he should

---

*Isocrates, *To Philip*, §17–23.
†Isocrates, *To Philip*, §24.
‡Isocrates, *To Philip*, §28.
§An intriguing second is Plato's *Theaetetus*. See Gurd, *Work in Progress*, 25–48.

change in this very *logos.** Isocrates expresses concern about how he will address all of those pressures and maintain compositional unity.[†]

His medium transcends Athens-bound voices and particularities discussed in the courts. Writing is a choice, but he does refer to being small-voiced and without swagger as justification for why he philosophizes about, works through, and writes out his thoughts.[‡] His themes are not cramped and private ones (*mikrōn, idiōn*) but large and public matters of the Hellenes, and rulers, and *poleis.*[§] The *Panathenaicus* celebrates Athenian contributions to Hellenic culture and contrasts them with Spartan.** At first, the *logos* is eminently timely, since Athenians are in the middle of the yearly Panathenaic festival. Having recorded his thoughts but not yet written a conclusion, Isocrates spends time going over them with three or four of his students, opting also to send for a former student who looks favorably on oligarchy and Spartan customs to read it and "to make visible [*dēlōseien*]" any falsehoods or infelicities that may have escaped Isocrates's notice.[††]

What Isocrates's current students find ready for finishing touches this former student finds in need of serious reconsideration. Isocrates responds harshly, correcting the corrector and making a teaching moment out of the whole disagreeable business.[‡‡] In the first quiet moment he gets after this editorial showdown, Isocrates dictates these developments to his scribal slave. Once the new words are committed to a wax tablet or spare papyrus scrap (he does not specify), Isocrates revisits and revises everything written up to that point, reading and going over it by himself after having let three or four days go by and some critical distance build up.[§§] By this point in the text, the *logos* destined to be *Panathenaicus* has been through a full course of editing. Still, Isocrates finds himself so torn by it—thinking the Athenian segments "well and justly written [*kalōs kai*

---

*Isocrates, *Panathenaicus,* §16 (Lyceum); Macedonian aggression is not explicitly treated; §200–265 (Isocrates and his students edit together).

[†]Isocrates, *Panathenaicus,* §24–25.

[‡]This is part of the framework of the argument structure Too calls his "politics of the small voice," or, placing the emphasis differently, his politics of the big pen. Too suggests that Isocrates's emphasis on vocal smallness is a way of criticizing the big mouths who dominated the democratic discourse venues of Athens. Too, *The Rhetoric of Identity in Isocrates,* 113–150.

[§]*Isocrates, Panathenaicus,* §11.

**Thebes was the dominant super-*polis* of the time, but Isocrates harkens back to the Athenian-Spartan leadership role in the Greco-Persian conflicts of the early fifth century.

[††]Isocrates, *Panathenaicus,* §200.

[‡‡]Isocrates, *Panathenaicus,* §203–230.

[§§]Isocrates, *Panathenaicus,* §231.

dikaiōs gegraphōs]" but the Spartan parts bitter and unsympathetic—that "many times I was about to white wash [*ezaleiphein*] or burn [*katakaein*] it, changing my mind out of pity for my old age and the labor [*ton ponon*] that had been spent on the *logos*."* He therefore opts to summon his students—including the former student—once again to assist him in choosing whether "to suppress [*aphanisteos*] it altogether or to turn it over to [*diadoteos*] whoever wishes to receive it."† The *logos* is then read aloud (by whom it is unclear), and the students roar with approval; well, all but one. The former student freely offers his editorial advice, proceeding as though Isocrates does not intend to neglect the *logos* as it presently stands, genuinely welcomes criticism on it, and did not invite them there just for applause and flattery.‡

The former student's criticisms pertain to the *logos*'s fate at the hands of others. Because Isocrates strives to achieve his very own idiolect—being like others humiliates and distresses him—his writing demands a lot of its readers.§ But, as Plato's Socrates reminds Phaedrus, writing cannot make demands. Indifferent readers will scan Isocrates's *logos* quickly, and only those who go over it precisely (*akribōs diexiousin*) will notice all the fine detail.** The wisest counselor, the former student continues, sometimes takes too long to arrive at a political point that even an inexperienced speaker could quickly make his audience understand, so he advises his teacher to be more explicit about what motivated his *logos* in the first place, for the sake of both Athenian and Spartan readers.††

This lack of directness is a marked problem with graphic rhetoric, which diffuses across time as the duration of its composition is drawn further and further out. Isocrates also needs to revise his writings to better suit the culturally diverse audience he hopes to reach. He recognizes that if he wants a *logos* on comparative politics to circulate widely, he must alter it; hence the anxiety that prompts him to call over his former students in the first place.‡‡ Spartans will read Isocrates not looking for advice on how to conduct their lives—they are too steeped in their own traditions for that—but to enjoy his rich treatment of their greatest deeds and exploits.§§ As it currently stands, however, *Panathenaicus* will

---

*Isocrates, *Panathenaicus*, §231–232.

†Isocrates, *Panathenaicus*, §233.

‡Isocrates, *Panathenaicus*, §245.

§Isocrates, *Panathenaicus*, §237.

**Isocrates, *Panathenaicus*, §246. At *Phaedrus* 264c, Phaedrus seems flattered that Socrates thinks Phaedrus can precisely (*akribōs*) discern Lysias's reasons for arranging his *logos* as he does.

††Isocrates, *Panathenaicus*, §248.

‡‡Isocrates acknowledges his two audiences at *Panathenaicus* §240, when he writes of a "double *logos* [*logous amphibolous*]."

§§Isocrates, *Panathenaicus*, §250, §253.

receive a mixed reception. Most Spartan readers will hate Isocrates, but the most sensible—who already have read and are amazed at certain *logoi* of his—will wrestle with it for a time, see the praise of Spartan achievements as justified, and come to charitably classify the barbs as misguided rather than deserving of hate.* If Isocrates's account of his former pupil's account can be relied upon, it seems Isocratean *logoi* did travel and receive hospitality in distant lands, something speeches delivered in and tailored to the Athenian assembly, for instance, could not do. Isocrates's graphic, philoponic rhetoric, then, has international currency. His words truly have cross-cultural political dimension and appeal.

The former student expresses confidence that Isocrates will achieve immortality, not the divine kind but that which lives on as a memory in those who are to come.† He will achieve that status not by burning or suppressing the *logos* under discussion but by revising and supplementing it before giving it to those who desire it and finally benefiting from all the time and pains spent upon its completion.‡ The spirit of Athens's political culture, too, will get a lift from it, even if Isocrates's competitors do not fully see that their work compares even less favorably to Isocrates's than Homer's imitators to his.§ Isocrates's other assembled students receive their predecessor's assessments with fervor, not able to emend any of his emendations.** The old man himself praises his former charge's "natural endowment" and "care" but says absolutely nothing about the accuracy of his judgments.†† That Isocrates does not chastise him, though, says something in and of itself, given that Isocrates did not hold back the first time his former student aired criticisms.

Isocrates incorporates this second round of editing into his text, which, he narrates, ended up taking three years to assume the form readers now see. It was not editorial queasiness, however, that caused the publication lag time but rather something more closely resembling actual queasiness.‡‡ A nasty illness, the sort that snatches up even the youngest and most fit, hit Isocrates hard, but he maintained his increasingly famous "*philoponia* [labor-love]."§§ Any time he did waver, friends who "had read many times the part of my *logos* that I had written up implored me and advised not to abandon it half-finished or put an

---

*Isocrates, *Panathenaicus*, §250–251.

†Isocrates, *Panathenaicus*, §260.

‡Isocrates, *Panathenaicus*, §262.

§Isocrates, *Panathenaicus*, §263.

**Isocrates, *Panathenaicus*, §264.

††Isocrates, *Panathenaicus*, §265.

‡‡Thucydides fell ill during the composition of his *History*. See Butler, *The Matter of the Page*, 28–36.

§§Isocrates, *Panathenaicus*, §267.

end to it altogether, but to work a little bit longer and apply my mind to what remained."* A sensible man, he allows himself to be persuaded by their pleas, even though he is in such a state that someone else in his place would not only refuse to write his own *logos* but would not act as a hearer to one "worked out" and "turned out" by another.†

Why, if everything turned out well in the end, would someone with such a tale of suffering, strain, and sickness want it represented in his final *logos?* Why, if it bears no resemblance to Isocrates's actual process, would he produce such a fiction? Isocrates reflects on this curiosity he has done plenty to nurture. In publicizing his numerous writing difficulties, he has made visible how a *logos* develops and has praised those readers and listeners (*tōn akroatōn*) who deem such *logoi* more serious (*spoudaioterous*), philosophical (*philosophōterous*), instructional (*didaskalikous*), and artistic (*technikous*) than words recorded for merely epideictic or agonistic purposes.‡ Isocrates demystifies his writing process not to reform skimmers who do an injustice to careful writing but to pitch his views against those who claim that writing is easy and ineffectual. The length of his *logos* and the harrowing composition narrative it contains evidence a clear awareness of the demands of textuality when it is done right and directed toward a public purpose. It also affords a view of how extensive and collaborative an editorial process can be: students, scribes, and friends helped Isocrates, offering assistance, correction, and encouragement.

Rhetoric Hardens: Demosthenes, Aeschines, Aristotle, Anaximenes

Isocrates was far from the only Athenian to apply his rhetorical artistry to the big picture. The most complete speech-sets surviving from the middle of the fourth century originate from ambassadorial activity that included Demosthenes and Aeschines, both of whom Athenians selected to negotiate with Philip on the basis of their public warnings about the threat he posed to their power in the region, even to their very *polis*. Demosthenes first spoke out in the Athenian assembly against Philip in 351 B.C.E.—the so-called First Philippic—and Demosthenes reports that Aeschines claimed to be the very first to rouse the assembly against Philip, though that speech has not survived.§ As mentioned, in 347 and again in 346 Athenian ambassadors petitioned Philip for peace, ultimately

---

*Isocrates, *Panathenaicus*, §268.
†Isocrates, *Panathenaicus*, §270.
‡Isocrates, *Panathenaicus*, §271. *Akouein* can mean to listen or to read. In his study of that verb, Dirk Schenkeveld cautions scholars not "to detect everywhere in the fifth and fourth century signs of oral culture." Schenkeveld, "Prose Usages of Ἀκούειν 'To Read,'" 138.
§Demosthenes, *On the False Embassy*, §10.

coming to terms more favorable to Macedon than to Athens. Uneasy about the agreement but unable to indict Aeschines promptly of flagrant wrongdoing, Demosthenes finally prosecuted Aeschines for *parapresbia* (embassy misconduct) in 343.

For a decade and a half, Demosthenes and Aeschines traded insult-dense oratory, pulling considerable invective energy from each other's purported rhetorical methods, mistakes, and miscalculations. Occasionally, an insult contained in one speech was so devastating that whatever prompted it is missing in the other, evidence of someone's editorial judgment at work, perhaps before the speech circulated on papyrus around mid-fourth-century Athens but perhaps long after.* In a speech dispensing with Timarchus, an early co-accuser with Demosthenes, Aeschines claims that "what I say is manifest and not fabricated [*enarges esti kai ou peplasmenon*]."† His speech merely puts into words what everyone sees; it does not use hidden arts to manipulate and manage matters. Demosthenes, on the other hand, is a *technitou logōn*, a craftsman of words, and a sophist.‡ Aeschines begins his defense against the *parapresbia* charge by immediately asking his fellow citizens to be mindful of "the arts and preparations [*tas technas kai tas kataskeuas*]" of his accuser, words that emphasize Demosthenes's rhetorical craft and craftiness.§ Aeschines teases Demosthenes for embarrassing himself during the first embassy to Philip: for all his rhetorical provisions, Demosthenes is ill-equipped for public service. During the journey to Philip, Demosthenes promised "founts of words" that would rush over Philip, sweeping him up without resistance.** So much did Demosthenes gush that word of his prowess—or just of his hyperbole (the Greek here is wonderfully ambiguous)—had reached even Philip's court.†† Being the youngest ambassador, Demosthenes spoke last. Allegedly he was so flustered by the lack of novel arguments available to him that he stuttered, fell silent, received some encouragement from Philip himself, started again, departed utterly from what he had written (*tōn gegrammenōn*), and broke down beyond recovery.‡‡ Across speeches, Aeschines calls Demosthenes a *logographos,* an accusation referring to Demosthenes writing out his own speeches before delivering them or writing speeches for others to deliver.§§ Taken together, the insults suggest Demosthenes speaks

---

*See, e.g., Aeschines, *Embassy,* §10.

†Aeschines, *Against Timarchus,* §128.

‡Aeschines, *Against Timarchus,* §170, §125, §175.

§Aeschines, *Embassy,* §1, see also §4.

**Aeschines, *Embassy,* §21.

††Aeschines, *Embassy,* §34.

‡‡Aeschines, *Embassy,* §35.

§§See, e.g., Aeschines, *Against Ctesiphon,* §173.

with confidence only when he is able to prepare his words in writing first and the situation does not shift beneath his un-spry rhetorical feet.

For his part, Demosthenes mocks Aeschines's background as a bit-part actor who has memorized many lines from tragedies and recites them within his speeches, for effect.* Demosthenes submits as evidence that Aeschines himself is a "logographer and sophist" an occasion when Aeschines crowed some obscure lines from Euripides and avoided reciting lines from Sophocles's *Antigone*, lines Aeschines himself had delivered on stage and that would have served as a reminder of the comportment his fellow citizens expected of him during the embassy.† "Are you not then a sophist? Yes, and a good-for-nothing one, at that. Are you not then a logographer? Yes, and one hateful to the gods, too. That with which you so often competed and knew precisely, you passed right over, and you sought that which in your life you never delivered and brought it into the middle of things to mislead your fellow citizens."‡ In preparing to speak, Aeschines ostensibly read all sorts of drama with which he was not familiar, seeking a few lines of verse that could justify his poor choices. Had Aeschines stuck with what he knew well—stayed on script, as it were—he might have avoided deviance.§

Though accounts of the editorial efforts Demosthenes expended on his public words antedate him considerably, he seems to have had a reputation in his own time for excessive preparation.** In a trial tucked into the long battle with Aeschines and usually dated to 348 B.C.E., Demosthenes prosecutes Meidias for attacking him while Demosthenes was serving in a public office. Near the end of the *logos*, Demosthenes predicts Meidias will call him a *rhētōr* in the hope that the jury will take it to be a dirty word.†† Demosthenes reckons Meidias will also say "that what I say to you now has been all planned out and prepared beforehand [*eskemmena kai pareskeuasmena panta*]. That I have planned it out [*eskephthai*], o men of Athens, I freely say, and I do not deny it, or to have spent all possible care [*memeletēkenai*] on it. For surely I would be pitiful if the experiences and happenings that have befallen me left me careless of what I was going to say about them to you. Yet it is Meidias who really wrote my speech:

---

*Demosthenes, *On the False Embassy*, §245.

†Demosthenes, *On the False Embassy*, §246–248.

‡Demosthenes, *On the False Embassy*, §250.

§See Duncan, *Performance and Identity in the Classical World*, 58–89, and Worman, *Abusive Mouths in Classical Athens*, 213–274.

**Plutarch, *Moralia, Precepts of Statecraft*, 802e–f: the speech of a statesman "must not, as Putheas said of that of Demosthenes, stink of the lamp and sophistical over-elaboration, with pointed arguments and periods perfected by rule and compass." See also Plutarch, *Demosthenes*, §8.

††Demosthenes, *Against Meidias*, §189.

for he who has supplied the very deeds necessitating these arguments most fittingly bears that responsibility, not the one who planned, no, not the one who cared about this case being spoken now."* Demosthenes's preparation and care are signs of respect, for his fellow citizens, for their laws, and for himself. Demosthenes quickly shifts attention, however, to the author of the whole doing: Meidias. It is Meidias's scheming rather than Demosthenes's planning that should put his fellow Athenians on guard.

Against Meidias is a succulent (and truculent) example of the difficulty of discerning how much extant speech-texts resemble their orally delivered counterparts. There remains no consensus about how much Demosthenes may have edited it for textual publication or about whether he delivered an earlier, ear-focused form *at all.*† The ninth-century Byzantine bibliophile Photius estimated *Against Meidias* "to have been left in a solid form, but not thoroughly cleaned up for [or before] publication [*dio kai tines ephēsan heskeron logon en tupois kataleiphthēnai, alla mē pros ekdosin diakekatharthai*]."‡ Scholars have long presumed that Demosthenes would have tidied and tightened any text intended for public circulation and that a polished text would look—and sound—a particular way.

An exact contemporary of Demosthenes, Aristotle ventured south to Athens in 367 B.C.E. to study with Plato. After Plato died, Aristotle returned north and tutored Alexander, venturing back to Athens in 335, after Philip died. Aristotle regularly met with students in the *peripatos* (covered walkway) of the Lyceum, a public sanctuary just outside the city, featuring a gymnasium and a grove and thought for while to have contained Aristotle's extensive personal library.§ Though Aristotle wrote dialogues ancient readers deemed delightful, none survive, and he is not known for any forms of orality other than instruction and conversation.** For centuries, people have read Aristotle not to learn his manner but to learn the matter upon which he concentrated his classificatory powers.††

---

*Demosthenes, *Against Meidias,* §191–192.

†For a summary of the arguments and evidence, see Harris, "Demosthenes' Speech against Meidias."

‡Photius, *Biblotheca,* 491a–b. *Tupos* is often used of molds and statues and other material forms.

§For the little we know about the Lyceum at this time, see Hendrickson, "The Invention of the Greek Library," 377–379.

**Cicero, *Epistulae Ad Fam.,* 1.9.13; Cicero, *Academica,* 2.119. See, however, the reconstruction of Aristotle's fragmented dialogue, *Protrepticus,* undertaken by Hutchinson and Johnson.

††Innes observes, however, that "even in his textbooks he can on occasion rise to a more formal level, and we then find a greater smoothness, with little or no hiatus and clearly articulated short units with antithesis and balance." See Innes, "Aristotle: The Written and Performative Styles," 164.

Within his *Rhetoric* and *Poetics,* though, he explores matter (*logos, muthos*) *and* manner (*lexis*), since "it does not suffice to have something to say only, but it is necessary also to say it in the right way, and this contributes greatly to the speech [*ton logon*] seeming to be of a certain kind."* The textual variants of *Rhetoric* and *Poetics* that we possess make cross-references; for example, Aristotle points readers of his *Rhetoric* to *Poetics* for further discussion of metaphor and readers of his *Poetics* to his *Rhetoric* for further discussion of *dianoia* (thought).† The commonalities do not stop there.

Writing appears explicitly in this third book of the *Rhetoric* when Aristotle names and describes a *lexis graphikē* (written style).‡ Richard Graff has argued that the very naming of such a style is an "indicator of the generally bookish character of Aristotle's style theory and the *Rhetoric* as a whole."§ The distinctive property of the written style is *akribeia* (precision), the pursuit of which Alcidamas had deemed pathetically inappropriate to rhetors engaged in public struggles.** Isocrates used the word in *Panathenaicus* to describe careful writing *and* reading. *Akribeia,* then, has not just a textual tinge but an editorial one, too. Precision requires working and reworking written words. Aristotle connects the quality to the epideictic genre, whose required graphic preparations Plato had mocked in *Menexenus.*

Several poets and rhetors discussed in this chapter brought attention to themselves as writers, and Aristotle addresses the matter of revealing one's compositional labors. In *Rhetoric,* Aristotle advises that "one should try to escape notice when writing, and not to seem to speak artificially [*peplasmenōs*] but naturally."†† When they notice artifice, people become resentful, thinking they are being cheated or schemed. Alcidamas had made a similar warning.‡‡ Aristotle credits Euripides with being the first and finest to counteract his artistry by using everyday speech. In *Poetics,* Aristotle advises tragedians to keep out of their plays, since their intervention risks disturbing the *mimēsis* that their entire art is meant to structure and support.§§ Aristotle may have offered different advice in his second book-roll of the *Poetics,* which treated comedy and does not survive. It was comedy that showed poets at work, even *the* poet himself at

---

*Aristotle, *Rhetoric,* 1403b15–18. It seems to have occurred only to the Romans to stress that there is no such thing as a how-less what or a say without a way.

†For more on explicit cross-references see Kirby, "Aristotle's *Poetics:* The Rhetorical Principle," and Kirby, "Toward a Rhetoric of Poetics: Rhetor as Author and Narrator."

‡Aristotle, *Rhetoric,* 1413b4–5, 1414a5–17.

§Graff, "Reading and the 'Written' Style in Aristotle's *Rhetoric,*" 20.

**Aristotle, *Rhetoric,* 1413b9, 13.

††Aristotle, *Rhetoric,* 1404b18–19.

‡‡Alcidamas, *On the Writers,* §13.

§§Aristotle, *Poetics,* 1460a5–8.

work, as in Cratinus's *Wineflask*. The representation of poetic work makes audiences aware that they are seeing the result of artifice, jolting them out of their mimetic immersion and into a mode of critical evaluation. Poets who show their work—especially themselves working—are prepared to be judged for it.

The only other fourth-century rhetorical treatise to survive is the *Rhetorica ad Alexandrum* (the Alexander being the Great one). Though attributed to Aristotle during some points of its circulation, the rhetorical treatise has settled onto the shoulders of Anaximenes of Lampsacus. The criticism piled on them by several generations of scholars has been considerable.* It is only in the past decade that rhetoricians have taken an eager interest in *Rhetorica ad Alexandrum*.† Pierre Chiron, a champion of the humble treatise, dates it to 340 B.C.E., just before Macedon defeated Athens at Chaeronea.‡ Not much is known about Anaximenes. He seems to have tutored Alexander—when, in relation to Aristotle, is unclear—and written histories even while traveling with Alexander on campaign. According to the much-later Plutarch, Anaximenes joined Isocrates's famous pupils, Theopompus and Ephorus, in writing heavily rhetorical battlefield speeches with long periods, when, really, "no one is so foolish when near the iron."§

Toward the end of the treatise, Anaximenes provides rejoinders to several preparation-related accusations a speaker could face during judicial proceedings, including speaking from a manuscript, being trained in speaking, and coaching others in speech or outright composing speeches for them. Generally, Anaximenes recommends irony.** His leading examples pertain to the first two charges. The first response borders on the tedious: it is not illegal to speak from a written speech or from an unwritten one.†† The second steps up the snark: "Say also that 'my opponent thinks that he has done such a serious wrong that he does not think I could do a prosecution speech worthily unless I wrote it out and examined it for a long time.'"‡‡ It is a dodge, of course, but it also invites the jury to attribute to the speaker's opponent a complex nefariousness. The third

---

*See, e.g., Cope, *An Introduction to Aristotle's Rhetoric with Analysis, Notes, and Appendices*, 402.

†See the special issue of *Rhetorica* dedicated to *Rhetorica ad Alexandrum* and edited by Chiron. See Timmerman and Schiappa, *Classical Greek Rhetorical Theory and the Disciplining of Discourse*, 115–136, for a summary of critical dismissals and reasons to regard the text not as a rhetorical handbook but as a treatise on argumentation that can teach us a lot about the mid-fourth century B.C.E.

‡Chiron, "Relative Dating of the *Rhetoric to Alexander* and Aristotle's *Rhetoric*," 240.

§Plutarch, *Moralia, Precepts about Statecraft*, 803b.

**[Aristotle], *Rhetoric to Alexander*, §37.

††[Aristotle], *Rhetoric to Alexander*, §37.

‡‡[Aristotle], *Rhetoric to Alexander*, §38.

sounds very much like Demosthenes in *Against Meidias*: Anaximenes encourages those thought "to study and show care for speaking [*legein manthanein kai meletan*]" not to deny it and to insist that the only reason the litigation is under way is that the opponent is woefully unskilled in speech but plenty sneaky with the law.* Regarding the accusation of assisting others with their speaking, Anaximenes suggests "point[ing] out that everyone else, as much as he is able, helps friends by teaching and advising."† Such a reframing makes the giving of assistance seem common and socially motivated instead of rare (and thus meriting attention) and mercenary.

While it is certain that what was happening within and without Athens at a given time affected the verbal options of the major players featured here, it is questionable to consider textual polish primarily—and maybe even at all—as a reaction to a bad political situation. Throughout the fifth and fourth centuries, as poets and rhetors responded to the affordances of writing, they presented audiences and readers with a variety of forms ready for easy comparison and thus rank order. The body recommended itself as a critical thematic and schematic, because it can sustain dismemberment into small parts (*kōla*, limbs, for instance) or stay whole as an evaluable unit with an overall shape and state of fitness. Poets, in particular, pursued connections between writing bodies and their respective bodies of work, but Isocrates, too, purported to adjust the vigor and rhythm of his *Panathenaicus* to suit his increasingly feeble body.

Appellations such as "golden age" or "classical age" valorize the Athens of the period from the 490s, when Athens and Sparta overpowered the Persians, to 323, when Alexander died. Isocrates lived less than a year beyond the publication of *Panathenaicus,* perhaps electing to starve to death upon learning of Athens's defeat by Macedon at Chaeronea in 338. Joining Isocrates in suicide in 322, Demosthenes is usually considered the last "canonical" Attic speaker-writer, though Cicero sneaks in Demetrius of Phalerum, whom I present in the next chapter. Aristotle left Athens upon the announcement of Alexander's death, in 323, and to escape charges of impiety, dying of natural causes a year later. Alexander had stretched Hellenic dominion from northern Africa to current-day Afghanistan, placing a superstructure of cultural unity atop hundreds of cities and towns and establishing many new ones. The result, known to the Greeks as *hē oikoumenē* (the inhabited world), held together through various means of association, a variant of the Greek language known as *koinē* ("common") being a vital one.

---

*[Aristotle], *Rhetoric to Alexander,* §39.
†[Aristotle], *Rhetoric to Alexander,* §42.

The period subsequent to Alexander's death is known as "Hellenistic," from the German *hellenistisch*. Johann Gustav Droysen, who coined the name in the nineteenth century, did not seem to intend it as a slight, but many accounts of the Hellenistic period view it as a lesser, diminished, and derivative form of what proceeded it.* Given that so many rhetors who came to be classified as preeminent died as Athens lost power, it is easy to see how historians could regard the Hellenistic period with dejection, if not outright hostility. Alan Cameron has observed that "modern scholars have often posited a radical discontinuity between Hellenistic and earlier Greek culture—whence (they assume) all that editing, classifying and canonizing of what were now perceived as classics." He argues that Hellenistic-age writers and organizers did not view themselves as living through a "postclassical age" devoid of its own merits; that is, the kind of editorial work for which they are usually acknowledged did not reflect some kind of preservation zeal born of nostalgia and self-pity.† It is precisely because the Hellenistic period is associated with editing of the textual management kind that I attend to editing as the polishing of one's own written words in the next chapter.

---

*Droysen, *Geschichte des Hellenismus.*
†Cameron, *Callimachus and His Critics,* 27–28.

CHAPTER TWO

HELLENISTIC GLOSS

The Hellenistic age is best known as bookish. Indeed, it is probably clichéd to call that designation clichéd. When mentioned in the Hellenistic context, editing typically references the management of all those book-rolls, namely their collection, collation, and correction. Labors of unification and integration reconcile conflicting and conflicted copies, resulting in attempts at authoritative "editions" of the big names.* Item by item, the first lists of selected poets, orators, and philosophers advance. Acknowledging the significance of those organizational energies, Tim Whitmarsh orients his entire account of ancient Greek literature around the informational concept of the archive, tracing "the emergence (in fifth-century Athens), the building (in Ptolemaic Alexandria), and the manipulation (in Roman Greece) of an archival sensibility" that conjured from a plurality of texts written in Greek but across forms and dialects and centuries a notion of cultural unity.† Some Hellenistic writers broadcast their archivist inclinations. A now fragmentary work of the third century B.C.E., the *Grapheion* of Callimachus, could have been "a collection of epigrams on poets," or "a kind of literary criticism of poets," or "a work of a literary-historical nature."‡ Whatever it was, its title translates to *Registry* or *Archive*. The archival attitude and infrastructure of the Hellenistic period systematically preserved and perpetuated much of the textual material we possess about Greek culture before the Macedonian rise. Because of the predominance of this managerial kind of editorial focus, I see all the more reason to focus on the kinds of polishing practices used by writers of the period on their own texts.

It seems that, for the most part, book-rolls featuring words *conceived* during the Hellenistic age largely ceased being copied when the dominant textual

---

*There is still disagreement about what a Hellenistic *ekdosis* (edition) referred to, exactly, and what method an "editor" would have used to arrive at one. See Montanari, "From Book to Edition."

†Whitmarsh, *Ancient Greek Literature,* 227. Parentheses *sic.*

‡Trypanis, "Note," 231.

format changed from book-roll to codex in the second century C.E.* Earlier enthusiasms for Attic texts and for the dialect itself may be responsible. Such zeal registered in the Atticist movement of the mid-first century B.C.E., extended through the so-called Second Sophistic, and grew in strength during the Byzantine period.† It is one of history's many cruel ironies that Hellenistic copies of "classical" texts made those successive periodic vogues possible. As a result, none of the Hellenistic period's own oratory and little of its own poetry and philosophy survive. Several generations of modern scholars figured the material must have been deemed too inferior to merit copying, and that conclusion enabled a cascade of dismissiveness.‡ Poets and rhetoricians of the time have been cast as little more than the critical or deferential readers, organizers, and imitators of their predecessors. Reputationally, at least, philosophers have fared a little better, since the Peripatetic, Stoic, Academic, Cynic, and Epicurean schools continued to differentiate and define themselves during this time. When the twilight of democratic Athens specifically is seen as the end of the vibrant public life of the ancient *polis* generally, it becomes easy to imagine writers of all kinds—having been cut off from public roles and responsibilities—hunched and hushed over book-rolls and producing "new" work that was highly allusive at best, derivative at worst. The infamous fastidiousness of Hellenistic word-workers suggests they compensated for their subpar talents with superior efforts or that their talents could not flourish in conditions of diminished public life.

Scholarship of the past few decades has pressed hard on all of those assumptions and evaluations. Calling this chapter "Hellenistic Gloss," I fix attention on the stylistic sheen and so-called scholarly apparatuses of Hellenistic word-workers, just as scholars derisive toward those characteristics have done. Whereas they detect democratic decay, however, I see a continuation of commitments outlined in the previous chapter, and in political conditions less restrictive of public verbal activity than once thought. The two figures central to the first part of this chapter are Demetrius of Phalerum (c. 350–280 B.C.E.), a deme of Athens, and Callimachus of Cyrene (c. 310–240 B.C.E.), in northern Africa, both of whom practiced a learned aesthetic that polished or peeled away verbal roughness and, in Callimachus's case, reduced redundancy. Demetrius and Callimachus spent time in the northern African *polis* of Alexandria, a city founded by one of Alexander's generals and celebrated as a hub of Hellenistic culture. Demetrius is best known for his Peripatetic training and for his decade-long

---

*Callimachus's *Hecale* is one of the exceptions, since it was "read, copied, paraphrased and commented on up to the thirteenth century A.D." (Trypanis, "Note," 178).

†I return to the mid-first century B.C.E. neo-Atticist movement in the next chapter.

‡For a full account and redress, see Cameron, *Callimachus and His Critics*.

oversight of Athens, Callimachus for his polymetric poetry and his attempt to take stock of the entirety of Greek textual culture. It is no longer thought that Demetrius instructed Ptolemy II Philadelphus on the construction of the Alexandrian library or that Callimachus served a term as its head librarian.* Still, both of them read and wrote and presented themselves in public extensively, activities credited for the polish for which they are independently recognized. I highlight the editorial efforts—reducing, refining—they put into their own to-be-published work, rather than that which they devoted to preparing editions of the texts of others.

The abundance of extant writing-about-writing from the fifth and fourth centuries enables one to work within the limits of verse and prose original to the period. By contrast, one builds arguments about the textual culture of the Hellenistic period from a later excerpt or allusion here, an odd papyrus scrap there.† Evidence about Demetrius's book-rolls comes from much later writers. Moving into Roman texts is therefore unavoidable, and they contain critical assessments rather than excerpts. Cicero, for instance, communicates his ardent admiration for Demetrius in both his rhetorical and philosophical works, giving his impressions of Demetrius's usefulness to aspiring Roman orators and rightful place in the history of rhetoric's development. Of Callimachus's *corpus,* at least, parts remain, from quotations in the work of later writers to legible words on discarded papyrus strips. It is plain that Callimachus developed the physiological vocabulary of earlier writers, especially Aristophanes, to establish his own poetic program. Callimachus's poems and poetics shaped the projects of Roman poets such as Catullus, Propertius, Vergil, Horace, and Ovid.‡ The smoothness of Demetrius and Callimachus did not result from their sticking their noses into books because they were unwelcome elsewhere. Both had public profiles from which Roman writers learned and borrowed.

The swath of time between Callimachus and Cicero saw an unknown number of book-rolls from all manner of contributors to culture, most of them lost completely or absorbed by later writers.§ Moving into second-century Roman texts, which are also incomplete, affords a view of writers given places of honor

---

*See Bagnall, "Alexandria: Library of Dreams," 349–351, and Hendrickson, "The Invention the Greek Library." A papyrus list of librarians was found in the garbage heap at Oxyrhynchus.

†We do have the entirety of some version of Apollonius of Rhodes's epic, *Argonautica.*

‡For an overview of "Roman Callimachus," see Barchiesi, "Roman Callimachus."

§For overviews of rhetoric during this period, see Pernot, *Rhetoric in Antiquity,* 57–82; Walker, *Rhetoric and Poetics in Antiquity,* 45–70; Kremmydas and Tempest (eds.), *Hellenistic Oratory;* Porter (ed.), *Handbook of Classical Rhetoric in the Hellenistic Period 330 B.C.–A.D. 400.*

in first-century genealogies of Roman rhetoric and poetics but described as rough. The two writers upon whom I focus are the orator Cato Maior and the poet Gaius Ennius Lucilius. My readings suggest that neither Cato nor Lucilius were as atechnical and harsh as some later Romans made them out to be, but neither of them relished compositions smoothed down to the level of the clause. The latter part of this chapter turns to the oldest surviving Roman rhetorical handbook to cover all five *partes* of rhetoric, the unknown *auctor's Rhetorica ad Herennium.* However one marks the boundaries of the Hellenistic period, Roman rhetorical education was thoroughly Hellenistic in its structure and much of its contents.* The handbook offers a compression and Romanization of native Hellenistic texts and teachings that have disappeared. Of particular interest is the *auctor's* approach to stylistic categorization within the fourth book-roll of *Rhetorica ad Herennium,* wherein he draws upon the body language that had been one of rhetoric's central creative and critical metaphors since the take-up of the papyrus book-roll in fifth-century Attica. As textual culture continued to accumulate, polishing and pressing written words came to be forms of the management of plentitude across rhetoric and poetics, across oratory and poetry, and across types of prose style.

Polis *Power in the Hellenistic Period*

Discerning what "political" (relating to the *polis*) and "democratic" (relating to the power of the people) denote in the Hellenistic period is not uncomplicated. But it is precisely the assumption that such terms are meaningless in the period that has been offered as an explanation for why no Hellenistic-age oratory survives: oratory flourishes in democracies only, the Hellenistic age was undemocratic, ergo there were no speeches worth preserving. Quality oratory—public speech that could *do* something and sound great, too—died with Demosthenes. The same goes for poetry. The so-called Old Comedy of democratic Athens took on matters of civic substance, and boldly. The survival of paltry bits of poetry native to the Hellenistic period is marshaled as evidence that its verses turned inward on themselves, growing increasingly metapoetic and myopic. Such smallness was deemed unworthy of preservation by later copiers and editors.

---

*Starting and ending points for historical periods are scholarly impositions that become a matter of consensus. That the Hellenistic period begins with the death of Alexander in 323 is a clean enough claim, but establishing where it ends is less so. Because Cleopatra was of the Ptolemaic line, her suicide is the usual endpoint, but one could argue that the Hellenistic period ended when Rome conquered Macedon in 148 B.C.E. One could also argue that the Hellenistic period continued during Roman domination and threaded into the Byzantine.

The best place to start troubling those assumptions is Athens. Any insistence that Athens's Macedon-forced transition from full democracy dimmed the light of the *polis* across the grid of Greece betrays not only an Athenocentrism but also a simplification of complex circumstances preserved in fragmented form, whatever medium one chooses to investigate. Those looking for something redeeming about Athens's nosedive from its pedestal note that Athens's loss of full autonomy—as well as that of Thebes and other super-*poleis*—made for a different distribution of influence across Greece and Asia Minor, and one that served smaller *poleis* well. The democratic Athens of the so-called classical period could be brutal in its subjugation and exploitation of less powerful *poleis,* an ugly and recurrent dynamic of the twenty-six-year-long Peloponnesian War. Some rhetoricians have dealt with the perceived democratic lull by pointing toward the development of the genres and protocols of ambassadorial and epistolary rhetoric, through which the powerful were addressed and petitioned.*

Increasingly, however, scholars of the Hellenistic period are challenging the decline narrative of Athenian democracy and of democracy as a constitutional form across Greece during this time and of the *polis* itself.† Even those, such as Paul Cartledge, who cannot bring themselves to surrender declinist language concede that "the life of democracy in the Hellenistic period presents much scope for interpretive confusion."‡ There is a great deal of time and land to cover, and epigraphy from the period has often been passed over for textual evidence from later periods. The essential point, which even Cartledge endorses, is that the *polis* as a unit of governmental and communal organization "retained its legitimacy and vitality" throughout the Hellenistic period.§ That seems to be so from the beginning of Macedon's management of the rest of Greece. A term of the League of Corinth designed by Philip after Chaeronea and honored by Alexander was permission for all involved *poleis* to maintain the constitutions they had; Athens, therefore, remained a democracy. Macedon established garrisons in several *poleis* but not in Athens (until 322, about which more later). In terms of control over its internal policies and practices, Athens remained democratic, though qualifications for inclusion in the *dēmos* fluctuated. Athens could no longer enlarge its dominion, and some of its interstate relations required Macedonian approval, but that check on Athenian autonomy ought not to be mistaken

*See, e.g., Walker, *Rhetoric and Poetics in Antiquity,* 45–55; Pernot, *Rhetoric in Antiquity,* 67, 120, 190. Demetrius's *Peri Hermēnias* (*On Style*), an early to mid-third century B.C.E. handbook, features the first attention to epistolary rhetoric (4.223–235).

†For more on Hellenistic democracy in general, see Grieb, *Hellenistische Demokratie.*

‡Cartledge, *Democracy,* 244. His treatment of Demetrius of Phalerum is abysmally dismissive (242).

§Cartledge, *Democracy,* 244.

for a total lack of sovereignty. As Andrew Bayliss wryly observes, it is odd that scholars should think Athens ceased to be a democracy just because it could no longer be "an expansionist, imperialist state."* Abundant inscriptions marking decisions made by the *dēmos* suggests that "democracy was a customary form of political organization" in *poleis* across Greece and Asia Minor during the Hellenistic period until the rise of Rome.† Eric Gruen maintains that inscriptions "document a sense of civic pride in the community, a locus of loyalty that continued to be centered in the polis."‡ Of the super-*poleis* of Greece, Josiah Ober estimates that they saw a "political fall" but that their fall was contemporaneous with the "robust persistence of economic growth, federalism, and democracy in a transformed ecology of city-states."§ These substantial revisions to the traditional understanding of the Hellenistic period put Demetrius of Phalerum and Callimachus in contexts not antithetical to democracy or to the power of the *polis* as an organizer of identity and agency.

The situation across northern Africa, the location of the monarchical Alexandria, differed politically, but cities boasted distinctive and agentive civic cultures that were celebrated and perpetuated during festivals and contests. Attempts to place Callimachus in context, for instance, have emphasized his participation in the construction or further enrichment of site-based tales, probably for civic festivals and competitions. What were previously categorized by scholars as obscure geographical details and glosses in Callimachus are now being read as keen attention to local traditions and origin tales that give pride of place to places other than super-*poleis*. As Benjamin Acosta-Hughes and Susan Stephens put it provocatively, that level of detail "is pedantic—if by pedantry we mean interest in people, places, and events not familiar in Athenian texts (or to us) though relevant to the world in which he lived and celebrated."** The makers of subsequent celebratory poetry and oratory could pull from his verses, continuing a verbal strain unique to and evocative of that place. Callimachus also endowed Alexandria with a civic topography that, being newly founded and before that probably a military installation, it did not have.†† The old belief that Callimachus wrote "for the book rather than fellow citizens" seems insupportable.‡‡ A lot of

---

*Bayliss, *After Demosthenes*, 1.

†Carlsson, *Hellenistic Democracies*, 17. Richard Leo Enos has urged rhetoricians to take a keener interest in Athenian epigraphy. See Enos, "Writing without Paper: A Study of Functional Rhetoric in Ancient Athens."

‡Gruen, "The Polis in the Hellenistic World," 345.

§Ober, *The Rise and Fall of Classical Greece*, 262.

**Acosta-Hughes and Stephens, *Callimachus in Context*, 203.

††Acosta-Hughes and Stephens, *Callimachus in Context*, 163–168.

‡‡Cameron, *Callimachus and His Critics*, ix

presiding assumptions about Hellenistic *poleis* and democracies have been challenged in the past twenty years. Reevaluations of major figures of the period are
increasingly available, and mine pairs the revised view of Hellenistic decline
with an orator and a poet whose editorial smoothness was deemed by earlier
scholars to be emblematic of the fallenness of public life.

In the Middle: Demetrius of Phalerum

Demetrius grew up in the echoes of Demosthenes, and not only of Demosthenes's major speeches. The noise of the sea roaring and breaking at Phalerum
offered Demosthenes an acoustic environment analogous to the din of a crowd,
and there he was known to have strengthened his projection and stamina.* The
two were contemporaries, though far enough apart in age to have grown up in
different political conditions; Demosthenes grew up in an Athens that had been
subdued by Sparta, Demetrius in an Athens subdued by Macedon. From opposite directions, then, Demetrius and Athens toddled together toward awkward
semiautonomy: Athens lost to Macedon at Chaeronea in 338, when Demetrius
was nearly a teenager. Aristotle returned to Athens a few years later, lecturing
regularly in the Lyceum. There is wide agreement in ancient sources that Demetrius was a student of Aristotle's student, Theophrastus, a dimension of Demetrius's way with words to which I return later.†

Meanwhile, Demosthenes, Hyperides, and Demetrius's brother, Himeraeus,
spoke out against what they perceived to be Macedon's stranglehold on Athenian freedom. Alexander's death, in 323, and the subsequent disarray in the
Macedonian ranks catalyzed the rhetors' rebellious energy: Athenians joined
with other unsatisfied Greek *poleis* to challenge Macedonians in what is called
the Lamian War.‡ They lost badly. The victorious general, Antipater, with whom
Aristotle was friendly, summoned each state to talk terms. Demetrius served in
the Athenian embassy that negotiated peace with Antipater, who was determined
to be more meddlesome in internal Athenian affairs than his predecessors had

---

*Cicero, *De Finibus*, 5.2.5.

†Demetrius may have purchased a parcel of land for a school upon Aristotle's death, in
322, something that non-Athenians would not have been able to do. Once it had land of
its own—the Lyceum was a public shrine and could not be owned or permanently occupied—a Peripatetic school could get under way. Fortenbaugh and Schütrumpf, *Demetrius
of Phalerum*, contains all the ancient sources about Demetrius of Phalerum, so I will
include references to that work alongside the ancient works. See Fortenbaugh and
Schütrumpf, *Demetrius of Phalerum*, 8 for a list of sources attesting to Demetrius's association with Theophrastus. On the parcel of land, Diogenes Laertius, *The Lives of the
Philosophers*, 5.39 (Fortenbaugh and Schütrumpf, *Demetrius of Phalerum*, 10).

‡The historical sketch here follows the broad strokes of O'Sullivan, *The Regime of Demetrius of Phalerum in Athens*, 1–44.

been. Antipater offered to restore *philia* (friendship) and shared governance, but he had conditions. Among them: the Athenians had to pay reparations, submit to a garrison in the Piraeus, limit democratic participation to property owners with an amount of yearly income beyond that of most Athenian laborers, and surrender the firebrand orators. Demosthenes took flight and killed himself when cornered, purportedly biting down on a pen he had filled with poison.[*] Demetrius, by stark contrast, found himself appointed by Cassander, Antipater's son, to oversee the administration of Athens, a position he held from 317 to 307. Aristotle had maintained his close relationship with the Macedonian court and its major figures, and that association imbued—or tainted—the early Peripatetic circle with a pro-Macedonian air. Aristotle's ties could account for the choice of Demetrius.

As Lara O'Sullivan sees Demetrius's task, "Demetrius was called upon to balance the demands of his Macedonian hegemon with the imperatives of domestic Athenian concerns."[†] How and how well he struck that balance was and remains contested, but a fixture of scholarly debates about Demetrius's administration of Athens is curiosity about the role played by his Peripatetic training. Claude Mossé describes Demetrius's leadership as a "philosophical tyranny," suggesting an undemocratic imposition of his philosophical teachings and their instantiation into law.[‡] O'Sullivan argues that Demetrius's philosophical *and* rhetorical-political prowess, "contradicting as it did the assumed conflict between the two ways of life, no doubt encouraged Demetrius's enemies to highlight his philosophical endeavors to undermine his political life. It ought not simply beguile us into seeing Demetrius as a philosopher-king."[§] Demetrius was forced from Athens when another Demetrius (Poliorcetes) claimed to restore democracy in 307. Whatever "restoration" means in this context, something about Demetrius of Phalerum or his methods of administering was unpopular with factions powerful enough to effect his ejection.

Though establishing a chronology of his works is impossible, Demetrius wrote a lot, suggesting productivity spanning several decades. Diogenes Laertius, the third-century C.E. biographer, reports in his *Life of Demetrius* that "in plentitude of book-rolls and sum of lines, he surpassed almost all the members of the Peripatos of his day; he was well-educated [*eupaideutos*] and widely

---

[*]Fortenbaugh and Schütrumpf, *Demetrius of Phalerum*, 13A and B. Demetrius's brother was present and died, too, though not by his own hand.

[†]O'Sullivan, *The Regime of Demetrius of Phalerum in Athens*, 7.

[‡]Mossé, *Athens in Decline*, 108.

[§]O'Sullivan, *The Regime of Demetrius of Phalerum in Athens*, 240. See also Gottschalk, "Demetrius of Phalerum."

experienced [*polupeiros*] beyond anyone."* Laertius provides an inventory of Demetrius's writing that spans forty-five titles and fifty-eight book-rolls, including two book-rolls *Peri rhētorikēs* (*On Rhetoric*), one *Peri kairou* (*On Kairos*), and several collections of speeches, maxims, and Aesopian fables. Demetrius also spoke a lot. Laertius writes that Demetrius, "through his speeches [*dēmēgorōn*] to the Athenians, led the city for ten years."† *Dēmēgoria* refers to public speaking in the context of mass deliberation. Demetrius is, therefore, the only Peripatetic thinker from the early days of that philosophical school to speak for the *polis* in public, administering internal democratic matters—and in consultation and deliberation with the *dēmos*, recently delimited by Antipater, though it was. And we do not have to take Laertius's chronologically distant word for it: epigraphic evidence from this period indicates that the *dēmos* maintained decision-making power.‡

None of Demetrius's own words survive. But for one line, we do not even have quotations or paraphrases of them in later writers. The line appears toward the end of *Peri Hermēneias* (typically translated *On Style*), a treatise on characteristics of style composed by yet another Demetrius. I agree with Grube, Edwards, and de Jonge that evidence internal to the work supports a composition date of the early to mid-third century B.C.E., and thus not chronologically far from Demetrius.§ In the portion of *Peri Hermēneias* about the necessity of using figured language (*schēmatos logos*) to censure someone one does not want to offend, whether a friend or a tyrant, Demetrius provides an example from the Phalerean. When the latter was received haughtily by a powerful Macedonian and treated as a suppliant rather than as an ambassador, he obliquely called out the Macedonian.** According to this account, at least, Demetrius of Phalerum could deftly manage situations of status asymmetry, and far, far away from the breezy colonnade of the Lyceum.

Copies of Demetrius's demegoric speeches may have made it as far as Cicero's time. Historical people play an important role in Ciceronian self-fashioning, which operates largely by the forging of intellectual lineages, but it is unlikely that Cicero distorted Demetrius beyond recognition by Cicero's contemporaries. Demetrius appears across works composed during Cicero's inky decade of the mid-50s through the mid-40s. That the two men had similar arcs goes far to

---

*Diogenes Laertius 5.80 (Fortenbaugh and Schütrumpf, *Demetrius of Phalerum*, 1).
†Diogenes Laertius 5.75 (Fortenbaugh and Schütrumpf, *Demetrius of Phalerum*, 1).
‡See Carlsson, *Hellenistic Democracies*.
§Grube, "The Date of Demetrius 'On Style'"; Edwards, "Dionysius and Isaeus," 48; de Jonge, Review of Nicoletta Marini. *Peri Hermēneias* was attributed to Demetrius of Phalerum for some time (and cannot be ruled out entirely).
**Demetrius, *On Style*, §289 (Fortenbaugh and Schütrumpf, *Demetrius of Phalerum*, 12).

explain Cicero's frequent appeals to him: they were born to unestablished families, were bookish, rose to political prominence marked by rhetorical excellence, were exiled, and returned to their studies since the rhythms of their days had changed. They both served their states in trying, transitional times. Though Cicero did not enumerate such parallels explicitly, it is not unreasonable to suppose he expected some readers to do so.

Cicero evaluated Demetrius's rhetorical style with critical language taking a sensual form and culminating in praise for Demetrius's polish. Demetrius held for Cicero positions of significant firsts. Cicero seemed to push against a view held by his own contemporaries that Demetrius came from an Athens whose purity of Attic diction had been compromised by foreigners. Cicero credited Demetrius with a kind of speech that is soft and sweet but also superlatively learned and polished, those first two qualities keeping the second two from being too severe. In *De Oratore* (55 B.C.E.), Cicero's version of Marcus Antonius names Demetrius and Demosthenes's nephew as the first practitioners of a style "more soft and more loose [*molliora ac remissiora*]" than that of previous generations.* Antonius pronounces Demetrius "superlatively polished [*politissimus*]," which seems to indicate a sophisticated, spacious kind of polish that presses together abundant learning rather than an etched and precious type.

In *Brutus* (46 B.C.E.), his account of eloquence's historical development, Cicero deems Demetrius "the most learned [*eruditissimus*]" of his respective contemporaries and emphasizes his emergence from the "shade of Theophrastus" rather than from the sun and sand of the forum. Cicero recounts that the name Theophrastus (Divine Speech) is a nickname admiringly given to the student by his teacher, Aristotle; Theophrastus's birth name was Trytamus.† How much of Demetrius's own way with words comes from his Peripatetic training and his closeness with Theophrastus in particular is a measurement impossible to take. Diogenes Laertius reports from the third century C.E. that Theophrastus authored book-rolls on matters ranging from rhetoric to advice to slander.‡ Laertius's inventory of Demetrius's works shows his similar range. Something Theophrastus never did, though, was deliver speeches to the Athenian *dēmos,* and that crucial difference is what brought Demetrius to Cicero's attention in *Brutus* and elsewhere.

---

*Cicero, *De Oratore,* 2.23.95 (Fortenbaugh and Schütrumpf, *Demetrius of Phalerum,* 120). Sutton and Rackam, the translators of the Loeb *De Oratore,* translate the Latin here as "less spirited and lazier," a testament to past classicists' dismissal of the oratorical quality of Hellenistic rhetors (Sutton and Rackam, trans., Cicero, *On the Orator,* 269).

†Cicero, *Orator,* §127; Cicero, *Brutus,* §119–121.

‡Fortenbaugh, *Theophrastus of Eresus,* 463.

Cicero establishes Demetrius as the change agent of oratorical style: "Here, first, he altered oratory and rendered it soft and tender [*mollem teneramque*] and he preferred to seem sweet [*suavis*], as he was, rather than heavy [*gravis*]; in fact, he preferred an oratory with sweetness [*suavitate*] so as to flow through [*perfunderet*] the mind rather than to fracture it [*perfrigeret*], and leave a memory of its neat combinations [*concinnitatis*] . . . ."* This marks the second appearance of "softness," and Cicero's insistence on this word is noteworthy. In both Athens and Rome, the language of softness was gendered, and Demetrius's mollification of oratory could be read as feminizing. The style he pioneered broke from the harshness and hardness of his predecessors, but the break is explained by his Peripatetic provenance rather than by insufficient manliness. For Romans other than Cicero, however, those two characteristics may not have been mutually exclusive.

In *De Officiis*, composed two years after *Brutus*, Cicero encourages his son and other young Romans to read his philosophical works. He describes them as not much different from Peripatetic writings, since they all claim a kinship with Socrates and Plato.[†] Where Cicero does part from the Peripatetics is in his oratorical prowess. "And I see no one among the Greeks" who has joined together the philosophical and the oratorical, "unless perhaps Demetrius of Phalerum can be included in that number, a refined [*subtilis*] arguer and too little vigorous orator, but so sweet [*dulcis*] that you can recognize him as a student of Theophrastus."[‡] It seems clear, then, that Cicero thinks Demetrius pulled Theophrastean traits into oratory, publicizing a style that is usually reserved for conversationalists strolling in shady colonnades: expansive, forgiving, inviting.[§] Returning to the *Brutus* passage, Cicero pairs softness with tenderness, emphasizing the pliable properties of Demetrius's prose. The oppositional pair of suavity and density recalls Aristophanes's scales in the *Frogs;* words have sensible, measurable qualities that achieve different effects. *Suavitas* indicates a sustained sweetness, while *concinnitas* suggests a trim elegance resulting from a sense of what pairs with what. Demetrius does not clang with aggressive boisterousness or twang with incongruity.

In his other rhetorical work of 46 B.C.E., *Orator*, Cicero dwells on a tripartite taxonomy of *oratio*. The middle *genus* contains "a minimum of strength

---

*Cicero, *Brutus*, §37–38 (Fortenbaugh and Schütrumpf, *Demetrius of Phalerum*, 121).
[†]Cicero, *De Officiis*, 1.2 (Fortenbaugh and Schütrumpf, *Demetrius of Phalerum*, 119).
[‡]Cicero, *De Officiis*, 1.2.
[§]For more on how and why Cicero recommended that young Roman orators cultivate a conversational style in public, see Kennerly, "*Sermo* and Stoic Sociality in Cicero's *De Officiis*."

[*nervorum*] but a maximum of sweetness [*suavitatis*]."* Demetrius is Cicero's sole representative. His speech is sedate and placid but shimmers with *stellae* (stars), by which Cicero means flashes of figurative language.† Above all, the intermediate style "is certainly a remarkable and flowering *genus* of speech, painted and thoroughly polished [*expolitum*], in which all words and all thoughts are bound up with charm [*lepores*]."‡ All these little stars and blossoms represent short bursts of departure from the rest of Demetrius's prose, grabbing attention or senses. Cicero explains that most "middle" speakers come from philosophical schools, though the sophists are the original source.§ These origin points indicate an intense concentration on language, including listening and wide reading. Philosophical listening and reading can have, Cicero believes, a softening effect, especially so in regard to the Peripatetic model of those practices.

During Demetrius's decade of public service to Athens, he brought Lyceum learning into a cultural form—oratory—that had fascinated Aristotle and Theophrastus but that they themselves had not practiced. He also left behind a legacy in speech-texts that Romans, or at least some Romans, appreciated. His philosophical learning softened his speech, but his political experience gave his speech a bright vitality. While none of the titles in the inventory of Demetrius's work suggest he wrote explicitly about preparing written words for publication, his reception in the work of Cicero places him in the middle of debates about the value of pursuing various registers of style and about the challenge of speaking as one writes and writing as one speaks. Occupying the broad middle between hefty and dainty speech, Demetrius is for Cicero an *exemplum* of someone with speech smoothed by the application of extensive learning; it polishes, but not to a small, sharp point. Cicero deems Demetrius pleasant to read and seems also to imagine he was pleasant to hear.

Upon his ejection from Athens, Demetrius settled in Alexandria, established by one of Alexander's Greek generals, Ptolemy, begetter of the Ptolemaic dynasty, which ended with Cleopatra. Demetrius may have helped Ptolemy I Soter, as he is known, (r. 305–283 B.C.E.) get Alexandria's legal codes in order. Greeks of the fourth century were well aware of Egypt's comparative antiquity and venerable textual culture.** To attract and keep Greeks in Alexandria, Ptolemy II Philadelphus (r. 285–246 B.C.E.) leveraged that tradition, but he Hellenized it. His effort to procure a copy of every known book-roll considered "Greek" yielded an abundance of *bibloi* in the Library-Mouseion, which drew poets,

---

*Cicero, *Orator*, §91 (Fortenbaugh and Schütrumpf, *Demetrius of Phalerum*, 124).
†Cicero, *Orator*, §92.
‡Cicero, *Orator*, §96.
§Cicero, *Orator*, §96.
**See, e.g., Plato, *Phaedrus*, 274c–275b; Plato, *Timaeus*, 23a1–5.

rhetoricians, and philosophers from far and wide. He also sponsored the translation of the Septuagint into Greek. Ancient sources have it that Demetrius helped
Ptolemy I design the space, scaling up what he had learned about book-roll
accumulation and storage from Aristotle's texts at the Lyceum.* On chronological
and technical grounds, those sources have been challenged, but the third century broadly saw new ways of thinking about places for book-rolls.† The extensive holdings of the library enabled a bookishness of unprecedented magnitude
and necessitated systems of selection and organization (both plural processes)
that would bring the abundance to order. Demetrius and Callimachus, the poet
with whom I pair him, likely resided in Alexandria at the same time, drawn and
contributing to the wide range of knowledge domains under development there.

Callimachus, through Thick and Thin

Hailing from Cyrene, a lively Greek city whose ruins persist near present-day
Shahhat, Libya, Callimachus brought to the Ptolemaic court and the institutions
it supported an insuppressible taxonomic and aesthetic meliorism. He strove to
make that which was good better still: to his sensibilities, better usually meant
tighter in form. Callimachus belongs among a select few who could be celebrated
by both librarians and poets for contributions to their respective ways of order-
ing words and worlds. During his time in Alexandria, it is likely that book-rolls
were continuing to arrive at the Library-Mouseion by the caseload, stretching the
stamina of copiers, the ingenuity of organizers, and the curiosity of all manner
of learned people assembled there. How the trove of texts was verified, organized, and tracked before he arrived and during his time there is not known.
Zenodotus of Ephesus, an early head librarian (*bibliophulax*, literally "guardian
of books"), likely made some organizational advances beyond merely affixing
sullaboi (book-roll title-tags), but he also tapped into the talent pooling around
him to innovate and improve techniques of information management.

For his part, Callimachus produced the *Pinakes* (*Lists/Tables*). Its name suggests tablets hanging from book nooks and functioning like tables of contents,
aids to researchers and reshelvers alike. But the reference guide is reported
to have unfurled more than 120 book-rolls; by comparison, Homer's *Iliad* and
Odysseus combined span 48. What Callimachus produced was no proto-card
catalogue. The operating fantasy of the *Pinakes* was that they enabled reference
and gesture to the totality of Greek textual culture, or at least that sizable part
that had been logged to date. In a massive effort of quality and quantity control, Callimachus gauged the provenance and authenticity of texts and of texts

---

*For a good summary, see Blum, *Kallimachos*, 99–104.
†For a full treatment, see Hendrickson, "The Invention of the Greek Library."

mentioned within texts, provided locational and biographical background on writers, and summarized the contents of their works and the contents of works cited therein, thereby establishing "a broader documentary basis for literary criticism."* Essentially, Callimachus's "work as a scholar consisted of the transmission and dissemination of information from the literature and about the literature."† He endowed texts with contexts.

His command of those texts and contexts meant that Callimachus had robust if not complete knowledge of what had already been attempted when he composed his own verse, and it shows. Marco Fantuzzi and Richard Hunter stress the demands Callimachus's poetry placed on its readers: "an extraordinarily easy familiarity with the Greek literary heritage and with the various levels of literary and non-literary Greek," from rare and archaic words to banal words in common circulation.‡ Of course, readers do not have to catch every hint of allusion or whiff of competition with predecessors to appreciate a work or *the* work of poetry, but poet and reader must share some "consciousness of tradition."§ Callimachus's challenge—and achievement—was to craft poetry aware of its heavy inheritance but not weighed down by it. Though he wrote in several different meters and genres, his poetry reads as suggestively compressed across them. Every word knows its weight.

Callimachus enjoyed a lively afterlife, but little of his work remains. Daringly, then, the contents of several excerpts and fragments have been deemed programmatic—and agonistic. His poetic principles take form in contested aesthetic terms, most of which are clearly somatic. Among the qualities he values are *leptos* (slender), *toros* (sharp), *atriptos* (not worn out); among those qualities he disavows are *pachus* (thick), *platos* (wide), and *megas* (big, bulky).** Though there is little scholarly consensus about how totalizing or damning Callimachus was in his poetic contentiousness, it is largely agreed that he contrasted his poetry and poetics with those of Antimachus and Apollonius, the former of whom is most famous for his epic *Thebais* and his elegiac *Lyde,* the latter for his epic *Argonautica* and for becoming head librarian at Alexandria. Their poetry is no so much bad as it is invariably *big:* they have only one scale, only one stylistic register. Invariable bigness offends Callimachus's sensibilities because it risks

*Blum, *Kallimachos,* 237. See also Krevans, "Callimachus and the Pedestrian Muse," 173, and Krevans, "Callimachus' Philology," 121–126.

†Blum, *Kallimachos,* 246.

‡Fantuzzi and Hunter, *Tradition and Innovation in Hellenistic Poetry,* 43.

§Fantuzzi and Hunter, *Tradition and Innovation in Hellenistic Poetry,* 75.

**Callimachus, *Prologue to Aetia; Hymn to Apollo* 105–113; fragment 398 (Pfeiffer, *Callimachus, Vol. 1,* 325); epigram 27 (Pfeiffer, *Callimachus, Vol. 2,* 88).

an echoing emptiness if it is too spacious and a thick cacophony if it absorbs everything. The resonance of that which is taut can be better managed.

In a fragment of the prologue to the catalogic epic *Aetia* (Causes), Callimachus twice uses variants of *leptos* (slender): first when addressing critics who dismiss his small poems as unmanly and then when quoting advice given him by Apollo. The poet first expresses his preference for the *leptos,* however many perfectly decent poets may heed the *megalē gunē* (big lady). *Leptos* seems, then, a term of corporeal opposition and the big lady a fleshy or bulky Muse. The poet then reports the origin of his preference: Apollo urged him the very first time he "placed a writing tablet on my knees" to "feed the victim to be as thick [*pachiston*] as possible but, my friend, keep the Muse thin [*leptaleēn*]."* Apollo seems to endorse weighty themes but also their constrictive poetic presentation. Writing, too, is immediately implicated, and on a wax tablet, a medium of temporary writing that may be rubbed out.

In Aristophanes's *Frogs,* Euripides had flaunted that same pared-down aspect of his poetics, as I showed in the previous chapter. Aristophanes made that very word—*leptos*—emblematic of Euripides's laborious and bookish method and its lightweight results.[†] The ancient mind did not necessarily link a fondness for books with bloated verse or prose. *Leptos* may originate from *lopos* (shell, husk, peel), meaning it could evoke that which has been husked or peeled, or even a brightness resulting from the removal of a rough layer or surface. Either way, *leptos* indicates that slenderness has been painstakingly maintained or excess has been shed. *Pachus* (thick), the antonym of *leptos,* appears also in Callimachus's assessment of Antimachus's *Lyde:* "*Lyde* is thick [*pachu*] and not sharp [*ou toron*]."[‡] In her analysis of this teasing fragment, Nita Krevans points out that *pachus* also can be considered an intellectual slight—just as the English word "thick" can be—and in later poetic and rhetorical criticism can mean "florid" or "rough."[§] It is always framed as a stylistic flaw. *Toros* refers to sharpness or distinctness, such that its negation (*ou*) suggests a perceptual vexation that makes fine details difficult to discern or suggests they were absent in the first place. Callimachus values the stylistically contained, controlled, and crisp.

This stripped-down aesthetic is immediately contrasted with that which is tramped down. Apollo also exhorts Callimachus to seek untrodden paths

---

*Callimachus, *Prologue to Aetia,* 23–24.

†Aristophanes, *Frogs,* 956.

‡Callimachus, fragment 398 (Pfeiffer, *Callimachus, Vol. 1,* 325). As I discussed in the previous chapter, Euripides refers to Aeschylus's poetic art as "word-heavy [*rhēmatōn epachthōn*]" during their debate at the end of Aristophanes's *Frogs.*

§Krevans, "Fighting against Antimachus," 173.

(*atriptous keleuthous*) rather than those that are chariot-worn and broad (*platos*) from much passage. To pursue novel paths purposefully and nimbly, one has to know the territory, and there were few who would have known it better than Callimachus the Cataloguer. Novel paths are also potentially narrow ones: few if any have passed through before, and not many can squeeze through after. All the more reason to keep one's Muse thin.

In his *Hymn to Apollo,* Callimachus personifies Envy (Pthonos), who whispers in Apollo's ear that it "does not like the singer whose song is not as big as the sea." Apollo kicks Envy and counters that "the stream of the Assyrian river is great [*megas*], but it carries much [*polla*] refuse of earth and much [*polla*] filth in its waters."* That which is big sweeps, carries, collects, churns and is not choosy about what it picks up. Callimachus thinks a poet should wield a very fine filter. Extending the aqueous language in the verses, Ahuvia Kahane has argued that this poem evidences "not a case of personal mudslinging, but a broad, positive flow of ideas within a community."† Callimachus damns large outpourings not necessarily to abuse his rivals but to offer the possibility that epic need not be thick, clogged, and sloppy; he offers a generic corrective. "A big book amounts to a big evil [*to mega biblion ison ... tōi megalōi kakōi*]" is likely the most famous snatch of Callimachus that aligns with his fondness for the compact.‡ *Megas* is not a material designation, however, but an aesthetic one. A later scholiast refers to "the four books of the very substantial [*megistōn*] *Aetia,*" the aforementioned catalogic epic in which Callimachus accounts for his loyalty to *leptotēs* (thinness).§ Estimated at seven thousand lines, it is not small. Callimachus could (and did) write long poems and sizable collections, but he maintained in each element a svelte form and feel. Callimachean poetics would come to inform Roman poetry and his poems to be read by its orators.

Rome Rises

Rome's stories of its own foundation and ascension resound with calls for and cries of violence. The very word *Roma* smacked of aggression to Greek ears, since the Greek word *rhōmē* means force. It makes a certain kind of sense, then, to presume that such a bellicose people would be relatively defenseless against the alluring accumulations of Hellenistic culture. Brutality cannot defeat beauty; warriors and wordsmiths wield incommensurable weapons. For instance, George

*Callimachus, *Hymn to Apollo,* 105–113.

†Kahane, "Callimachus, Apollionius, and the Poetics of Mud," 132. See also Farmer, "Rivers and Rivalry in Petronius, Horace, Callimachus, and Aristophanes."

‡Callimachus, fragment 465 (Pfeiffer, *Callimachus,* Vol. 1, 353).

§*Callimachus, Testimonium 23 (Pfeiffer, Callimachus, Vol. 2, xcviii–xcix).*

Kennedy submits that "Romans first became conscious of methods of persuasion in the late third or early second centuries B.C. when their city had become not only the most powerful state of the Italian peninsula but also the greatest power in the Mediterranean, and they found themselves the object of every subtlety Greek rhetoricians could devise."* But such an account does not entertain the possibility of savagery and suavity coexisting in Rome prior to its clash with Greece.

Romans would—and did—contest an origin story of Roman rhetoric that did not begin with their own native roots and that framed their rhetorical culture as merely reactive to or defensive against Hellenistic formations. Acknowledging Rome's "growing pains" during the late third through early second centuries, Eric Gruen insists that "the Romans were by no means boorish rustics, awestruck and intimidated by Hellenism, gripped by an inferiority complex that produced a mix of clandestine acceptance and ostensible rejection." Instead, Romans "engaged in [the] adaptation, modification, and manipulation" of that tradition to suit their purposes and situations.† Still, written evidence (textual and epigraphic) from early Rome is scarce and that from second-century Rome not substantively more abundant.‡

Echoing the earlier pairing of Demetrius and Callimachus, this section briefly pairs an orator and a poet, Cato Maior (234–149 B.C.E.) and Gaius Ennius Lucilius (c. 180–102 B.C.E.). Like those of Demetrius and Callimachus, their speeches and poems survive in fragments; unlike Demetrius and Callimachus, they became known for their rough language, especially at the compositional level of the clause (*membrum*, literally "limb"). Cato became an important figure for the Roman-oriented rhetorical histories and theories of Cicero and Quintilian, and Lucilius loomed large for Horace. Neither, however, was as generally atechnical as later writers made them out to be. Cato and Lucilius belonged to what has been called the Scipionic Circle, a group of cultured Romans and Greeks with the famous general Scipio at its titular core and most famous for adapting strains of Hellenistic philosophy to Roman *mores*. Cato and Lucilius knew Greek, and they both displayed their knowledge of rhetorical art while distancing themselves from it; in fact, they publicly criticized themselves for that very knowledge.

Cato's contributions to the development of Roman prose style are now being explored in book-length studies, but Romans even a century after him

---

*Kennedy, *Art of Rhetoric in the Roman World*, 4.

†Gruen, *Studies in Greek Culture and Roman Policy*, 1.

‡For more on early Roman rhetoric and "literature," see Fantham, *Roman Literary Culture*, and Habinek, *The Politics of Latin Literature*, 34–68.

recognized him as a pioneer, however rough.* Cornelius Nepos, a first-century B.C.E. historian, related that Cato "put together speeches from the time of his adolescence [*ad adulescentia confecit orationes*]."† This youthful zest for speech-craft adumbrates a lifelong interest. He seems to have published some of his speeches in written form, but only portions have reached us. A lengthy frag-ment permits a view of how Cato incorporated trappings of rhetorical and textual culture. During his time as censor, Cato was sued for living beyond his ostensibly—perhaps ostentatiously—modest means. In *De Sumptu Suo* (*On His Own Expenses*), Cato purports to describe how difficult it was to decide on a defense strategy and how useless it was to draw upon any of his previous speeches. He relies upon repetition based upon the imagery of wax tablets, upon the surfaces of which were written a speech (*mea oratio scripta*) he had deliv-ered previously to the Roman people. An unnamed person, likely a scribal slave, reads to Cato arguments and appeals from that speech that bear also on his current case. Again and again, Cato tells the unnamed person to delete, erase, and rub the wax until he reaches the wood frame of the tablet itself: none of those persuasive means will work. Reflecting on the present rhetorical useless-ness of his good deeds done for the *res publica*, Cato concludes glumly: "Thus it has been brought about that it is possible to do harm with impunity [*male facere inpoene*], but not to do good with impunity [*bene facere non inpoene*]."‡

Cato seems to know the rhetorical convention of shoring up goodwill (*benevolentia*) with reference to one's honorable ancestry and one's own good works, and he does so at the beginning of the passage, while at the same time deeming those details of no interest to his fellow citizens in their current mood. The series of passings-over (*praeteritiones*) permit him to protest the irrelevance of some public contribution or another *after* airing it; they function like correc-tives, but they add even while they ostensibly subtract. This play of inclusion and exclusion takes a graphic form, with Cato using the language of rubbing out what has been written in wax. George Kennedy urges readers to "note that Cato does not pretend that his defense is extemporaneous, and that he expects his audience to have a certain interest in the process of composition, another sign of growing rhetorical sophistication."§ It *could* be that Cato offers a view of his

---

*See Gruen, *Culture and National Identity in Republican Rome*, 52–83, for Cato the par-adox (a proud Roman well versed in Hellenistic culture). The full-length study is Sciar-rino, *Cato the Censor and the Beginnings of Latin Prose*.

†Nepos, *Excerpt from the Book of Latin Historians*, 24.3.3.

‡Cato Maior, XLIV, *De Sumptu Suo* (a.164), 173.1–24 (in Malcovati, *Oratorum Romano-rum Fragmenta, Liberae Rei Publicae*, 70–71).

§Kennedy, *The Art of Rhetoric in the Roman World*, 44.

speech-crafting process because he thinks listeners will be interested in those details. It is more compelling, however, to consider his recurrent references to writing on wax tablets an analogical dramatization of the impermanence of that which has been pressed into public memory. References to memory as "the wax tablet of the mind" have their origins in Plato and became idiomatic in Roman rhetoric.* Again and again, Cato has acted uprightly for the *res publica,* building a record of service. Now, he dramatically presumes Romans will deny the depth and durability of that service, item by item. If what he did left no lasting impression on them, then reminders will only irritate. "Rub it out to the very wood," Cato instructs his scribal slave, and we see Cato resigning himself—but not totally—to the *tabulae rasae* that his personal archive, peers, and the *populus* have become. The antithesis that closes the passage suggests Cato is not entirely minimalist in his style. It is also an early variant of the *sententia*—a rhetorical form for which Cato is famous—that "no good deed goes unpunished."† Cato cleverly incorporates tools of rhetoric and of writing to say—and, so he says, to take away—what seems to be a usual though situationally unavailable means of persuasion: doing well by one's fellow citizens. The memories of citizens are no more permanent in what they hold than a wax tablet put to frequent use.

Cato's junior by nearly half a century, Lucilius hailed from the upper echelons of Roman society. As I detail in chapter 4, Horace judged Lucilius to have been deficient editorially, willfully unmanaged in form, and too loose in content, too. Though Lucilius's *corpus* is in tatters, a few surviving lines have been deemed characteristic of his and his coterie's impatience with speakers and writers who seemed to be trying too hard. Emblematic are these verses from a hexametrical rendering of a defense speech of a friend, Quintus Mucius Scaevola, being tried for extortion by someone a bit too precious, Titus Albucius: "How tidily, like little tiles, are the words placed together, all artfully, as in a pavement and vermiculate emblem [*quam lepide lexis compostae ut tesserulae omnes / arte pavimento atque emblemate vermiculato*]."‡ Scaevola compares Albucius to a painstaking setter of mosaics. Each of his tile-like words draws attention to itself as an individual unit, whereas mosaics and speeches both appear to best advantage when their piecemeal construction is not apparent. Albucius's verbal mosaics

---

*See, e.g., Plato, *Theaetetus,* 194c–d, for wordplay between *kēr* (heart) and *kēros* (wax) in reference to the imprint-holding soul and retentive memory of the wise; Cicero, *De Partitione Oratoria,* 7.26; Quintilian 11.2.4. See also Small, *Wax Tablets of the Mind.*

†See, e.g., discussion of the so-called Cato's *Distichs,* a collection of maxims dating to late antiquity (Crane, "*Intret Cato*").

‡Lucilius 2.84–85.

seem worm-wiggly (*vermiculatus*) because he draws others in too close to its composition.* *Lepidus,* which I have translated as "tidy," is the Latin rendering of *leptos* (peeled, thin), the quality so dear to Euripides and Callimachus. In the next century, Roman writers across genres would use *lepidus* to signal concern with sophistication, wit, and polish, who demonstrates possession of those qualities, and when.† Here, it takes on a finicky connotation: Albucius has done painstaking work, and he wants others to see it. *Lexis* (words) and *emblēma* (emblem) are Greek, and their application to Albucius's rhetorical method marks that method as Hellenic. Of course, that Lucilius used those Greek terms means he, too, knew the lingo. Not everyone who read Lucilius thought there was not something to aspire to within those teasing verses. Allusions to or quotations of those lines appear in Cicero's *De Oratore, Brutus,* and *Orator,* three of his mature rhetorical works, and in Quintilian's *Institutio Oratoria.*‡ Cicero and Quintilian joined Lucilius in belittling those who dedicate themselves to delicate and minute placements and patterns of words.

Given the punishing *ponos* and polish of Isocrates, discussed in detail in the previous chapter, Lucilius's invocation of him is worth a closer look. Leaving a portion of this poem untranslated highlights the mix of Greek and Latin words, which we saw in the Scaevola verses, too. Here, too, the Greek words smack of opprobrium. Chiding a friend who did not visit him while Lucilius was sick, Lucilius teases: "you wish that man to have passed away whom you would not [*nolueris*] come and see when you should have [*debueris*]. If this 'would' [*nolueris*] and 'should' [*debueris*] gives you little pleasure because it is *atechnon et Eisocration lerodesque simul totum ac sit meiraciodes,* then I will not waste my effort, if you are going to be like this."§ Lucilius characterizes his friend as someone who could be turned off by even a simple and likely accidental homoteleuton: the same -*ueris* ending on *debueris* and *nolueris.* Such jingles are judged "artless, and Isocratean, and foolish, and boyish," all Latinized Greek words. Though Lucilius is likely exaggerating his friend's verbal sensitivities to taunt him, these fragments demonstrate that, as early as the second century, Romans were already negotiating their relationship to famous rhetorical figures of democratic Athens. And in verse. Isocrates, it seems, has been deemed unworthy of emulation by one of Lucilius's associates. Lucilius protests—again, likely in jest—that

---

*A mosaic is like a Monet in that distance is required for the representation to take form. Up close, a mosaic can look like a segmented worm.

†For a detailed treatment of *lepidus* in the middle of the first century B.C.E., see Krostenko, *Cicero, Catullus, and the Language of Social Performance,* 64–72 and 94–99.

‡*Cicero, De Oratore,* 3.171; *Brutus,* §274; *Orator,* §149–150; Quintilian 9.4.112–113. See analyses by Butler, *The Matter of the Page,* 42, and Fitzgerald, *Variety,* 71–2.

§Lucilius 5.186–193.

he has no time for someone unforgiving of momentary Isocrateanisms. Though Lucilius does not represent his own habits of composition or publication in any surviving poem, it seems unlikely he would have wanted anyone to dwell on visions of him mussing or fussing.

Roman Rhetoric Takes Textual Form

Cato Maior and Lucilius likely read copies of Hellenistic rhetoric handbooks that circulated around Rome aplenty, but, other than the *Peri Hermēneias* of Demetrius, we possess none compiled between those of Aristotle and Anaximenes in the fourth century and those of the *auctor* in the first. *Rhetorica ad Herennium* is typically dated to the first two decades of the first century B.C.E. It bears Hellenistic imprints, however much the *auctor* Romanized and individualized what he had read and heard. *Rhetorica ad Herennium,* the oldest complete rhetorical handbook in Latin, survived largely because of its spurious attribution to Cicero, but its serviceability ought not to be discounted. The *auctor* covers all five *partes* (parts) of rhetoric, but in the atypical order of invention, arrangement, delivery, memory, and style. Evidently, young Cicero intended to write about each *pars* individually, but he never returned to the project in that form.* My interest lies primarily in the *auctor*'s use of body language, which he invokes to set up his configurations of style.

The *auctor* opens the *opus,* his response to the titular Herennius's incessant and ardent wish for rhetorical instruction, by stating his preference for pursuing philosophy when he has any time at all for leisure (*otium*) and closes the first book-roll by promising that he will make up for in diligence that which he cannot provide in sheer working hours.† Throughout the handbook, the *auctor* frames his effort as a good deed gladly but not easily done. He approves of Herennius's will to learn, because "copiousness of speech and agreeableness of oratory [*copia dicendi et commoditas orationis*] do not bear fruit unless managed by appropriate knowledge and a bounded moderation of mind."‡ The *auctor* discloses that he has avoided arrogant or inane subject matter (*res*) generated by Greek writers attempting to make their art seem hard to master; instead, he has taken (*sumpsimus*) only that which is pertinent to one who wants to help others learn the art.§ The *auctor* purports to write not for financial or professional gain

---

*See, e.g., Cicero, *De Inventione,* 1.9, 2.178. Cicero's *De Inventione* is conventionally dated to 91 B.C.E. and the *Rhetorica ad Herennium* to 86–82.

†*Rhetorica ad Herennium* 1.1.1, 1.17.27. It seems Herennius are blood relations (4.55.69), though the precise nature of their familial affiliation is unknown.

‡*Rhetorica ad Herennium* 1.1.1.

§*Rhetorica ad Herennium* 1.1.1.

or for glory, "in the manner as the others who have written," but only to oblige his eager friend.*

Throughout the preface to the fourth book-roll, which is dedicated solely to style, the *auctor*'s metaphors roam from the athletic to the aquatic to the somatic. As I have shown, the body figures prominently in classical Greek rhetorical composition and criticism and in Hellenistic ones thereafter. Corporeality features plentifully in Roman rhetoric and poetics. The first decade or two into the first century B.C.E., nowhere is that corporeality more on show than in the *auctor*'s treatment of what he uniquely calls *figurae*, figures or forms.† By Quintilian's time, *figura* referred to "figure of speech" and translated the Greek word for a verbal structure, *schēma;* for the *auctor*, however, *figura* seems to have functioned as a classificatory term, like the Greek *eidos* (form).‡ The *auctor* offers a tripartite set of stylized figures: *gravis* (heavy, weighty), *mediocris* (moderate, average), and *extenuata* or *adtenuata* (thinned out).§ These three forms are sometimes translated less literally as grand, middle, and simple and attributed to Theophrastus.** According to the *auctor*, one achieves the *gravis* figure with "weighty words with a smooth and equipped arrangement"; the *mediocris* figure "from a more grounded, yet not the bottom and most common, rank of words"; and the *adtenuata* figure with words "lowered even to the very most used and customary to conversation [*sermonis*]."†† An orator should use all three figures, since "by means of variety, satiety is more easily avoided", for speaker and listener both.‡‡

To supply Herennius and other readers with a visual of the undesirable forms that result from a zealous commitment to a given *figura*, the *auctor* fleshes out his metaphor. A too-eager pursuit of the thinned-out style sucks speech dry, leaving it "arid and bloodless [*aridum et exsangue*]" and deserving of the adjective *exilis:* meager, feeble, depleted, emaciated.§§ The *auctor* calls flailing attempts

---

*Rhetorica ad Herennium 1.1.1.

†It is the noun form of the verb *fingere*, to form or fashion, usually with the hands. *Figura* often refers to a figurine or statue.

‡Quintilian 2.13.9, 9.1.11.

§*Rhetorica ad Herennium* 4.8.11.

**Since the rhetorical works of Theophrastus are in tatters, it is not clear whether he relied upon and extended the occasional body language Aristotle used to describe what we would call sentence construction or whether Theophrasus maintained Aristotle's distinction between a *lexis agōnistikē* (style for competitive speaking) and *lexis graphikē* (style for writing). The *auctor* does not make that distinction. For speculations about the contributions of Theophrastus to style theory, see Kennedy, "Theophrastus and Stylistic Distinctions," and Innes, "Theophrastus and the Theory of Style."

††*Rhetorica ad Herennium* 4.8.11.

‡‡*Rhetorica ad Herennium* 4.11.16.

§§*Rhetorica ad Herennium* 4.11.16.

at the middle style "slack [*dissolutum*]," because without "sinews and joints [*sine nervis et articulus*]," or "flopping," because drooping here and there without firmness or virility. Such an effort fails "to hold [*tenere*] the audience's attention [*adtentum auditorem*] because it is too loose [*diffluit*]" to keep a solid grip on it.* Overdoing the grand style is a particular fault of exuberant novices and results in a "bloated, swollen [*sufflata*]" style that bulges like a tumor: "for just as a tumor often resembles a good condition of the body [*ut corporis bonam habitudinem*], so, to those who are unskilled, turgid [*turget*] and inflated [*inflata*] speech often seems weighty [*gravis*]."† The *auctor* also relies on the body to explain why he cannot provide a short example of the rhetorical practice of dwelling on a point (*commoratio*): "it is not isolated from the whole case like some limb [*membrum*], but rather, like blood [*sanguis*], is spread through the whole body of the speech [*per totum corpus orationis*]."‡ Such corporeal language courses throughout the so-called Atticism-Asianism debates of the midcentury.

All three styles must satisfy demands of *elegantia* (chic concision), *compositio* (cohesion), and *dignitas* (suitability) in order to be "agreeable and finished [*commoda et perfecta*]."§ *Elegantia* results from purity of Latin and precision of diction; that the *auctor* refers readers curious for further explanation to his *ars grammatica*—which has not survived—points to a lack of contestation though still a separation between rhetoricians and grammarians on this matter.** *Compositio* "is the arrangement of words, which makes all parts of the *oratio* more equally and thoroughly polished [*perpolitas*]."†† All three *figurae* attain "suitability [*dignitas*]" from what the *auctor* calls *exornationes*, with which *figurae* are fitted or kitted out.‡‡ Like what would later be called "figures of speech and of thought," *exornationes* are of words or of matter, with the distinction that the former pertains to the "thorough polish" of the words themselves and the latter to the suitability of the matter.§§ What follows is the oldest surviving taxonomy and inventory of rhetorical equipment and adornment, totaling sixty-four terms. A few *exornationes* do not result "without labor and pains [*sine elaboratione et sumptione operae*]" and must be used cautiously.*** The *auctor* also translates into Latin body-based sentence parts present in works such as Aristotle's *Rhetoric*

Rhetorica ad Herennium 4.11.16.
†*Rhetorica ad Herennium* 4.10.15.
‡*Rhetorica ad Herennium* 4.45.58.
§*Rhetorica ad Herennium* 4.12.17–18.
**Rhetorica ad Herennium* 4.12.17.
††*Rhetorica ad Herennium* 4.12.18.
‡‡*Rhetorica ad Herennium* 4.11.16.
§§*Rhetorica ad Herennium* 4.13.18.
****Rhetorica ad Herennium* 4.22.32.

and *Poetics* and Demetrius's *Peri Hermēneias*, including *kōlon* (limb) to *membrum* (limb) and *komma* (a cut-off piece) to *articulus* (joint).* The *auctor* encourages Herennius to apply diligence in his pursuit of "perfect style [*perfecta elocutio*]." Art and work, both hidden, of course, will ensure that no invented material presents itself in a form "nude and unequipped [*nuda atque inornata*]."†

Attention to and the management of textual abundance, both the archive of the past and the growing contributions of the continuous present, are hallmarks of the Hellenistic period. The softening polish of Demetrius and the squeezing compression of Callimachus resulted from their extensive and intensive learning, gathered in either a philosophical school renowned for its collection of book-rolls or in a *polis* amassing book-rolls from throughout the known world. The smoothness or density of prose or verse index the ability of a writer to filtrate and concentrate a lot of learning. Choices of inclusion and presentation are editorial in my operationalization of the concept insofar as they pertain to what should stay and what should go within works meant to travel beyond earshot, that is, on book-rolls. The polish of fifth- and fourth-century Athens was a response to a papyrus-prompted awareness of what one could achieve through texts and learn through the study of texts deemed worthy of perpetuating because of their quality. Hellenistic polish, within Athens and without, was a response to that response, but it has wrongly been deemed derivative rather than accretive. Those accretions—and novelties, besides—were put to public and communal use by rhetors and poets who participated with others in discussions of the terms of shared life and, thanks to Alexander, of shared language and shared culture.

The Roman statesman Cato Maior and the poet Lucilius knew the Greek language and its textual culture, including, it seems, handbooks of rhetoric. They both wrote, and, in one case, at least, Cato unabashedly spoke publicly about his use of writing to prepare for speaking. He even managed to turn his writing tools against those who might have been suspicious of them, comparing his hostilely forgetful audience to a wax tablet scraped down to its wooden frame. Lucilius and his readers judged the painstaking word-placement efforts of Isocrates and Titus Albucius to be beneath them, either juvenile or too artisan-like. A speech or poem should not be minutely managed. That attitude was challenged by the writers that followed.

The *auctor ad Herennium* does not name a single Greek rhetor or rhetorician in his work. His body-based stylistic classification of weighty, moderate,

---

***Rhetorica ad Herennium* 4.19.26.
†*Rhetorica ad Herennium* 4.56.69.

and thinned-out does not place editorial polish with any one *figura*. Instead, the *auctor* extends an editorial burden across the style spectrum. In whatever style one works, one must strive for "thorough polish" and "suitability."* Words dispatched without subjection to such considerations are bare and often unbearable. Overdoing it, however, results in bodies of work that look and sound unhealthy.

Rhetorica ad Herennium 4.12.18.

CHAPTER THREE

TALES AND TOOLS OF THE ORATORICAL *TRADITIO* IN CICERO

Cicero knew his way around a book-roll. Accordingly, he lavished attention on writings and writing in his rhetorical works. That attention must be indicative of the fallen state of speech only if the purpose and purchase writing had enjoyed in rhetorical pedagogy and oratorical production long before Cicero's time wrongly go unacknowledged, an error I hope the previous two chapters have made less difficult to commit. A crucial difference between Cicero and most earlier orators and rhetoricians, however, is that he had a keen and not at all antiquarian interest in tracking down speech-texts and handbooks ranging across several centuries.* The plentiful texts that reached him, some of them dozens of copies removed from their earliest iterations, must have been material proof of the value of textually publishing his speeches, his opinions about rhetoric, his reflections about philosophy, and even his (notoriously bad) poetry. He also regretted not having texts he knew to have existed and speeches of past orators that were never textually published. Memory's losses are large, but Cicero pursued what remained with a *furor tabularii* that astounded even his best friend, a scrupulous historian.† As Richard Leo Enos estimates, "Cicero's abilities in speaking and writing"—and I interject to add "and reading"—"functioned as confluent talents which raised his level of expression beyond any Roman standard."‡ He achieved his elevation of eloquence through editorial means, which he took no pains to conceal.

---

*He had help, in the forms of: his associates and their private libraries; his beloved scribe, Tiro; and his dearest friend, Atticus, who had a flair for acquisition. Bookshops existed in Cicero's time, but "he himself was hardly more likely to set foot in a bookshop than in a butcher's shop" (White, "Bookshops in the Literary Culture of Rome," 274). It is widely agreed that the first public library did not open in Rome until the mid-30s B.C.E., well after Cicero's death.

†*Furor tabularii* is my attempt to translate Jacques Derrida's "archive fever" into Latin. See Derrida, *Archive Fever*.

‡Enos, *The Literate Mode of Cicero's Legal Rhetoric*, 91.

Throughout *De Oratore* (55 B.C.E.), his second public text about rhetoric (after his youthful *De Inventione*), Cicero repeatedly recognizes reading, writing, and "turning the *stilus*"—idiomatic for rubbing out with the flat end of the *stilus* something written into a wax tablet with the pointed end—as indispensable enablers of that ready eloquence through which public matters are negotiated.* Discussions of writing in *Brutus* (46 B.C.E.) tend more toward its being a preservative of oratorical prowess. By publishing a speech-text after its oral delivery, orators contribute to the rhetorical record, allowing others to trace their culture's rhetorical development, use their speeches as critical benchmarks or artistic models, and keep their name and fame alive with every reading. Not only writing but also editing are tools of an orator's trade and of the oratorical tradition that permit a handing down of speech-texts and reputations, both individual and national. Loose speech-notes or speech-texts that do not read well are not of much use to any person or people.† In *Orator* (also 46 B.C.E.), Cicero combined the productive and preservative capacities of writing, arguing that rhythm—that most oral, aural, social, and influential of qualities—is best achieved with the point and paddle of the *stilus*. From upfront editorial work emerges an energy that makes the same speech both worth hearing when it is initially delivered *and* worth reading thereafter: words are raw material "thoroughly polished [*expolitio*]" by rhythm to communicate moods, whether in an urgent moment or on a more patient page.‡ I say "the same speech" boldly, and not without qualification. It seems highly likely that an orator would not have delivered orally every word worked out in writing beforehand and would not have said every word later represented in a textually published speech-text. It seems unlikely, though, that an orator who thought highly enough of his reputation—and its reliance on his heard words—to circulate speech-texts would issue forth ones that differed *greatly* from their oral precursors, unless it was to pursue some purpose other than memorialization. A constraint on major deviations as a case moved from speech to book-roll seems to have put pressure on the orator to bring polish forward, out of the textual, into the oral, and back again.§

The mid-first century B.C.E. saw a large-scale "cultural contest" over "style in its broadest sense."** Between the publication of *De Oratore* and that of *Brutus*

---

*See, e.g., Cicero, *De Oratore*, 2.96, 3.190.

†Though ancient Romans certainly could and did read silently (see, e.g., Parker, "Books and Reading Latin Poetry"), Cicero describes his friend Marcus Marius as having a slave read one of Cicero's speeches aloud (*Epistulae ad familiares*, 7.1.3).

‡Cicero, *Orator*, §185.

§For emphasis on the deep enfolding of writing within Cicero's rhetorical process, see Enos, *The Literate Mode of Cicero's Legal Rhetoric*, especially 31–35, 46–58, 88–93.

**Batstone, "Dry Pumice and the Programmatic Language of Catullus 1," 13, n. 32.

and *Orator,* the struggle seems to have gained intensity and clarity as it coalesced around ownership of a particular modifier: *Atticus,* meaning of or pertaining to Attica, whose chief city was Athens. Roman orators laid claim to the adjective explicitly or to verbal qualities they attributed to Attic writers, including *limatus* (filed), which could mean either trim and minimalist or smooth and sophisticated, depending upon who wielded it.* Regardless, it is a textual word. This contest is commonly known as the Atticism-Asianism debate, where Asianist—that is, redolent of Asia Minor, that is, perceived to be bombastic, garish, and too rhythmically regular—was conferred upon opponents but claimed by no contestant.† It is hard to miss the cultural snobbishness in this construction of Asianism. The ugliest depiction of the two rhetorical forms features in the preface to Dionysius of Halicarnassus's *On the Ancient Orators,* wherein he describes a pure, contained Attic Rhetorica and a loose, spreading Asian Rhetorica. Dionysius credits Augustan-age Romans for restoring Attic Rhetorica to its rightful place and ousting the Asian Rhetorica, who had clawed "her" way out of an Asiatic pit and into Attic Rhetorica's position in the *polis.*‡ Dionysius's depiction exaggerates the language of purity and rightfulness used in the Atticism debate roiling a few decades before he wrote, the chronological focus of this chapter.

Atticus, then, was a quality desired by all contestants, but there was no agreement about which Athenian writer best exemplified it or what type of Latin *oratio* came closest to approximating it. This fad for the Attic came at the expense of Hellenistic writers, particularly non-Athenian ones, and especially those from the eastern places into which Alexander had pushed Hellenism. It was the Hellenistic age that had chosen and copied the writers with whom some Romans now wanted to be associated, but texts original to that period were passed over in favor of a more distant past. Though writers of this time had not

---

*There was a similar hefty-dainty debate happening in Roman poetry and poetics, but "thin" poets embraced certain Hellenistic poets, whereas "thin" orators passed over the Hellenistic period completely. A prime example of a poet practicing a thin aesthetic is Catullus (see especially c. 1 and 95). Catullus and Calvus, one of Cicero's opponents in the Atticism contest, were intimates (see Catullus c. 49 [which is about Cicero], c. 50, c. 14; see also Dugan, "Preventing Ciceronianism").

†Wilamowitz-Möellendorff, "Asianismus und Atticismus." Wilamowitz was the first to suggest that that "Asianism" was not a movement but a term of opprobrium. Jakob Wisse wrote of an Atticist "movement," by which he meant "a fashion or a trend, based on a set of only more or less coherent ideas that is shared by a number of people." Wisse, "Greeks, Romans, and the Rise of Atticism," 65, 70–71.

‡Dionysius of Halicarnassus, *On the Ancient Orators,* §1. Dionysius celebrates Rome. Being highly cultured, Rome's leaders administer and keep order well, and writers of all genres have composed works worthy and redolent of the old Rhetorica, he writes (§3). Still, Dionysius retreats to fourth century B.C.E. Athens for the purest exemplars of Attic Rhetorica's influence.

quite worked out this vocabulary, the new Atticists seem to have been positing a distinction between the classical and the merely old, the one eternally glossy and the other irredeemably hoary.* Fixated on diction (Attic/a was a dialect of Greek as well as a part of Greece), it was a movement of linguistic-rhetorical purity based on the purgation of everything that had accumulated within the rhetorical record since Lysias.†

The debate seems to have been carried out largely through corporeal language, which stretched back at least to Aristophanes but which more recently had structured the tripartite stylistic division of the *Rhetorica ad Herennium* and appeared in the rhythm sections of the third book-roll of *De Oratore*. The body had a grip on the critical imaginary because it was a trope familiar to those who knew techniques and technicalities of rhetoric and poetics and was easy for anyone else to picture and understand. Cicero's main argument against the group he calls the new Atticists (*novi Attici*) is that they are not availing themselves of the full range of Attic *genera* (types).‡ That means they are either not reading very extensively in the archive or are intentionally confining themselves to only one *genus,* the one Cicero calls *tenuis* (thin). Above all, they restrict themselves to the Attic orator Lysias, who featured in Plato's *Phaedrus* in textual form as a book-roll that Phaedrus read to Socrates and whose prose Socrates called "clear and compact, and precise."§ Lysias is best known for his logography, or speeches written for others caught up in minor lawsuits. Since Lysias wrote for others, his prose is impersonal, minimal, and serviceable; it was designed to do just enough to win a given lawsuit and to beat the water-clock. A striking feature of Cicero's response to those who have a thin approach to Atticism is his judgment that their prose may read well on the roll but will fail to impress in the air and will not hang around long in either form. (Lysias's *corpus* might beg to differ.) As textual as Cicero may have been, he knew how to write for the ear; indeed, he had mastered a singular though multifarious rhetorical form that warmed up during his written preparations, flared in the heat of the moment, and read well even after the situation had cooled off.**

*I return to the concept of "the classical" in the Conclusion.

†O'Sullivan, "'Rhetorical' vs 'Linguistic' Atticism: A False Dichotomy?"

‡Cicero, *Orator,* §89.

§Plato, *Phaedrus,* 234e.

**Temperature language plays an important part in Cicero's rhetorical works, since he applied heat-related words only to those styles of which he approved, and especially to his own; *Orator* §132 is representative. These are styles responsive to situations and appropriately attuned to the emotions and agitations of people involved in a case (broadly conceived) or invested in its outcome. For a recommendation of heat and passion as rhetorical terms, see Hawhee and Holding, "Case Studies in Material Rhetoric," 268–278.

Cicero's rhetorical works from the middle of the century—namely, *De Oratore, Brutus, De Optimo Genere Oratorum,* and *Orator*—contain evidence that editorial language was becoming absorbed into Latin taxonomies and terminologies of style.* That absorption resulted from an open recognition among Cicero and his contemporaries of the role of writing in rhetoric and oratory, from training during education, to preparing for major speeches, to publishing speeches in textual form thereafter. All three items in that sequence have clear if different orientations toward and importance for public life. Editing-based style terms also followed from a fascination with the speech-texts of ancient orators, which, by virtue of their very form as written objects, encouraged a text-based form of critical language through which to evaluate them.† That critical language was then applied to contemporary oratory, but preferences were not at all uniform.

Cicero wrote his mature rhetorical works between his return from a one-year exile from Rome during 58–57 and the assassination of Julius Caesar in 44. Because the Atticism debate took hold after the publication of *De Oratore,* I focus on three rhetorical works from 46: *Brutus, De Optimo Genere Oratorum,* and *Orator.*‡ The last few years of Cicero's life were prolific; he composed a lot of other writings besides and served as an advocate or prosecutor in several high-profile cases.§ Also included among Cicero's writings from this time are hundreds of letters, some of which detail the circumstances of the composition of his rhetorical works, even down to where Cicero sat as he composed them: usually the book room in his country villa at Tusculum.** The three works from 46 were written quickly, and a defensive energy emanates from them. His efficacy and legacy were under an attack with generational and situational dimensions. The push of his younger contemporaries for "pure" and "pared down" diction might have been an attempt to distinguish themselves from Ciceronian *furia* and *copia,* but it coincided with a perceived influx into Rome of provincials and foreigners whose Latin was thick or overdone, which may have provoked

---

*Cicero conceives of style broadly as how an orator manages the relationship between matter and manner. He tends to use the phrase *genus dicendi* (kind/type of speaking).

†As I showed in chapter 1, Athenian speaker-writers themselves battled over terms of style. For orators, a key question was which types of style were worth pursuing orally and which textually (or both, or neither).

‡I do not include *De Partitionibus Oratoriae,* which Cicero addressed to his son, Marcus, which may have come from this same year. Its date is not secure, however, and it does not hold much in common with the workings of this chapter.

§One speech-text, *Pro Milone* (52 B.C.E.), proves especially interesting from an editorial perspective.

**Cicero's letters contain many details about his collaborative editorial practices, which I do not address here. For a lively study, see Gurd, "Cicero and Editorial Revision." I focus on the sociality of editing in chapter 5.

this tight network of aristocratic native Romans to regard all but the finest, thinnest Latin with suspicion.* Cicero set the new Atticists against all of the oratorical, rhetorical tradition, both Greek and Roman. If it was an Attic form of prose they wanted, then they needed to understand its various contours and demands. If it was Latin removed from foreign influence that they wanted, then they needed to understand the early Roman textual tradition. He demanded of them the purity to which they lay claim.

Et tu, Brute? *Stylistic Disagreements between Cicero and Brutus*

Brutus evokes the must and dust of the archive.† The archive and talking about it with knowledgeable friends offer a sweet retreat during an anxious time. In early 46 B.C.E., in which *Brutus* is set, Rome awaits news from northern Africa, where Cato and other Pompeians have mustered to battle Caesar.‡ Brutus is Cato's nephew, and he and Cicero's closest friend, Atticus, seek out Cicero in his reconstructed house on the Palatine for some conversation to occupy their idle hours. *Brutus*, then, contains what it purports to be: a discussion among Cicero, Atticus, and Brutus about the birth and rise of oratory. Cicero begins the work, however, deep in remembrance of his great oratorical rival, Hortensius, who had died four years earlier. With a glum sort of faux envy, Cicero marks how fortunate Hortensius was to pass away before the political situation declined so seemingly irretrievably.§ Cicero credits the succor arising from the "memory and recollection [*memoria et recordatio*]" of people such as Hortensius with helping him through this time of heavy care.** That acknowledgment serves as a segue into the *sermo* and also introduces the dominant theme of memorial and archival complexity. Though *recordatio* does not mean "record" in Latin, it does

---

*See, e.g., Cicero, *Brutus,* §258. Cicero enumerates his teachers in *Brutus;* many of them were not Roman, and some of them were from Asia Minor, where Cicero went for training. It is likely that many or all of those Romans to whom Cicero referred with *novi Attici* had had non-Roman teachers—Brutus certainly did (e.g., *Orator* §105)—but being taught by heads of Athenian philosophical schools does not mean one will have welcoming feelings toward other *alieni*. It bears emphasizing that Cicero himself was not from Rome, which native Roman aristocrats never let him forget.

†In his introduction to his translation for Loeb, G. L. Hendrickson asserts that Cicero (or his scribes) did not go researching, which I think must be wrong (5–6). He sees in *Brutus* evidence of compositional hastiness and a "lack of revision," which he judges to impart "reality and vivacity" to the discussion (10).

‡After losing the battle in April, Cato opted to commit suicide rather than accept the clemency Caesar was sure to offer. Other than being able to place *Brutus* in the spring of 46, we cannot be more precise, so Cicero may have written this work with knowledge of Cato's death. Cicero mentions his laudatory *Cato* in *Orator* §35.

§Cicero, *Brutus,* §1–2.

**Cicero, *Brutus,* §9.

index a process of retrieval. *Brutus* is largely about how one pulls from the past, an especial challenge when the object one traces—*oratio,* speech—is by nature ephemeral. Though that is, perhaps, its nature, speech had possessed artistic and preservative strains for several hundreds of years by the time Cicero is writing. The word for those strains is rhetoric. For Cicero, rhetoric is indisputably present only when orators are using writing before and after the delivery of a speech and the speech-text has a gloss or glimmer (*nitor*) about it—and not one that has been added ex post facto but one that made the speech worth hearing in the first place and preserving thereafter.

Throughout *Brutus,* Cicero is at pains to locate rhetoric's emergence in Rome and track it thereafter. The pains arise from materials, and a lack thereof, since Cicero needs speech-texts or poems or histories that preserve names and oratory-relevant descriptions of any person beyond the reach of living memory. He and Atticus collaboratively contest the authenticity of several historical speech-texts.* As Cicero slogs through registries of Roman names in an attempt to provide a complete-as-possible account of the development of Roman oratory, he includes Romans who are "held to be" orators. Reputation informs his choice of whom to include, even if he does not personally agree with the judgment. At play, then, in his narrative is a mix of memory and monumentality, the latter coming from the word Cicero and his interlocutors use to describe a speech-text (*monumentum*).† The memory of an orator may exist without a textual *corpus* or may not match up with one that does exist, in the opinion of current Romans, anyway.

Brutus is doubly teleological, first tracing the maturation and perfection of oratorical form in Athens and then doing the same in Rome. But, of course, Cicero is not tracing; he is constructing. Atticus, a historian known for his rigor, jokes that orators permit themselves "to fabricate [*ementiri*] history, so as to give more shrewdness to what they say."‡ Yet all of the materials Cicero mentions throughout *Brutus*—the 150 speech-texts of Cato Maior he has "found and read," for example—anchor his account deeply in the documentary.§ The texts make a claim: Cicero is not conjuring a tale, as orators lacking his industry and scruples might do, but presenting a trove of textual evidence that he himself has

---

*Cicero, *Brutus,* e.g., §99–100; §205.

†Cicero also refers to Atticus's history as a *monumentum* at §28. Atticus calls it a *memoria* at §19.

‡Cicero, *Brutus,* §42. *Ementior* (fabricate, falsify) resembles *emendo* (emend, correct, revise), and the two may share a common root. Given that Atticus covered what Brutus called "all of memory" in just one book-roll, it is obvious that Atticus compressed and cut, too (*Brutus* §13–14).

§Cicero, *Brutus,* §65.

dug up. Cicero connects published, polished speeches with the attainment of oratorical perfection. Their relationship is directly proportional: the more polished speeches an orator has published, the more perfect he can be considered to be. It is, of course, a self-serving definition.*

Explicit attention to the new Atticists does not appear until the final third of *Brutus,* which accords with its two-layered chronological orientation. It is with them that the two chronologies—one Athenian, one Roman—intersect; more specifically, the Athenian loops back in, and teleological tracks that Cicero had held separate collide. The new Atticists are striving for a Latin Atticism that marks oratory's Athenian peak of perfection with Lysias and ignores everything and everyone else. As Cicero sees it, the historical arcs and fine points of oratory are being hotly contested, and he actuates his talent for accumulating and marshaling evidence to support his case. The archive has become very active.

The dialogue begins when Brutus and Atticus find Cicero pacing nervously around his colonnade. He receives them warmly, telling them how much the writings they recently sent him have buoyed his sinking spirits. Brutus's work is likely his *De Virtute,* whereas Atticus's work is a tight history known as the *Liber Annalis* that, as Brutus puts it, "envelops all matters of memory very briefly and, if I may give my view, very diligently."† Cicero regrets that he cannot repay Atticus for the salvific novelty and utility of that singular *liber.* His stores are empty, and "the flower that once promised abundance has dried up, that used to open to the sun, has been blocked."‡ Atticus sees, however, that Cicero seems less depleted than usual and decides to call in his debt: Atticus proposes Cicero write something. His *stilus* has been static since he "published [*edidisti*]" *De Re Publica* five years prior, the very work that had inspired Atticus to write his concise history.§ Brutus prevails upon Cicero to speak if he cannot write, enjoining Cicero to repeat and complete the inchoate *sermo* about "orators, when they made a beginning, who they were and of what sort" that Atticus had told him Cicero and Atticus had begun recently at Cicero's Tusculan villa.** The occasion for that original conversation was wonder and worry about Brutus's "exquisite learning and singular industry [*exquisita doctrina et singularis industria*]" and how he would fare given the "sudden" collapse in *civitas* that has seen eloquence

---

*Cicero, *Brutus,* §122–123; see later discussion. At *Orator* §108, he boasts of having published more speeches than all the Greeks combined who wrote during peacetime/leisure time (*otium* can mean either).

†Cicero, *Brutus,* §13–14.

‡Cicero, *Brutus,* §16.

§Cicero, *Brutus,* §19.

**Cicero, *Brutus,* §20.

muted.* The three sit down under a statue of Plato, and Cicero begins a lengthy narrative that, in Platonic fashion, is only periodically interrupted by questions or exclamations from his interlocutors.

Cicero uses Atticus's *liber* for his chronological framework and builds upon it through additional research. That Cicero's account of Greek oratory is Atheno-centric is a function of evidence extant at the time: Athens "shines out" for being "the first city in which the orator emerged and *oratio* began to be entrusted to texts and letters [*monumentis et litteris*]."† Cicero emphasizes that the lack of *memoria* of eloquence before Solon and Pisistratus does not mean speech did not have a *vis* (power) worthy of preservation; Homer would not have praised the verbal power of Ulysses or the sweetness of Nestor or "have been elegant in speaking and clearly an orator" if eloquence had not been honored even in his time.‡ Cicero passes through all the big names preserved by Hellenistic copyists, sometimes in name only: Pericles, several sophists, Isocrates, Lysias, Demosthenes, Hyperides, Aeschines, Lycurgus, Dinarchus, Demades.§ Isocrates "wrote much [*scripsit multa*] very excellently and taught others" and made prose rhythm *de rigueur.*** Lysias wrote for others who were engaged in forensic action, and he was "an especially delicate [*subtilis*] and elegant [*elegans*] writer."†† For perfection, though, for one "from which nothing at all is missing," none best Demosthenes. In a very long sentence, Cicero gushes: "it is possible to find nothing sharp [*acute*] in those cases that he wrote up [*scripsit*], nothing, if I may say so, cunning [*subdole*], nothing sly [*versute*], that he did not see to; nothing said delicately [*subtiliter*], nothing pressed [*presse*], nothing precisely [*enucleate*], that one could make it more filed [*limatius*]; nothing contrary to the grand [*grande*], nothing rousing [*incitatum*], nothing ornate [*ornatum*] or with heft [*gravitate*] in either words or thoughts, that one could say it any higher [*elatius*]."‡‡ This description features every adjective and adverb that appears across the stylistic registers Cicero parses in *Orator,* written a few months subsequently. With the repetition of "nothing [*nihil*]," Cicero expresses Demosthenes's amplitude negatively. Nothing can be taken away, nothing added; it is thoroughly self-sufficient.

---

*Cicero, *Brutus,* §22.

†Cicero, *Brutus,* §26. At *De Oratore* 1.13, Cicero describes Athens as the place where oratory had been *inventa et perfecta* but notes that he prefers native examples to Greek ones.

‡Cicero, *Brutus,* §39, §40.

§No writings remain from Pericles or Demades.

**Cicero, Brutus, §32–33.*

††Cicero, *Brutus,* §35.

‡‡Cicero, *Brutus,* §35.

In the next sentence, Cicero describes the age of Demosthenes as effusively copious but posits that "the juice and blood of oratory were uncorrupted up to this age, in which, what was, was natural, not reliant upon dye [*sucus ille et sanguis incorruptus usque ad hanc aetatem oratorum fuit, in qua naturalis inesset, non fucatus nitor*]."* Cicero uses the language of purity, nature, and the healthy circulation within an oratorical body to credit Athenians even late into the fourth century with qualities that separate them from what follows. Within this Athenian segment of his chronology, the only attention Cicero affords to "Asianist" orators amounts to crediting their zeal for oratory, which kept "the name orator" not only alive but also in high regard. He seems to personify *eloquentia* to track "her" as "she" sets out from Piraeus and into the Hellenistic dawn: "she traveled to all the islands and trekked around the whole of Asia, becoming sullied by foreign ways and losing that healthfulness of Attic diction and, as it were, soundness and nearly forgot how to speak." Though he does not think *Asiani* orators ought to be condemned, he does agree with the observation that they speak quickly and copiously and are too little pressed and too greatly redundant. Cicero mentions that Rhodes held closer to the Attic than the Asian.†

Cicero then transitions to Rome, acknowledging, as he did for Athens, that nothing in those earliest days was done without *oratio* but that none of it remains. The first orator he includes is Brutus's famous ancestor, Lucius Brutus, no doubt a heavy inclusion given that the paterfamilial Brutus drove out the king in the sixth century B.C.E.‡ Moving ahead a few centuries, he affords more attention to Cato Maior than to any other second-century figure, mainly because Cato's oratorical *corpus* is sizable but also because Cicero (probably not entirely seriously) fancies Cato as the Roman Lysias.§ That classification is a dig at the new Atticists for ignoring Rome's own roster of trim figures. Atticus calls Cicero out on the absurdity of that analogy later in the dialogue, but Cicero did earlier concede that Cato's language was "more archaic" and "more shaggy" than current custom permits.** But Cicero is unwilling to cede Cato's utility as a learning tool. In fact, Cicero proposes to "change" Cato, updating him for this age, adding rhythm and tightening up how the parts of his *oratio* fit together.††

---

*Cicero, *Brutus*, §36, §37. Cicero squeezes Demetrius of Phalerum into the Attic bracket and praises him as "the most learned of them all." Demetrius's inclusion here among orators suggests that Cicero considers Demetrius to be, above all, an orator, since Cicero treats philosophers in a separate section (§119–120).

†Cicero, *Brutus*, §51.

‡Cicero, *Brutus*, §53.

§Cicero, *Brutus*, §63–69.

**Cicero, *Brutus*, §292–294; §68. Picking up another Platonic element, Cicero has Atticus call him an *eirōn* (ironist).

††Cicero, *Brutus*, §68.

Struck by Cicero's difficulties in assembling a record-based narrative, Brutus asks why more orators do not write. Cicero provides several reasons. The first is "inertia, since some orators do not want to add a domestic labor to their forensic one, for most orations are written once a speech has already been given, not so that they might be given; others are not willing to work to get better—for no thing contributes so much to speaking as writing [*scriptio*]; others do not desire to a memorial of their talent for posterity," preferring to enjoy a temporary acclaim that could be diminished were their speech-texts judged harshly; and then there are others, "who think they speak better than write, these being men of great talent but little learning."* Those who pursue a "more filed [*limatius*] type of speaking" seem better able to capture their performance on the page thereafter. Those who heat themselves up to deliver a speech are at a disadvantage, since time, "as it were, extinguishes the oratorical flame."† Not many orators write, then, and the book-rolls of those who did are becoming harder to find amid what Cicero calls "this crowd of new volumes [*hac turba novorum voluminum*]." Brutus jokes that Cicero's publications alone are crowding out other texts.‡ Cicero does not disagree.

Twice, Cicero and Brutus debate the necessity of slogging through the work of so many orators, including ones who are unremarkable but for having left a trace of themselves in some medium of memory.§ When Brutus goads Cicero to hurry up and get to the good stuff, Brutus means for Cicero to move into the new and the now. Though Cicero did not plan to speak about any of his contemporaries, even ones not still alive in 46 B.C.E., he tentatively enters his own time. He surveys all of the orators featuring in *De Oratore,* but Brutus insists on hearing about currently active orators, being particularly eager to hear Cicero's opinion on Caesar and depriving Cicero of the excuse of bashfulness about registering his opinion, since everyone knows Cicero admires Caesar's "*ingenium* [talent, genius]."** Later biographers of Caesar report that he studied rhetoric and philosophy with Molo of Rhodes, one of Cicero's teachers, too.†† Caesar was intellectually formidable. Cicero does not speak up about Caesar, so Atticus takes the lead.

He gushes that of all the orators Caesar speaks Latin the very most elegantly. Caesar has attempted to perfect "speaking well [*bene loquendi*]" through diligent study. The result, which Atticus refers to as *De Ratione Latine,* is carefully

*Cicero, *Brutus,* §91–92.
†Cicero, *Brutus,* §93.
‡Cicero, *Brutus,* §122–124.
§Cicero, *Brutus,* §137–138 and §176–182.
**Cicero, *Brutus,* §251.
††Plutarch, *Caesar,* 3.1.

written and dedicated to Cicero, whom Caesar hails as "nearly the founder and inventor of *copia* [verbal abundance]."* Cicero doubts Caesar means that as a compliment.

Atticus goes on to explain that the "foundation of oratory" is "correct speech and Latin [*locutionem emendatum et Latinam*]."† Knowing how to achieve them is therefore vital. Caesar wrote *De Analogia,* what Atticus called *De Ratione Latine,* in response to the small section of book-roll three of *De Oratore* about *Latinitas,* from which I quoted in my introduction.‡ Perhaps listening to everyday conversations when at home or out and about used to be a sufficient way to gain *Latinitas,* but no longer: "for as into Athens, so into this city, there has been an influx of many impure speakers from diverse locales. That demands a purging of language [*sermo*] and a turning to system [*ratio*] as a touchstone, and one not able to be changed, unlike the crooked ruler of common usage."§ Caesar's rulebook "emends" faulty and corrupted habits and establishes usage that is "pure and incorruptible."** Brutus jumps in to say that he has read Caesar's orations, finding them "commendable," and a few of the *commentarii* Caesar has written and published while on military campaign. At this, Cicero scoffs: Caesar's orations and observations are not "commendable," they are "nude."†† Caesar provides bare essentials only. For its part, a *commentarius* is meant to be loose, lax, unpolished, thrown together. A military man of Caesar's caliber ought to be providing sprawling raw material for historians to tame and smooth. Instead, what Caesar sends back has been subjected already to his own rigor and discipline. It is immaculate. Not a hair out of place. The bad historians will have nothing to curl, declares Cicero, and the good ones will have nothing to remove.‡‡ Caesar is a one-man show. In that way, Caesar is the mirror image of Demosthenes as Cicero described him earlier in the conversation: Demosthenes wants for nothing out of abundance, whereas Caesar wants for nothing out of austerity.§§

Cicero began *Brutus* with a reflection on the passing of Hortensius, several years back. More recently, however, a young orator of promise, Calvus, had died.

---

*Cicero, *Brutus,* §253.

†Cicero, *Brutus,* §258.

‡For more details about Caesar's *De Analogia,* see Hendrickson, "The *De Analogia* of Julius Caesar," and Garcea, *Caesar's* De Analogia.

§Cicero, *Brutus,* §258.

**Cicero, *Brutus,* §261.

††Cicero, *Brutus,* §262.

‡‡One wonders if Cicero is playing here with this hair language to tease Caesar, who was bald but whose name means, literally, "luxuriant locks." For more on Caesar as orator, see Leeman, "Julius Caesar, the Orator of Paradox." For more on Caesar's speeches and writings, see Gurd, "Cicero and Editorial Revisions" and *Work in Progress,* 49–76.

§§Cicero, *Brutus,* §35.

That Cicero did not begin the dialogue by reflecting on the passing of Calvus may be significant. Cicero deems Calvus's speaking to have been careful, exquisite, elegant, driven by inquiry and observation, and yet sacrificing its "true blood" due to fear of failure. The result was oratory so delicate that learned listeners savored it but "the multitude and the forum, for whom eloquence was born, devoured it."* Brutus volunteers that Calvus's having fancied himself "Attic" was the reason for his industrious pursuit of "slightness [*exilitas*]."† Cicero is well aware but asserts that Calvus "erred and caused others to err" by narrowly defining the Attic: "if being dried-up and sucked-up and without resources—however polished [*polita*], however urbane, however elegant—are put down as Attic, that is correct [*recte*], to a point; but because there are in the Attic *genus* other and better qualities, one must see and not ignore the gradations, and the differences, and the vim, and the variety of those from Attica."‡ Cicero proceeds to compare many of them, performing his point that there is no one Attic type. If Cicero had to choose, though, he would select Demosthenes, whom the whole of Greece would come to hear. Crowds and hearing are central to that description; "when the new Atticists speak, they are abandoned not only by the circle of odd-and-end listeners, but, what is worse, also by their supporters."§ They offer no variety and thus also no utility.

As the dialogue draws to a close, Cicero circles back to Hortensius, giving a ring composition to the work. Cicero splices himself in, but ostensibly only because Brutus insists. Cicero ventures measured autobiographical details about his own reliance on the *stilus,* obliging Brutus's wish to know "the whole me [*totum me*]" and "all of his body [*corpore omni*]," from the earliest days of his oratorical practice.** At the start, Cicero would bring into court speeches he had "diligently worked out and composed by lamplight [*diligenter elaboratas et tamquam elucubratas*]" and proceed to orate them without vocal variety, straining his voice and his body, much to the worry of his friends and physicians. Alterations are in order.†† Cicero travels first to Greece and then to Rhodes, where he pairs up with Molo, an advocate, logographer, and teacher best known for "marking up and noticing faults."‡‡ Molo makes Cicero his project, focusing on Cicero's redundancies, superfluities, youthful lack of restraint, and tendency to spill over bounds. Cicero returns to Rome after two years, "not only better

*Cicero, *Brutus,* §283
†Cicero, *Brutus,* §284.
‡Cicero, *Brutus,* §285.
§Cicero, *Brutus,* §289.
**Cicero, *Brutus,* §312–322.
††Cicero, *Brutus,* §312, §313.
‡‡Cicero, *Brutus,* §316.

trained but nearly transformed," both his body and speech better defined for the unrelenting demands of public speaking.* Cicero credits his ceaseless exercises, especially with the *stilus,* with imparting to his *oratio* an exquisiteness well beyond the prevailing standards of speech. When added to his tirelessness and industry in pleading cases, his speech grabs ears with its attention-turning novelty.†

Upon his return to Rome, Cicero adopts Hortensius as a model, though the two are frequently rivals in major cases. Hortensius has mastered the two primary species of the Asianist *genus*: one sententious and squeezed, the other rapid in its flow but not without ornate and witty words.‡ Cicero judges both species to befit a younger man better than an older one—there is something unsustainable about them—and Cicero watches as Hortensius's rich oratorical hues subtly dull and fade over time. Now that Hortensius is dead, men like Cicero and Brutus must guard "orphaned eloquence," protecting her purity as if "she" were "a virgin come of age" and hounded by "impetuous lovers."§ Given the way Cicero describes the new Atticists (bloodless, slight, thin), it does not seem to be they who give him worry. That is not to say they do not worry him, however.

What troubles Cicero about the new Atticists is that they threaten to make *tabulae rasae* of all of the archival *tabularii* of Rome's rhetorical history that he has painstakingly consulted, including his own contributions. It is not in Cicero's character to erase. Instead, he corrects (and himself has been corrected), making minor adjustments and updates to tradition's texts that preserve the animating spirit of an earlier orator but give it a body suitable to a new time and taste—that is precisely what he demonstrated with lines from Cato and Hortensius.** Cicero packs so many Roman speakers, even the mediocre ones, into his narrative to show just how much the new Atticists would wipe out with their petulant disregard and ignorance. He considers their historical erasure puerile: "Not to know what happened before you were born is to be a child forever," he points out.†† Brutus says repeatedly throughout the dialogue that, having been convinced by Cicero's appraisals of Rome's earlier orators, he will now read what he had previously looked down on, modeling the kind of behavior Cicero deems mature

---

*Cicero, *Brutus,* §316.
†Cicero, *Brutus,* §321.
‡Cicero, *Brutus,* §325.
§Cicero, *Brutus,* §330.
**Cicero, *Brutus,* §68, 298, 319. see also *Orator,* §155 and §232–233. It is fascinating that Cato himself recognized how quickly Romans forgot about contributions to their culture and commonwealth, and he used the language of a rubbed-out wax tablet, as I discussed in chapter 2.
††Cicero, *Orator,* §120.

and respectful.* Above all, Cicero hopes Brutus will heed the record of his illustrious ancestry.† Cicero remains tactfully tacit about which familial actions or orations Brutus should emulate, but the lack of specificity is suggestive.

Incomplete and Inedita: De Optimo Genere Oratorum

The historical illiteracy and flippancy of his young contemporaries bothered Cicero, but he knew that attitudes can be adjusted. After completing *Brutus,* he set about preparing a translation into Latin of Aeschines's *Against Ctesiphon* and Demosthenes's *In Defense of Ctesiphon* (better known as *On the Crown*), delivered in Athens in 330 B.C.E. Cicero's *De Optimo Genere Oratorum (On the Very Best Kind of Orator)* seems to be a preface for the translation, which has not survived, if Cicero even made it. His *refutatio* of those who find a translation of speeches an odd prospect suggests that those who wanted to read Aeschines and Demosthenes did so in the Greek, though Cicero notes that Greek poetry has been translated into Latin and accepted without a fuss.‡ Cicero is not insulting the learnedness of the new Atticists by translating Greek speeches into Latin. As aristocratic élites, they would have known Greek, even if they, like Cicero, did not use it in public. What he offers them is a truly Attic Latin to their supposed one.

Cicero is forthright about the corrective motivations of his translation. The new Atticists have gained a measure of credibility, but he identifies a "great error" in understanding about their style of speaking and deems this work "useful to students, though not necessary for myself."§ Cicero's demonstrations of the error of their ways will serve as lessons for students observing the struggle over the Attic name. One more group, too, is pulled into the preface: "This work [*labor*] of mine seeks the following objective: that our people will understand what to expect from those who deem themselves *Attici,* and what rule of speaking, so to speak, to apply to them."** He intends for his translation to beef up the anemic Atticism adopted by Calvus and his friends, but he also hopes it will supply his fellow Romans with evaluative criteria to impose upon new-Atticist language and their claims about it, which, perhaps, are not aligning. Trusting and informing their powers of judgment, Cicero brings the Roman people into the debate.

Yet, this short, incomplete work does not seem to have circulated during Cicero's lifetime. G. Hendrickson calls it "a roughly hewn and abandoned block

---

*Cicero, *Brutus,* §123.
†Cicero, *Brutus,* §331–333.
‡Cicero, *De Optimo,* §18.
§Cicero, *De Optimo,* §11, §13.
**Cicero, *De Optimo,* §15.

from the workshop which produced the two larger treatises" of that same year, *Brutus* and *Orator*.* Cicero likely left it unfinished so that he could dedicate himself to the designing, chiseling, and filing of *Orator*. *De Optimo* is worth a look not because it entered into the Atticism debate but because it holds additional evidence of the uses to which Cicero puts corporeal, editorial, and evaluative language in the year 46.

De Optimo opens with Cicero seeking "the one genus" of oratory, and "it is the kind that flourished in Athens."† He contends, though, that "the power of the Attic orators from that place is unknown, their glory known. For many see one side, that nothing about them was faulty, but few see the other, that many things were laudable."‡ Avoidance of fault is, of course, a merit, but it is also a bare minimum. He uses an athletic analogy: "those who have achieved only this may be considered sound and sucked in at least, but they are as those who frequent the *palaestra* who are well able to stroll around the colonnade but do not lay claim to the Olympian crown."§ They are fit enough to avoid looking out of place in the gym. Cicero continues, "the prize-winners, though free from all fault, are not content with merely good health, but seek strength, muscles, blood, and even a certain suavity of *color*."** The optimal orator must build upon sound *sententiae* (thoughts), seeking the shape and definition that follow from their careful development and flushing with a *color* particular to his exertions. Mark Bradley maintains that *color* is a distinctly Roman contribution to rhetorical theory, practice, and pedagogy. He describes rhetorical *color* as "the 'gloss' or complexion put on an argument, [and] sometimes extended to refer to a speaker's personal 'character', behaviour or demeanour."†† *Color* infused and diffused throughout a speech instead of sitting on its surface, like paint or dye (*fucus, pigmenta*). This

---

*Hendrickson, "Cicero De Optimo Genere Oratorum," 109. More recently, Stephen Usher has called it "a rough draft (or a badly transmitted text)." See Usher, "*Sententiae* in Cicero *Orator* 137–9 and Demosthenes *De corona*," 100.

†Cicero, *De Optimo*, §7. Hendrickson (1926) reckons that the title, *De Optimo Genere Oratorum*, comes from a later editor and that a better title would be *De Optimo Oratore*, since Cicero believed "orators there are, worse better and best; but of orator there is but one genus" (109). See 113ff for support of Hendrickson's view that Cicero left *De Optimo* unfinished.

‡Cicero, *De Optimo*, §7.

§Cicero, *De Optimo*, §8.

**Cicero, *De Optimo*, §8.

††Bradley, *Colour and Meaning in Ancient Rome*, 111, brackets mine. See also Hawhee, "The Colors of Rhetoric." For his part, Hendrickson judges by its position in the sentence that the *color* remark was a "marginal jotting of Cicero himself" ("Cicero De Optimo Genere Oratorum," 117).

athletic analogy, then, sets oratory apart from cosmetics in a clever and chromatic way, taking a Greek trope and giving it a Roman twist.*

If it is "pure" and "thin" prose that one wants to imitate, and even that is not simple to do, then Lysias cannot be outdone. Yet, Lysias wrote speeches for people caught in inconsequential legal contests, "and he purposefully filed himself down [*limaverit*] to the profile of minute suits [*minutarum causarum*]. If anyone speaks in this manner without being able to use a fuller style [*uberior*] if they desire, he should be regarded as a sound orator, but of the minor sort."† The new Atticists ignore the situational reason Lysias applied the file so extensively: he ground down his prose so that it would be level with ordinary occasions. In considering Lysias's file the only rhetorical equipment they need, they render elimination and reduction a formal property without regard for its only occasional instrumentality. They mean to start where Lysias only left off. Their default mode is the thin and faultless, and Cicero wonders if they are capable of more: "Demosthenes could certainly speak humbly [*summisse*], but Lysias perhaps not highly [*elate*]."‡ An orator needs to strive to master all types of speaking, ranging up and down the vertical register of style. It is precisely to imagining— maybe, perhaps, presenting—that master orator that Cicero dedicates himself in the work he pursued after dropping *De Optimo Genere Oratorum*.

Writing Orator

Like *Brutus*, *Orator* teems with textual references: to lines from speeches of Cicero and Demosthenes, to its own written form, to a hefty volume that will have to be written to cover topics too large to treat sufficiently in the current work.§ Cicero composed *Orator* in the late summer or autumn of 46, and his letters from the time contain descriptions of how, when, and where he squeezed reading and writing into his days. It was written in conditions of relative leisure, if quickly. That, according to his own letters of the time, Cicero stole away to his *bibliotheca* to read and write strongly suggests book-rolls were present,

---

*Plato, *Gorgias*, 462d–465b.
†Cicero, *De Optimo*, §9.
‡Cicero, *De Optimo*, §10.
§E.g., Cicero: §102–103, §105, §107, §130, §167; Demosthenes: §26, §105, §132–139; "this writing/book-roll": §35, §112, §147–8, §23714 "*magnum volumen aliud*" all about decorum: §73. At 137–139, Cicero pulls thirty-four *sententiae* (figures of thought) from Demosthenes's *De Corona*, on which see Usher, "*Sententiae* in Cicero *Orator* 137–9 and Demosthenes *De corona*." Cicero did not write a large work dedicated exclusively to decorum, but large parts of *De Officiis* treat the topic (especially book-roll 1).

whatever their state of unraveling and whoever was doing the unrolling.* *Orator* represents many fewer texts than *Brutus,* but *Orator* is a bookish book-roll.

Its first two-thirds articulate *oratio* (speech) into three *genera:* the weighty, the thin, and the moderate. Cicero matches each of the three *genera* to one of the three *officia oratoris* (duties of an orator): the weighty moves, the thin proves, and the moderate delights. One cannot limit oneself to one *genus* without limiting oneself to a single rhetorical function, a clear violation of the tripartite terms of oratorical duty. He also pairs each *genus* with an exemplary Attic orator whose speech-texts survive, showing there is no singular Attic type of speech. The last third of *Orator* elaborates upon the dimension of oratory that appeals to and satisfies the demands of ears: rhythm. The sensibilities of the new Atticists often come at the expense of the senses and of other natural human endowments, such as sensitivity to the emotions of others.[†] To use rhythm rhetorically requires plentiful exercise with the *stilus.*[‡] Cicero compares those who ignore rhythm to those who do not attend to basic athletic training: their speech may be trim and occasionally nimble, but it lacks the strength and stamina required to tangle with other bodies.[§] Cicero guesses that the new Atticists have narrowed themselves to the thin *genus* exclusively because they cannot manage anything brawny or voluptuous. Theirs is a weakness masquerading as an aesthetic preference. If they could *write* something, anything—he will not even test their voices—in the manner of Isocrates or Demosthenes or Aeschines, then he would reckon "that they did not flee that [hefty] *genus* out of desperation but took refuge in this [thin] *genus* out of judgment."[**] He doubts they can.

Apparently, a persuasive failure propelled *Orator* into being: Brutus is unconvinced by the orientation and conclusion of Cicero's oratorical genealogy in the monologic dialogue that bears Brutus's name and that was completed

---

Bibliotheca is usually translated as "library," though Hendrickson takes issue with its unconditional translation as such ("The Invention the Greek Library"). See, e.g., *Epistulae ad Familiares* (Letters to Friends), vol. 2, 7.28.2, from August 46 and addressed to Manius Curius: "Once I have received the salutations of my friends, which are in even greater numbers than they used to be because they seem to see a thinking and feeling citizen [*sentientem civem*] as if he were a white bird, I hide myself away in my library [*bibliothecam*]. And so I produce works [*opera*] whose qualities perhaps you will perceive [*senties*]."

[†] Cicero, *Orator,* §168.

[‡] Cicero, *Orator,* §150. Though she focuses on Byzantine rhetoric, Vessela Valiavitcharska provides an overview of how a close study of rhythm helps us better understand rhetorical pedagogy and composition historically (*Rhetoric and Rhythm in Byzantium,* 1–21).

[§] Cicero, *Orator,* §229.

[**] Cicero, *Orator,* §235.

earlier that year. Brutus wants Cicero to be definitive about "the *genus* of *elo-quentia*"—*genus*, singular—he judges to be "the utmost and most perfect [*summus et perfectissimus*]."* Cicero's position is that there is no greater matter than to judge "the best species and as it were figure of speaking [*optima species et quasi figura dicendi*]," since "there is so much dissimilitude among good orators [*oratores bonos*]."† *Figura* here prefigures the body-based language of the critical concepts Cicero will use, and it also responds to Brutus's desire to see a singular, superlative embodiment.‡ Cicero's approach to this work differs from the one he described in his youthful *De Inventione,* but it shares a basis in sculpture and the bodily form. In that earlier work, he compared his method to that of the sculptor Zeuxis, who had stolen beauty from lots of women to arrive at the form of his Helen; in this work, Cicero compares his method to that of Phidias, who worked not from live models to sculpt his Jove or Minerva but purely from his imagination.§ What Cicero is up to is ideational in an explicitly Platonic sense: he will envision and attempt to describe the ideal form of the orator, a figure beyond sensual apprehension and nearly beyond mental comprehension.**

The singular title of the work as a whole, then, refers to this ideal: "no one [*nemo*]" is *the* orator.†† For that reason, Cicero worries that emphasis on the perfect will be the enemy of the good or even of the good enough; it will certainly discourage "the studies of the many," most of whom may attain a short-lasting mediocrity at best and will not be motivated by the absent-presence that is an unachievable ideal form.‡‡ What he proposes to seek, then, is a someone who has never lived and a something that sometimes appears: something that "shines out [*eluceat*]," some times, in some speakers.§§ Yet the *nemo* appearing here at the beginning of the work recalls the ten-times-repeated *nemo* at the end of *Brutus,* where the takeaway is "no one—*until me.*"*** Cicero's quotations in *Orator* may offer a clue. Though he mentions others, he quotes from only two orators: Demosthenes and himself. It is their range and multiplicity that recommend them;

---

*Cicero, *Orator,* §3.

†Cicero, *Orator,* §2.

‡Recall that *figura* at this stage did not yet refer to a "figure of speech." At *Orator* §83, Cicero translates the Greek *schēmata* as *quasi aliquos gestus orationis,* the *quasi* [as if] indicating that Cicero thinks the analogy needs softening.

§Cicero, *De Inventione,* 2.1–10; Cicero, *Orator,* §8–9.

**Cicero, *Orator,* §10. Cicero uses *ten-/hen-* verbs explicitly at §100.

††Cicero, *Orator,* §7. Latin's lack of an absolute article serves Cicero's purposes here.

‡‡Cicero, *Orator,* §3.

§§Cicero, *Orator,* §7. Recall that Cicero's typical word for what are later called "figures" of speech is *lumines* (lights, points of brilliance).

***Cicero, *Brutus,* §322.

they are many orators in one body. They are adaptability personified. Each is the orator which is not one.

Throughout, Cicero frames *Orator* as the fulfillment of an urgent obligation to an insistent friend who wants an answer to the toughest question, which should excuse errors should Cicero trip up under the burden of this heavy charge.* Whether or how much of that urgency is Cicero's fabrication is unknowable. The speed with which the work was composed—as well as what some take to be a lack of tightness and polish—suggests Cicero felt pressed. If Cicero wrote *Brutus* to respond to vocal challenges to what he presumed was his unanimous oratorical supremacy, then *Orator* suggests the challenges had not ceased. Cicero estimates that the work will circulate widely, which could be a sign of the gossipy liveliness of the debate.†

Cicero's most substantive response to Brutus—and to the *novi Attici*—comes in the form of three *genera dicendi*.‡ The trichotomy is an obvious point of resistance to the singularity Brutus ostensibly demands and also a departure from the two-part generic scheme Cicero offers in *Brutus* and *De Optimo*.§ Here Cicero wants to amplify an orator's range of options and combinations and modulations. He does not stick to one name for each *genus*, yet the three sets of adjectival assemblages differ enough from one another to avoid confusion. The first is *grandiloquens* (large-speaking) or *gravis* (weighty) or *vehemens* (intense), characterized by "ample thoughts and heavy and majestic words, being intense, varied, copious, and heavy, trained and equipped to move and change minds." It has two species: some speakers use a "rough, harsh, shaggy speech, not perfect and brought to a close," while others are "smooth and structured and close everything off." Its opposite is *tenuis* (thin) or *callidus* (clever), "tight, explaining and elucidating everything, not making anything more ample than necessary, using a delicate [*subtili*] and pressed [*pressa*] and filed [*limata*] kind of speech." It, too, has two manifestations, since some speakers are "clever but unpolished [*impoliti*] and deliberately resembling the untrained and unskilled," while others have "the same dryness but are neater, more touched up, even blooming and slightly ornate." Between the weighty and the thin lies the *medius* (medium) or *temperatus* (temperate) type, which lacks the shine and flash of the first type and the sharpness and sting of the second. Rather than being a mixture of the two,

---

*Cicero, *Orator*, §35; see also 1–3, 33–35, 140–141, 237–238.

†Cicero, *Orator*, §112.

‡Cicero, *Orator*, §21–23.

§As I showed at the end of the previous chapter, the *auctor ad Herennium* had offered three, thought to originate with Theophrastus: *gravis* (heavy, weighty), *mediocris* (moderate, average), and *extenuata/adtenuata* (thinned out) (4.11). Cicero himself offered three in book-roll 3 of *De Oratore*.

it enjoys its own "tenor," introducing nothing into speaking that is not "easy-going and even" and maybe tucking a flourish (*flos*) here and there. Through subcategorization and conceptual crossover, Cicero confounds the simple taxonomy of the new Atticists.

Before giving the genera a fuller treatment, he aligns each *genus* with a corresponding *officium oratoris,* duty or right action of an orator: "thin in proving, moderate in delighting, spirited in bending [*subtile in probando, modicum in delectando, vehemens in flectendo*]."* An orator who cannot—or will not—fulfill those offices falls short more than just aesthetically; he falls short essentially. He does not do all that he needs to do to be deserving of the name of orator, let alone *the* orator. He also does not practice or produce *eloquentia.* Cicero emphasizes the literal, oral meanings of the Greek *rhētōr* and the Latin *eloquens.*† If speaking were not essential to an orator's identity, another word would do, such as *inventor* (one who finds material), or *compositor* (one who puts together material), or *actor* (one who acts or enacts the material; literally, a doer). Necessary as it is, however, consideration of the oral is insufficient without that of the aural; an orator must learn how listening, attention, and attunement work.

Cicero returns to the *tria genera,* giving the *tenuis genus* the most space, since it is the *genus* the new Atticists claim is the only Attic one.‡ The incongruous impression cultivated by users of this *genus* is of "a not displeasing negligence [*non ingratum neglegentiam*]."§ It seems low maintenance, naturally neat, tidy. Cicero moves into the cosmetic strain of *ornatus* to find more language, and he leads with an image of a woman: "Just as some women are said to be not nothing when unornamented [*non nullae inornatae*], as if this itself becomes them, so this thin *oratio* delights, unadorned though it is; for there is a certain something in both instances that lends greater charm, but not so as to be apparent. At the same time, all conspicuous ornament, in the manner of pearls, will be set aside; not even curling irons will be applied; all paints, dyed white and red, will be pushed away; only elegance and neatness [*elegantia modo et munditia*] will be left."** The language of gender and sexuality does normative work within Roman rhetorical theory, policing appropriate style and delivery, above all, so that they remain within masculinity's approved cultural boundaries.†† With regard to delivery, such language monitors an orator's actual body, movement,

---

*Cicero, *Orator,* §69. See §101 for the matter-manner alignment.
†Cicero, *Orator,* §61.
‡Cicero, *Orator,* §75–99; *tenuis/subtilis* at §75–90.
§Cicero, *Orator,* §77.
**Cicero, *Orator,* §78.
††I deal with this matter more fully in chapter 6.

and voice; with regard to style, it scrutinizes a body of words and the bodies of words. *Mollis,* soft, is a good example. Cicero uses that adjective to describe the middle *genus,* but it is a risky word, since it is often associated with weakness and effeminacy.* To return to Cicero's analogy here, for him to compare neo-Atticism with an unadorned man would be odd, because unadorned men are the norm; Cicero pushes the limits of propriety in *Brutus* when he remains within a masculine register but refers to Caesar's prose as "nude," the most unadorned a person can be.† A purposefully unadorned woman departs from expectation, however, and especially one who stuns in her natural state and eschews what less attractive women rely upon and put on. Her beauty is in her bones and skin, in the basics of her construction. Still, that Cicero leads with an image of an unfussy woman indicates a certain level of mischief on his part.

Cicero borrows the four *aretai* (excellences) of *lexis* that Theophrastus enumerated in his lost treatise on rhetoric to describe how those who pursue this *genus* prioritize "talk that is pure and Latinate, speaking lucidly and plainly, and seeking what is befitting [*sermo purus erit et Latinus, dilucide planeque dicetur, quid deceat circumspicietur*]," lacking only "ornament that is sweet and flowing [*ornatum illud suave et affluens*]."‡ With this "pressing down"—the Latin is the root of our "suppression"—of *oratio* comes a compression of the voice that prevents it from being an instrument of energy, emotion, and power.§ Again, the new Atticists are incomplete.

The middle *genus* received mention in the previous chapter in reference to Demetrius of Phalerum, whom Cicero names the exemplum. It blooms, its words "painted and polished [*pictum et politum*]" and joined with "charming [*lepores*]" thoughts.** Its origin can be traced to the sophists. Cicero least explicates the *gravis* (weighty) genus, perhaps demonstrating his opinion that it is something better experienced than explained. The *gravis* orator is "ample, copious, weighty, ornate, and in him undoubtedly power [*vis*] is at its greatest."††

---

*See Edwards, *The Politics of Immorality in Ancient Rome,* 63–97.

†Cicero, *Brutus,* §262. Cicero also calls Caesar's prose *recti et venusti omni ornatu orationis tamquam veste detracta* and mentions that Caesar does not provide enough for historians to curl with their own devices.

‡Cicero, *Orator,* §79. Building on book-roll 3 of Aristotle's *Rhetoric,* Theophrastus's four *aretai* of *lexis* are correctness, clarity, appropriateness, and ornament. For an appraisal of Theophrastean strains in Cicero, see Fortenbaugh, "Cicero as a Reporter of Aristotelian and Theophrastean Rhetorical Doctrine."

§Cicero, *Orator,* §85.

**Cicero, *Orator,* §96.

††Cicero, *Orator,* §97.

Once Cicero has enumerated all three genera, he compares them using the criterion of danger:

> One who has worked thoroughly in the delicate and sharp *genus* so as to be able to speak cleverly and narrowly, and has not conceived of anything higher [*altius*], if he has perfected this one *genus*, is a great [*magnus*] orator, but not the greatest; and occupies ground so little slick, that, once he gets established, he will never fall. But he in the middle, whom I call moderate and temperate, if he builds himself up enough, will not fear the unsteady and uncertain contingencies of speaking; even if he is somewhat less than successful, as often happens, he will not be exposed to great danger [*periculum*]; for he cannot fall from very high. But truly this orator of ours whom we place in first position—weighty [*gravis*], piercing [*acer*], and burning [*ardens*]—if he is born for this one type alone, or trains himself solely in this, or shows zeal for only this *genus*, and does not temper his abundance with the other two genera, then he will be found greatly contemptible. For he who is the most lowly [*summissus*], because he speaks sharply and slyly, is already considered wise; the middle, sweet [*suavis*]; but this abundantly copious one, if he has nothing else, will regularly seem scarcely sane enough.*

These are not merely formal, aesthetic risks Cicero describes. When an orator fails, it is not only his art or himself that and whom he fails; it is a client, a friend, or the commonwealth. The orator of the third *genus* "can say nothing tranquilly, nothing softly, nothing divided up, definitely, distinctly, elegantly," and people can find him unintelligible and discomforting.† This third *genus*, when practiced exclusively, is off-putting. Using the usual Latinate English word to which the title of the treatise *Peri Hupsous* is typically translated, John Dugan calls this third *genus* "the Ciceronian sublime."‡ Cicero and the author of *Peri Hupsous* both throw thunderbolts, overrun riverbanks, and kick up Bacchic frenzies to describe this grandeur that *Orator* classifies as a particular *genus* of oratory and *Peri Hupsous* as a quality that can appear in any unit of prose or verse.§ There is growing scholarly support for considering *Peri Hupsous* (*On Height*), usually attributed to "Longinus," to have been written in the generation after Cicero. Longinus's work is a rejoinder to a treatise on *hupsos* (height)

---

*Cicero, *Orator,* §98–99.
†Cicero, *Orator,* §99.
‡Dugan, *Making a New Man,* 253, 315.
§For an extended comparison of the sublimities of Cicero and Longinus, see Porter, *The Sublime in Antiquity,* 610–617.

written by the Augustan-age critic Caecilius of Calaecte, which has not survived. Caecilius had supplied plentiful examples of verbal height, but he had not explained its basis or given any instruction on how one achieves it, rendering his account "trivial."* *Peri Hupsous* does both, naming five sources of height and tutoring readers in how to stretch toward each. Longinus also addresses errors that arise from missing the heights, such as swollen language, that is, language that thickens up rather than reaches up. "Swellings," he writes, "are just as unwelcome in words as in bodies."†

In the final sections of the work, Longinus addresses errors within those writers he had already deemed lofty. He scoffs that Caecilius preferred Lysias to Plato because the former "is immaculate and never makes a mistake, whereas Plato is full of mistakes."‡ Longinus finds such a view intolerable. He asks incredulously: "Which is better in poetry and prose, magnitude [*megethos*] with a few flaws [*diēmartēmenois*] or correct composition of moderate [*summetron*] quality, yet entirely sound and flawless?"§ Longinus elaborates, judging that those "with mighty natures are the least spotless" and that those messy spots should be regarded not as "willful mistakes but as oversights, let in at random and by chance by the inattentiveness of the huge-natured."** Longinus describes how poets and orators inclined to loftiness get carried away, lose themselves, and become inattentive to minutiae. Through *phantasia,* the ability or faculty or result of vivid imagination, a poet or orator is plunged into or pulled away to a scene while they craft it.†† In poetry, the effect of such scenes on the reader is "amazement"; in oratorical works, it is "reality and truth." In the section immediately prior, Longinus envisions a peculiar sort of visualization whereby a poet or orator reaching for the heights imagines how Homer or Demosthenes would say something or wonders what critical advice they would offer were they "present [*parōn*]."‡‡ The lofty are not above cheering on (or correcting) others.

---

*Longinus, *Peri Hupsous,* 1.1. Caecilius ran with the neo-Attic crowd.

†Longinus, *Peri Hupsous,* 3.4.

‡Longinus, *Peri Hupsous,* 32.

§Longinus, *Peri Hupsous,* 33.1.

**Longinus, *Peri Hupsous,* 33.2 and 33.4. For a comparison of Longinus's views on error and *hupsos* with those of the securely Augustan-age critics Dionysius of Halicarnassus and Pompeius Geminus, see de Jonge, "Dionysius and Longinus on the Sublime," 292–295.

††Longinus, *Peri Hupsous,* 15. Nowadays, in narrative theory, this phenomenon is called "immersion" or "transportation," to which I have alluded, respectively, with "plunged" and "pulled away."

‡‡Longinus, *Peri Hupsous,* 14.1.

Cicero seems uninterested in transporting Demosthenes to Tusculum to read over his shoulder.* Despite his obvious enthusiasm for Demosthenes, he makes the following admission to Brutus: "And I am far from admiring my own work, and am so difficult and fussy, that even what Demosthenes himself produced is not enough. He may be the one eminent among all in every *genus* of speaking, but still he does not always fill my ears; they are eager and capacious and so often desire something immense and infinite."† Cicero quotes from his own speeches to demonstrate his generic range, explaining that he would select even more exempla from his *corpus* were his speeches not known, notable, and easy to find to read.‡ Indeed, Cicero claims that he alone published more speeches than what remains of the output of the most celebrated Athenian orators between Athens's loss to Sparta in 404 and that to Macedon in 338, and he did not publish every speech he delivered.§

The final third of *Orator* pertains to prose rhythm, or what Cicero says one could call *compositio* or *perfectio* or *numerus*.** Since the language of sentence components is bodily, these sections are conspicuously anatomical and kinesthetic: limbs (*membra*) run and dance throughout. Cicero dedicates so much careful and technical attention to rhythm because each *genus* of speech limits or frees the voice in particular ways and because an orator who wants to intervene in urgent matters in his own time *and* to be read afterward needs prose that both rises to the original occasion and recreates certain dimensions of that occasion for readers. An orator must know how to manipulate pace to match sound with sense and emotion with expression: speeding up or slowing down a narrative, elongating or truncating an argument. This work is accomplished through patterns of vowel length, repetitions of words, the number of clauses, the size of sentences; a speech-text becomes a record of the orator's voice, a literal phonograph (voice-writing).†† The rhythm within a speech-text connects the reader to the orator's passion and pulse. It offers an approximation of them, not a reanimation of them, as Cicero points out, but it a powerful connection

---

*Still, that *Brutus* took place under a statue of Plato and that Brutus had a statue of Demosthenes suggests they liked looking upon and being looked upon by great Greek men. For more about Cicero's art collection, see Leen, "Cicero and the Rhetoric of Art." For more about the functions of busts of contributors to culture in private and public libraries, see Too, *The Idea of the Library*, 195.

†Cicero, *Orator*, §104.

‡Cicero, *Orator*, §102–105, §103, §132.

§Cicero, *Orator*, §108. On Cicero's *inedita* speeches, see Crawford, *M. Tullius Cicero*.

**Cicero, *Orator*, §149–236, §228.

††For more on this intriguing notion, see Butler, *The Ancient Phonograph*.

nonetheless.* As John Dugan observes, there is a two-way irony in the writing-rhythm relationship as Cicero sees it: "the artistry of the pen is required for an orator to appeal to the natural pleasures of the ear," and "rhythmical prose, achieved through careful writing, allows the text of an oration to overcome the limitations of its textual status."† This Ciceronian cycle shows how entangled orality and textuality could be—should be, in Cicero's estimation—and hints at the time, focus, and care required to produce a single speech worth hearing *and* reading. Cicero suspects many of the new Atticists are incapable of this sort of brutal industry, which is largely using art to envelope art. On the matter of hiding rhetorical art, necessary since "the tongue is suspect [*lingua suspecta*]," Cicero admits his curiously advantageous position: everyone knows he was a student of rhetoric and philosophy. "How could I—when I left home as a young man and crossed the seas for the sake of these very studies, and my house was filled with exceptionally learned men, and my conversation bore perhaps a note of learning, and my writings [*scripta*] were read generally [*vulgo*, perhaps "popularly"]—be able to hide what I had learned? What is there to blush about, unless, perhaps, because I have made small advances?"‡ Against the norm, Cicero's constant challenge may be put his well-known learning on show.

Throughout *Orator*, Cicero makes arguments for the work's own generic classification, and for his as its writer. Cicero claims to write as an *existimator* (critic) rather than a *magister* (teacher); he would not dare try (or stoop) to school Brutus and his well-educated but stylistically lackluster associates.§ All the same, Cicero offers them a correction course. First, they should get to know the Demosthenic *corpus* much better.** Among other benefits, reading him will help them recognize how contested the Attic designation is not only now but also historically, going all the way back to the very contests between Aeschines and Demosthenes.†† Since Brutus has a statue of Demosthenes at his own Tusculan villa, he must think the man worthy of recognition.‡‡ The disagreement between Demosthenes and Aeschines on rhetorical form is a lecture within a larger lesson: the new Atticists need to acknowledge that judgments and preferences differ,

---

*Cicero, *Orator*, §130. Where the Asianists goes wrong, in Cicero's estimation, is in their "slavishness to *numerus*," which results in a lack of *varietas* (§230–231). Unvarying patterns of rhythm work for poetry but not for oratory.

†Dugan, *Making a New Man*, 285.

‡Cicero, *Orator*, §146.

§Cicero, *Orator*, §112.

**Cicero, *Orator*, §23, §234, §235.

††Cicero, *Orator*, §26.

‡‡Cicero, *Orator*, §110.

among both orator-writers and their hearers-readers.* Among orator-writers, judgments and preferences must result from wide experimentation with language's possibilities. Cicero three times plays attempting (*conatus/temptatus*) against completing (*perfectus*): he is not perfect, but he tries, he strives, he takes risks.† Returning to his sublime language, he has far to fall if he fails, since he spends some time in the *gravis* and *altus* (heavy and high) mode. That is the only way to produce words that will remain on a page and in the air.

Several questions raised within *Orator* but present in similar forms in *Brutus* and *De Optimo* linger. What does the *auris civitatis* (ear of the community) want to hear in and around 46 B.C.E.?‡ How quickly are aural appetites sated on one style—though Cicero refuses to classify himself as using one *genus*—and then desirous of something different? How, if at all, do the ear's desires relate to the political situation, especially when the adjective Cicero applies to ear's, *civitatis*, can also mean "of the state"? And what role do speech-texts play? Cicero thinks ears want now what they have always wanted: calibrated ratios of calm and instruction, sweetness and delectation, and fury and motivation. As Cicero writes about them in *Brutus* and *Orator*, speech-texts preserve an orator's unique calibrations, giving readers a sense of how he sized up the situation to which a given speech purports to respond. Speech-texts preserve judgment and craft from which all manner of people can learn and will learn; Cicero certainly has future generations in mind.

The orator's—Cicero's—primary challenge is how to manage all the many resources and options available, and through the medium of *oratio*, which itself "is soft, and tender, and so flexible that it follows wherever you turn it [*torqueas*]."§ Yet the polished and the plentiful, for example, are not necessarily oppositional qualities. Often, that which is plentiful was even more abundant before the orator made choices of amplification and diminution, inclusion and exclusion. Everything from philosophy, to rhetorical commonplaces, to words themselves supply the orator with what Cicero calls *silva* (raw material; literally, a forest).** It is an orator's duty to cut, shape, and polish a wide swath of the raw material of his culture and community. This is eloquence.

Sounding much like his younger self when he wrote the opening of *De Inventione,* Cicero issues a challenge: if people suddenly consider eloquence dangerous to the city, then it needs to be thrown out; if they do not, then it cannot

---

*Cicero, *Orator,* §36.
†Cicero, *Orator,* §103, §132, §210.
‡Cicero, *Orator,* §106.
§Cicero, *Orator,* §52.
**For instances of *silva* as "raw material" in *Orator* and in two other rhetorical works of Cicero see e.g., *Orator* §12, §139; *De Inventione,* 1.34; *De Oratore,* 3.103.

be bad to learn it and live it.* The very social, communal virtue of decorum lies in making rhetorical alignments among "place, time, and audience [*locus, tempus, auditor*]."† A one-note orator who never adjusts or aligns does not deserve the name; he cannot even claim never to offend decorum, since doing anything too much—even doing too little too much—is indecorous. In certain situations, his restraint may be regarded as "prudent [*prudens*]."‡ And he may seldom fail to impress a tight group of self-styled experts with narrow preferences, but he will never compete in large-scale contests and win over multitudes.§ The new Atticists seem body-shy. If, as Cicero puts it, what is said is to *eloquentia* as an *animus* is to a *corpus*, then it seems that they are trying to slough off the corporeal.** They wish to inform without form. If what is uniquely the orator's is the "huge power [*maxima vis*]" that arises from the voice, bearing, gestures, and movements working in concert to perform rhythmic argument, then the new Atticists are enervating their own unique art.†† They are speakers or conversationalists, sure, but not orators. "In truth, the eloquent person [*eloquens*]," Cicero insists, "who ought to move others not only through approval but through admiration, acclaim, and applause, if it is possible, ought to excel in all things such that he would feel shame to have anything else watched or heard more willingly."‡‡ To presume that the new Atticists are turning inward—toward the narrow and pure and away from the capacious, and pleasurable, and popular—in advance of restrictions on the public voice and where, when, and how it may present itself is to endow them with clairvoyance. They are participating in the same public venues as Cicero.

In his three rhetorical works from 46 B.C.E., Cicero surveys the past and present sounds of eloquence. The vocabulary of *corpus* care bends to his service, as Cicero avails himself of athletics, cosmetics, dress, constitution, and more to demonstrate how ill equipped the neo-Attic cult of the pared-down and pure is for the demands of public live lived in language. Language is roomy, and the orator, above all, must know how to explore its expanses as well as to exploit its narrow nooks. The orator, a figure that in Cicero's estimation is always reading

---

*Cicero, *De Inventione*, 1.1ff; Cicero, *Orator*, §142.

†Cicero, *Orator*, §70. For more on the sociality of decorum in Cicero's other writing from this time period, see Kennerly, "*Sermo* and Stoic Sociality in Cicero's *De Officiis*."

‡Cicero, *Orator*, §236.

§Cicero, *Orator*, §183–189.

**Cicero, *Orator*, §44. Recall what Cicero said about Calvus's delicate body being gobbled whole by the people. If that is the way the popular ear eats, then Cicero's generous portion sizes are especially designed to slow people down so that they might enjoy their meal.

††Cicero, *Orator*, §61.

‡‡Cicero, *Orator*, §236.

and writing, must start from a place of plushness and plentitude and then pull back what will not be necessary or welcome in a given situation. This pullback is editorial, since it pertains to how an orator manages material he intends to make public. Cicero's flair was figuring out ways of speaking that would sound good and do well on the day of delivery and continue to be sought out in textual form by people years removed. He did not imagine later editors struggling to sort out textual variants of his speeches, but he did jokingly fancy "all the boys learning him" at school.*

Cicero's *rhetoricae* from the year before Caesar's assassination may leave readers with an image of an aging has-been, admonishingly brandishing his fraying book-rolls, many of which are his own works. Pushed far from his glory days by the passing of years and the scheming of his contemporaries, he retired to the country and philosophy. Yet Cicero was not the retiring kind. His final year and a half of life saw a frenzy of writing and speaking, including the fourteen items grouped together as *The Philippics,* only one of which he did not delivery orally; the raucous Second circulated as a pamphlet only.† Cicero's own generativity hastened his finality: he was assassinated on the road from Formiae in December 43, his name having been added to the proscription list by Marcus Antonius, the cause and aim of the *Philippics.* These speeches thus paid the ultimate homage to Demosthenes, similarly hunted down by those who deemed his fluency inimical to the new order of things. Cicero's contention that polished, published words had public purpose, however, did not die with him.

---

*Cicero, *Epistulae ad Quintum Fratem* (Letters to Quintus), 3.1.11. This letter is dated September 54.

†John Ramsey writes that "Like C.'s *Verrines* or *Catilinarians,* the *Philippics* form a corpus having a unity all its own, and yet the *Philippics* are unique in being the only speeches of C. to receive a title inspired by a Greek model. The decision to give them this title was made relatively late, after the majority of them had already been written and put into circulation. Presumably those speeches had originally been known simply as the *oratio prima* (*secunda,* etc.) *in M. Antonium,* after the fashion of C.'s four speeches against Catiline." They take on the title of *Philippics* in two letters Cicero exchanged with Brutus in April 43 (*Ad Brut.* 2.3.4, *Ad Brut.* 2.4.2). Ramsey, "Introduction,"16. Seneca the Elder names "Anthony Promises to Spare Cicero's Life if He Burns His Writings: Cicero Deliberates Whether to Do So" (*Suasoriae* 7) a popular student persuasive speech topic, as does Quintilian, 3.8.45.

CHAPTER FOUR

FILING AND DEFILING HORACE

In October 42 B.C.E., less than a year after the assassination of his father, Marcus Cicero found himself in a sticky marshland, in arms. He had joined up with Cassius and Brutus, whose force finally met that of Octavian and Antonius at Philippi in Macedon. The conditions made for combat that was cruelly intimate. Losing major battles there, Cassius and Brutus took their own lives; their soldiers who did not join them in death fled to Sextus Pompey in Sicily and, when peace was negotiated a few years later, were allowed to return to Rome under conditions of amnesty. Joining Cicero in that awkward position was an officer named Quintus Horatius Flaccus, or Horace, to later generations.* The two young men may have met in Athens two years prior while completing educations in rhetoric and philosophy financed by their fathers.† It was there that Brutus had recruited them. Upon their return from war, Cicero entered public service, serving as co-consul with Octavian in 30 and holding the governorship of Asia in the 20s. Horace began work at the Treasury. He also pursued poetry. Clearly, he had a way with *numeri* (numbers, rhythms).

In a poem from a collection published several decades after Philippi, Horace records that he found himself after the lost battles "humbled [*humilem*], with wings clipped, and without the resources of my father's / home and farm"— which were most likely confiscated by Octavian and Antonius—and thus "compelled" by "bold poverty to write verses."‡ Poetry, though, was not lucrative, in itself. *Humilis,* the root of "humiliation," is a not insignificant dimension of Horace's hexametrical poetics.§ Horace's poetry is ground-bound: it walks rather

---

*For a sensitive treatment of Horace's careful deployment of war stories in his poetry, see Citroni, "The Memory of Philippi in Horace and the Interpretation of *Epistles* 1.20."

†Cicero wrote *De Officiis* for and dispatched it to his son during this time. Horace writes about his philosophical training in "the groves of Academe" at *Epistulae* 2.2.45–46.

‡Horace, *Epistulae,* 2.2.49–52.

§His Muse is *pedestri* (pedestrian, *Sermones,* 2.6.17), his poems *repentis per humum* (*Epistulae,* 2.1.250–251), and poets *serpit humi* when a storm threatens (*Ars Poetica,* 28). The pedestrian nature of his Muse is reflected in the title and analysis of Freudenburg, *The Walking Muse.*

than soars. Yet Horace was not a lowly poet. In 38 B.C.E., Octavian's friend Maecenas, a patron of the arts, welcomed Horace into his generous patronage after meeting him through Horace's fellow poets Vergil and Varius.* Horace received an approving nod from Octavian, too. Without any hand-wringing about the intractably difficult matter of Horace's "true" feelings toward Octavian (he did not receive the title of "Augustus" until 27 B.C.E.), one can marvel at the turn of events through which an officer in Brutus and Cassius's fighting force came to take up this plush, powerful position in the circle of Maecenas only four years later.† The change in Horace's fortunes, whatever his allegiances, has typically been attributed to his entertainment value for Maecenas and to his propaganda value for the *princeps*. Accordingly, one can view Horace's situation from at least five perspectives. One, he was a sellout, a traitor to the republican principles for which he fought and many died at Philippi. Two, which is a more cynical version of the first position, he was a free rider, a barnacle attached to Augustus's ship of state, riding it solely to get ahead and spread his own reputation. Three, he was a genuine convert to the order arising out of the chaos. Four, he was a double agent, for, if one reads suspiciously enough, one can find a sneer underlying all of Horace's flattering gestures to the *princeps* and his so-called *pax*. Five, which is my position, Horace's writings show such complexity and sensitivity—they were, after all, written over a thirty-year span—that no one-faceted appraisal of his motives or moods suffices. Rather than being simply adopted or co-opted during a low period in his life, Horace actively and continually adapted to personal and political circumstances that were changed utterly by a grisly civil war and the subsequent flux of affairs, Rome's and his own.

Throughout his poetry, Horace insists upon the necessity of editing. The editorial tool to which he explicitly refers is the file (*lima*), which, above all, eliminates. Horace characterizes bad poetry—and lots of it—as the scourge of his age. As Rome's internal political conditions stabilized, innumerable élite Romans, no matter their talent and work habits, scribbled verses. Horace lodges this complaint from his first work, *Sermones,* to his last, *Ars Poetica.*‡ The poetic excesses and deficiencies he observes are something other and bigger than the faults of a few individuals ignorant of the demands of writing *recte,* an adverb meaning both "correctly," a technical consideration, and "suitably," a rhetorical consideration.§ These bad poets, he asserts, are embarrassing not only themselves but

---

*Horace, *Sermones,* 1.6.52–64.

†See Kennedy, "'Augustan' and 'Anti-Augustan': Reflection on Terms of Reference," where he shows such qualifiers to be unhelpful and simplistic heuristics.

‡Some even challenge him to poem-offs or brag on the stamina of their pens as he walks down the street (*Sermones,* 1.4.13–21, 1.9.23–24).

§Horace, *Sermones,* 1.4.13; *Ars Poetica,* 309. I treated this term in the Introduction.

also Rome. Further, Horace describes a publication push, a mounting public pressure for poets to make their work widely available, that is, to recite their work in public venues or submit it to the stalls of booksellers. Entertaining a crowd, especially *viva voce,* does not interest Horace in the least. More than that, he claims to feel defiled—his hard work effaced, his person tainted—by mere contact with the masses.* Such high-mindedness aligns with Horace's sights on Rome's position now and his in the long run.† The kind of poetry he prefers to write *will* be popular, but only with certain people.

Though it is fruitless to deny that fear (*metus*) dwells in meticulousness, it is less unrewarding to argue about what kind of fear drove Horace to value filed poetry so highly. Did he cleave to editing tools with the nervousness of a writer nursing perfectly healthy reception worries or with the timorousness of a writer in censorious times? Was the file his only protection against the exposure of his uncensored thoughts and the resultant counterblow of powerful men? By tracing the trail of Horace's meticulous file across his hexameter works (*Sermones, Epistulae,* and *Ars Poetica*), I push against a prevailing view on Horace's strictures on the *stilus:* that he "made a literary virtue out of a political necessity," as Emily Gowers puts it, the "necessity" being the need to watch one's words as the imperial period gained force.‡ As my arguments in this book thus far have demonstrated, an insistence upon editing or an enthusiasm for traits thought to result from editorial attentions can be something other than a survival mechanism in totalitarian times. How well that moniker fits Augustus's age is highly contested, besides.§ Instead, a zeal for editing signals a commitment to refinement that is central to, even definitive of, well-developed textual culture.

Horace's endorsement of the file (*lima*) constituted a civic act as well as a statement of poetic principle, since he placed himself at the vanguard of contemporary Roman literary dominance—as compared to the productions of ancient Greeks, ancient Romans, and modern poetasters—and ultimately pitched this dominance as a necessary complement to Rome's military might.** Horace

*Horace, *Sermones,* 1.6.18; *Odes,* 1.1.32, 2.16.41, and 3.1.1; *Epistulae,* 1.1.70–80 and 1.19.35–49.

†See, e.g., Horace, *Odes,* 3.30.

‡Gowers, "The Restless Companion," 48. Similarly, Freudenburg argues that Horace lacks both the highborn status and the "political luxury" of bluntness that Lucilius enjoyed, "so he [Horace] introduced an aesthetic refinement that the genre previously did not know or respect: the use of the eraser. Horace packages personal self-limits as aesthetic refinements expressed 'in conversation' that keeps within strict bounds of decorum, in tone, topic, meter, and so on" ("Introduction," 10–11). See also Gurd, *Work in Progress,* 77–103.

§See, e.g., Lamp, *A City of Marble.*

**Horace, *Ars Poetica,* 289–290.

appealed to the competitive civic pride of Augustus (and of overreaders) when he emphasized the irony that "captive Greece" captured feral Rome and brought Greek *ars* into what had been an uncultivated land.* It was high time Roman letters did the dominating. Though Horace occasionally peered beyond the horizon of Rome to scope it out for his own work, he was plenty interested in the city.† He disavowed the textual culture of the streets, but that is not to say he abjured being at least somewhat publicly available. Augustus's famous building projects included several libraries, the most glamorous one nestled next to his dwelling on the Palatine Hill, and Horace appealed to its shelves and the importance of filling them with worthy materials.‡ Augustus was uniquely suited and situated to give poets the impetus they needed—promised patronage, wide distribution of their work—to create book-rolls worthy of his assorted emendations to Rome.

For Horace, "good poetry is the product not just of writing but also of reconsiderations, constant erasures, and rewritings," as Yun Lee Too asserts.§ That process yielded poems worthy of the touch of the few (rather than suited to the sweaty grab of the many) and the growing glory of Rome. If Horace promoted the file solely out of fear for his well-being, he would not have pointed so often at the stylistic shabbiness and editorial failings of his predecessors and contemporaries. Diagnosing bad writing as an aesthetic, social, and political ill, Horace acted as "an honest censor [*censoris ... honesti*]" of unbefitting verbal conduct.** As censors do, he made notes and took names: *nota* is Latin for a corrective editorial notation or the black mark of a censor. When located within the history of ancient textual culture, Horace's attempts to enforce the rectitude of writers testify to the perennial political, interpersonal, and creative tensions between decorous restraint and the freedom to let it all hang out: loose, hairy, and uncensored. There are different kinds of "free" verse and "free" speech, and Horace's efforts to rein in the willfully unmanaged kind reflect an artistic choice rather than an autocratic imposition.

Poetry as Conversation

Often translated as "Satires," the title of Horace's first published poetry collection from 35 B.C.E. is *Sermones* (*Conversations*). Of all rhetorical forms, *sermo* is

---

*Horace, *Epistulae*, 2.1.156–157.
†Horace, *Epistulae*, 1.20, and *Ars Poetica*, 345–346.
‡Horace, *Epistulae*, 2.1. For a fuller treatment of how Roman poets relied on libraries to make poetic points, see Marshall, "Library Resources and Creative Writing at Rome," and Horsfall, "Empty Shelves on the Palatine," 62–65, for attention to potential display within the library as a goad for Roman writers.
§Too, *The Idea of Ancient Literary Criticism*, 164.
**Horace, *Epistulae*, 2.2.110.

the chattiest. Usually translated as "conversation," *sermo* can have a moralizing dimension, as in our contemporary advisory announcement "I think we need to have a little chat." In *Sermones,* Horace accentuates that advisory aspect, but he also explains how a writer bends the flexibility of *sermo* to his situational needs, being "at times harsh, often joking, / upholding the function of either a rhetor or a poet, / or occasionally of an urbane wit, conserving his strength / and minimizing it with deliberation."* Years before, Cicero had put the following words about *oratio* (speech) into the mouth of Crassus in *De Oratore:* "nothing is as tender or as flexible or follows so easily wherever you lead it as *oratio.* From it comes verse [*versus*], from it comes irregular rhythms; from it also comes loose and varied measures and many types; for not only are the words for conversation [*sermo*] the same as those for competitive speech, but we also do not take from one kind for use in daily life and another for the stage and parade; but we pick them up, lying about, right out of the middle of things, and we form them and shape them to our design like the softest wax."† Language bends.

Sermo, like verse, is a subset of *oratio.* It appeals to Horace because it does not fasten him exclusively to one function (for example, teaching, exhorting, delighting) or fashioner (for example, rhetor, poet, philosopher) of speech; it bends to his will. As reader reactions to his "chats" start to reach him, Horace learns that the sneering consensus seems to be that he spares no one with his tedious sermonizing. "He has hay in his horns [*cornu*]: run away!" they apparently say of him, referring to the custom of using hay to mark out defective cattle, a custom that should perhaps be extended to hazardous book-rolls.‡ *Cornu* were decorative knobs on the end of the rollers onto which papyrus sheets were wound for ease of unwinding during reading and winding up for storage. Horace again uses the horn-of-the-bull image (*cornu tauris*) to liken his natural defense mechanism when attacked to that of a bull.§

In his defense, Horace defines his communicative position. First, he denies himself the title of poet: "for merely rounding off a verse / you would not deem sufficient, nor would you think anyone who writes anything so near to *sermo,* as I do, / to be a poet."** He simply talks in meter. Horace urges readers to take a verse, any verse, and to disassemble and scramble the parts and see for

---

*Horace, *Sermones,* 1.10.11–14. Compare these lines and the next few with Cicero's advisements about *sermo* in *De Officiis,* especially §134, 136, and 137. See Kennerly, "*Sermo* and Sociality in Cicero's *De Officiis,*" and Oliensis, who fruitfully compares Cicero's *De Officiis* and Horace's *Ars Poetica* in *Horace and the Rhetoric of Authority,* 198–223.

†Cicero, *De Oratore,* 3.176–177.

‡Horace, *Sermones,* 1.4.34.

§Horace, *Sermones,* 2.1.52.

**Horace, *Sermones,* 1.4.39–42.

themselves that "you will not find the limbs of a dismembered poet [*disiecti membra poetae*]."* A. M. Keith has argued that the bountiful presence of body parts in Roman poetry attests to the "wide literary diffusion" of earlier Roman oratorical terminology in the corporeal idiom.† As I detailed in chapter 1, this idiom is actually much older and was shared by poetics and rhetoric. Horace seemed primed to provide a grand lesson in genre theory (*genus; genus hoc scribendi*) when he snaps his attention back to the other critical matter: whether his conversations merit the "suspicion" of his detractors.‡ He is no petty informant, taking cruel delight in tattling on others; moreover, he does not supply his *libelli* to pubs or pillars—where book-rolls are displayed and where "the hands of the crowd can sweat on" them—nor does he read them out to anyone except his friends, and only when they force him.§ (Horace offers no account of or apology for how these sheets come to leave the security of his small reading group.) He does not cast aspersions far and wide, and in no way are these critics right who accuse him of carrying out his office with perverse relish. No one who knows him can authorize such an attack against him, Horace claims. "That such viciousness be far from my sheets [*chartis*] / and, first off, from my mind, if anything I promise / can be regarded as true, I promise," he pledges.**

His final flourish involves his father, a freedman. "If I am more free [*liberius*] / in what I say, if perhaps more jocular [than is seemly], this [looseness] you will justly afford goodwill," since his father taught him to turn observances of the foibles and vices of others into instructions for living uprightly himself.†† Force of habit makes Horace think and "talk" as he does. Appealing to the traditional Roman intolerance for goofy behavior also endows his "chats" with the patina of wisdom. This is not to say, however, that Horace does not suffer from even minimal vices. He closes the poem with an anecdote about his odd habit of privately and publicly debating with himself through "shut lips [*compressis labris*]" about all manner of interpersonal behaviors and modes of comportment.‡‡ One gets the sense that his sealed lips indicate a self-searching introspection that arises from an idiosyncrasy rather than point to external constraints on *oratio*. Whenever he frees up a bit of leisure time, he plays around with his sheets (*illudo chartis*) and refines his unspoken debates.§§ If people have a problem

---

*Horace, *Sermones*, 1.4.62.
†Keith, "Slender Verse," 42.
‡Horace, *Sermones*, 1.4.24, 65.
§Horace, *Sermones*, 1.4.71–73; see also 22–25.
**Horace, *Sermones*, 1.4.100–103.
††Horace, *Sermones*, 1.4.103–105.
‡‡Horace, *Sermones*, 1.4.130–131.
§§Horace, *Sermones*, 1.4.139.

with that, then they will have to answer to the many poets who will come to Horace's aid and try to convert his critics to fellows.*

Editing is the seemingly paradoxical feature of his "chats" that Horace claims distinguishes him from his Roman sermonic predecessor, Lucilius, whom we met in chapter 2, and from many Romans who were versifying in his own time. Horace does not seem troubled by the apparent incongruity of a carefully edited conversation. He tells us his sheets record the polished results of his playfully agonistic conversations with himself about moral issues. More importantly, the sermonic mode entails neither vapidity nor unsophisticated blather but should be thought of as the tidy expression of a well-ordered soul. For precisely that reason, Cicero had emphasized *sermo* as no less worthy of rhetorical study and practice than oratory in his *De Officiis*.† Horace, in the second bookroll of *Sermones,* explains that a true *sermo* involves not "villas or homes of other men, / or whether Lepos dances well or not," but matters that are of greater pertinence and about which it is bad to be ignorant, including writing *recte*.‡ *Sermo* should not be a trade in trashy gossip.

Editing a *sermo* seems to be a relatively new activity, however. Though "witty and *emunctae naris*"—literally, "of refined nose," meaning having good taste—Lucilius "composed harsh [*durus*] verses."§ His gushing compositional current is to blame. "Often in a single hour, / as if a big deal, he would dictate two hundred lines while standing on one foot; / and as he flowed along turbidly [*lutulentus*], there was much you would like to toss out; / he was wordy [*garrulus*] and unwilling to bear the labor [*laborem*] of writing, / of writing well [*recte*]: as for writing much [*multum*], I care nothing for that."** Compositionally, verses gushed forth from Lucilius and were recorded by a fast-scribbling *amanuensis* without filtering out his impurities. Horace's use of the general second-person singular imputes to any refined reader a desire to sift through Lucilius's muddy gunk to get to the good stuff. Lucilius did not tidy his torrent before publishing.†† Horace does not heap any further critique upon Lucilius in 1.4, but what he opines here seems to rile up readers with a taste for the traditional.

Beset by admirers of Lucilius, Horace defends his judgments about his forepoet in 1.10, the last poem of *Sermones* 1. The poem ends with Horace telling one

---

*Horace, *Sermones,* 1.4.141–143.
†Cicero, *De Officiis,* §132.
‡Horace, *Sermones,* 2.6.71–73.
§Horace, *Sermones,* 1.4.8.
**Horace, *Sermones,* 1.4.9–13.
††This is Horace's uptake of Callimachus's *Hymn to Apollo,* treated in chapter 2. See Farmer, "Rivers and Rivalry in Petronius, Horace, Callimachus, and Aristophanes."

of his slaves to "go, boy, and quickly append these words to my little book-roll."* Horace gives the final impression of working under a strict deadline, as if his book-roll had already been prepared for his chosen few readers but he could not resist a retort, one to which his detractors will not get a chance to respond before it, as we say, "goes to press." (The debate continues in *Sermones* 2.1, however.) Likely punning on his earlier depiction of Lucilius as dictating on one foot and not composing with elegance, Horace launches into this ostensibly last-minute poem with a provocation that incorporates reader responses: "Of course I said the verses of Lucilius run clumsy foot [*incomposito pede*]. / Who is such a mindless fan of Lucilius, / that he would not acknowledge this? Yet that same Lucilius, because he rubbed down [*defricuit*] the city with much salt, / is praised on the very same sheet [*charta*]."† Horace's critics think they have caught him in a contradiction, since in 1.4 he both critiques Lucilius's composition choices and compliments Lucilius's appropriate handling of astringency.

Horace displays restraint in his elaborated assessments of Lucilius, even professing to fall short of Lucilius's example and not to dare dislodge the much-deserved crown that "sticks" on his predecessor's temples. Lucilius in his time poked fun at his own predecessors, and Horace inquires into Lucilius's methods by wondering whether his little verses are not "more well-done" and "more soft [*mollius*]" because of a fault in either the man or his "rough" subject matter.‡ Had Lucilius written in hexameters, his thoughts would have flowed better, but even then he probably would have spouted out "two hundreds verses before dinner and one hundred verses after." In short, his problem does not lie solely with his feet. Horace then inserts a quick tale about a poet whose compositional flow so ran over that his scroll cases (*capsis*) and book-rolls (*librisque*) provided enough suitable material for his funeral pyre. That deviously said, Horace willingly concedes "that Lucilius was polite [*comis*] and urbane, and that he was more filed [*limatior*] / than one might expect of an author of a song as yet undeveloped [*rudis*], untouched even by the Greeks, / and more filed than the crowd of older poets: but he, / if he had fallen by fate into our age, / would rub away [*detereret*] much, would cut back [*recideret*] everything that / dragged on beyond perfection, and in making verses / he would often scratch his head and gnaw his fingernails to the quick [*vivos et roderet unguis*]."§ This final description of an editorial body closely resembles Carolyn Marvin's depiction of the typically unseen body behind a text: "in addition to putting pen to paper or finger

---

*Horace, *Sermones,* 1.10.92.
†Horace, *Sermones,* 1.10.1–4.
‡Horace, *Sermones,* 1.10.56–58.
§Horace, *Sermones,* 1.10.64–72.

to key, skin is pulled and scratched, nails, lips, and mustaches are bitten, noses, ears, and faces are picked, fingernails are peeled, hair is plucked and twisted."* In Horace's depiction of the editorial body, Lucilius's *amanuensis* is out of the picture; there are only a poet and the page.

Lucilius pioneered a genre—and most beginnings are rough ones—but finishing a poem is a rough business also. If transported into "our time," he would no doubt wear down both of his *corpora* in the pursuit of perfection. What about Horace's age would compel Lucilius to be more careful, even chewing away nervously on his nails? How one interprets this recontextualization of Lucilius depends wholly on how one assesses Horace's comfort level and reasons for editing. The peek at his own body at work that Horace offers in *Sermones* 2.3, which I will come to shortly, reveals a great deal. But that Horace begins to bring 1.10 to a close by shifting into second-person sermonizing mode shows there are reasons—not limited to himself exclusively—that one should edit: "often you must turn your *stilus* [*stilum vertas*], if you want to write something worthy of repeated readings, / and you must not work [*labores*] for the amazement of the crowd, / but be content with few readers [*paucis lectoribus*]."† To write in a way that will earn one successions of or even generations of readers is phrased in terms of a negative: "turning the *stilus*" is idiomatic for and descriptive of the act of rubbing out words provisionally etched into a wax tablet. Ultimately, a writer should direct his editorial efforts toward a more permanent medium and toward choosy readers. Such lofty aims, especially when so haughtily expressed, bring trouble for a writer. All sorts of people try to drag Horace down—*moveat* (move him), *cruciet* (crucify him), *laedat* (rub him open)—but so long as Maecenas, Vergil, and similar men with high standards approve (*probet, laudet*) of his poems, Horace will keep at it. And so he does.

Horace opens the second book-roll of his "chats" by ostensibly seeking out some legal advice about his writings. He tells the lawyer Trebatius: "there are some who think I come off as too sharp [*nimis acer*] in my satire and / stretch [*tendere*] the work beyond lawful bounds [*lege*], while the other contingent thinks everything I have composed to be without sinew [*sine nervis*], / and that verses like mine / can be produced at rate of a thousand per day. Trebatius, / what should I do? Advise me."‡ Horace wonders if he is reaching beyond what is permitted or whether he lacks the backbone to do so. He worries that his verses seem effortlessly produced in the worst sense. Kirk Freudenburg has argued that this poem is a discussion less about morality or legality than about

---

*Marvin, "The Body of the Text," 132.
†Horace, *Sermones*, 1.10.72–74.
‡Horace, *Sermones*, 2.1.1–5.

forms and norms of composition, undertaken with choice stylistic terms whose sexual nether meanings Horace teases out.* For example, many of the verbs and adjectives in lines 1–2 can also refer to sexual virility, and Horace even plays around with the penile implications of his cognomen, assuring himself that the words of Flaccus (Flaccid One) will do their job when the time is right (*dextro tempore, Flacci / verba*).† Freudenburg demonstrates convincingly that concepts suggestive of sexual potency continue to flex and relax in later rhetorical works, such as Quintilian's *Institutio Oratoria* and Tacitus's *Dialogus de Oratoribus*.‡

Trebatius first advises Horace to cease writing altogether or, if he cannot abstain, to channel his energies into writing epic verses in celebration of Caesar's varied achievements, as "wise" Lucilius did of Scipio, the great republican general and litterateur. That would be a much *rectius* (more appropriate, correct, erect?) use of Horace's talents.§ But Horace claims to be insufficiently strong (*vires / deficiunt*) for such a big job, stuck in his ways, and delighted with Lucilius's satire.** Lucilius gives so freely of himself in his book-rolls, treating them like buddies to whom he can display "his whole life, as if on a votive tablet."†† Horace credits or blames his being from Venusia for why he cannot resist poking with his *stilus* anyone who lays a finger on him: "to cut a long story short: whether tranquil old age / awaits me or death flies around me with black wings, / wealthy or without resources, in Rome, or if such a thing were ordered, in exile, / whatever the color of my life, I will write."‡‡ When Trebatius warns of the certainty of accusations, Horace acknowledges that he lacks the protective distinction of Lucilius's social rank and trifling playfulness, even though he "lives among the great." The poem closes as Horace and Trebatius pun on *mala* and *bona* poems and suppose that so long as Caesar judges the recipient of a *mala* poem of Horace's to have deserved it and Horace to have maintained his integrity (*integer*), Horace will evade the reach of "the law."§§

According to most estimates, five years elapsed between the circulation of the first book-roll of the *Sermones* and the debut of the second. During that time, the second triumvirate lost two *viri:* Octavian, of course, was left standing. Also

---

*Freudenburg, "Horace's Satiric Program and the Language of Contemporary Theory in *Satires* 2.1." The words upon which he focuses can be found in *Rhetorica ad Herennium*, Cicero's rhetorical works, Quintilian, Tacitus, and Pliny the Younger.

†Horace, *Sermones*, 2.1.18–19.

‡Those concepts will appear clearly in chapters 6 and 7.

§Horace, *Sermones*, 2.1.21.

**Horace, *Sermones*, 2.1.12–13.

††Horace, *Sermones*, 2.1.33.

‡‡Horace, *Sermones*, 2.1.57–60. Both *exsul* and *color* appear in Ovid's very first poem from exile, *Tristia* 1.1.

§§Horace, *Sermones*, 2.1.85.

during this time, Maecenas bestowed upon Horace a sizable farm in the country, a place to scudder about like a country mouse and nibble on book-rolls, as such creatures do.* The self-satisfied tone ringing out at the end of 2.1 becomes more of a dinning as the rest of the text unfurls. As Ellen Oliensis, among others, has noticed, each installment of this second sermonic book-roll pits Horace against the grating voice of another's reason, and Horace uses their chattiness as a medium through which to talk through his recent status boost.† For instance, while visiting Horace at his country house, a bearded Stoic friend called Damasippus sees that Horace is having a hard time writing and projects a verbal reflection of what he sees back to Horace: "So rarely do you write, that not four times in a whole year / do you call for parchment [*membranam*], and reweaving [*retexens*] all that you have written, / you grow angry with yourself, because even when full-up on wine and sleep / you still produce not one worthy *sermo*. / What will happen? / And you fled here from the Saturnalia itself? / Since you're sobered up, say something worthy of your promises: / start. Nothing presents itself: / in vain your pens [*calami*] are blamed, and the undeserving wall gets a workout [*laborat*], / seemingly born to take the anger of gods and poets."‡ As Damasippus sees it, Horace spends most of his time working out the same pattern of words over and over, hesitating to move from wax to a more permanent medium. Even here and now, fully relaxed and removed from the bustle of city life, Horace cannot produce. Frustrated, Horace barks at his tools and pounds the wall in a fury fit for Jupiter. He has even hauled his favorite book-rolls with him out to the country as good and goading company, but to no avail. Before turning to philosophy, Damasippus had been an evaluator of art objects, so his aesthetic opinion counts for something, and even Horace exclaims that this wise guy knows him well.§

Why all the mussing and fussing? Why does not Horace just let himself flow like Lucilius? Framing this breakdown as representative of what writers suffer in times of political clampdown as they censor themselves into silence does not comport with the evidence: Horace has managed to squeeze out the very item from which one might draw that conclusion, and it is the longest satire in either book-roll. Not only its very state of being but also its conclusion encourage a different view. Damasippus—by Horace's design—diagnoses Horace as suffering from, in essence, short-man syndrome: "Listen up. First, / you are building

---

*Horace presents the fable of the city mouse and the country mouse at the end of *Sermones* 2.6.

†See Oliensis, "*Ut arte emendaturus fortunam*"; Freudenburg's "Introduction," 11–12; Gowers, "The Restless Companion," 57–61.

‡Horace, *Sermones*, 2.3.1–8.

§Horace, *Sermones*, 2.3.17.

[*aedificas*], this is to say, you are imitating tall [*longo*] men, even though / at most altogether you measure two feet, and all the same, / as if you were bigger in body [*corpore*], you laugh at Turbo in his armor, / spirited and strutting: how are you less ridiculous than he is?"*

Damasippus then recites the Aesopian fable of the ox and the frogs, wherein a mama frog, in her panicky efforts to demonstrate with her body the size of the great big ox that has stomped her babies, nearly bursts. Horace's general behavior these days approaches that of the mama frog in self-aggrandizement, but his poems are really what puff him up to the point of popping.† Horace needs to deflate himself and resume his proper dimensions; as he himself teasingly concedes in *Sermones* 2.1.18, he *is* Flaccus, after all. Moreover, Damasippus pokes at Horace's raging temper and *cultus maiorem censu,* cultivation or flair greater than his station. It is a potshot, perhaps, at Horace's background as the son of a freedman, but all the more possibly it is a dig at Horace's preoccupation with editing a genre of poem that is supposed to be harsh, improvisational, and provocative, all qualities a Stoic like Damasippus would value highly.‡

A Man of Letters

The *Epistulae* (*Letters*) are written objects through and through. Horace opens the first *epistula* by resting his voice, as it were, and taking up pen and paper again. Letters are the primary means of keeping in touch over distance, a distance Horace struggles to maintain, since he keeps being pulled from his retreat. Comparing himself to a retired gladiator or an aging racehorse one contest away from blundering (*peccet*), Horace tells Maecenas it is time Horace put aside his "verses and other playthings" and turn his care to what is "true and decorous."§ In his typical doubling way, Horace uses verbs that also pertain to

---

*Horace, *Sermones*, 2.3.308–311. Compare this building language to that in the poems that book-end book-rolls one and three of his *Odes*. At the end of *Odes* 1.1, Horace asks Maecenas, to whom the poem is addressed, to "insert" (35) him among the Greek lyric greats. Joseph Farrell has emphasized the materiality of this request, that is, that Horace asks Maecenas to insert Horace's physical book-rolls in the same bookcase as those of Sappho and Alcaeus ("Horace's Body, Horace's Books"). Horace gasps excitedly that being in such company will buoy him up such that his head hits the stars; he is the first skyscraper. *Odes* 3.30 opens with Horace's most famous use of monumental language. For an analysis of the architectural and construction language in *Odes* 4, see Jones, "*Ut Architectura Poesis.*"

†Bursting from stretching beyond one's limits occurs again in *Epistulae* 1.19.15–16, where Horace describes the orator Iarbitas as "bursting [*rupit*]" because of his straining efforts to be considered urbane and eloquent.

‡Horace, *Sermones*, 2.3.324.

§Horace, *Epistulae*, 1.1.9–11.

composition—*condo et compono*—to describe how he is "storing up/writing" and "putting together/composing" philosophical learning that he can soon draw upon, rather than producing verse.* The *Epistulae* themselves both underline and undermine that inward retreat. An attitude of withdrawal and of attempting to draw strength from philosophical stores from within rather than seeking accolades from without pervades the first book-roll. Horace dramatizes the voices that disturb him—such as Maecenas beckoning for him, the reader criticisms that reach him, and even the book-roll that asserts a will of its own—all tugging him out of philosophical peace and quiet.† It bears emphasizing that Horace was studying philosophy when he was recruited into military service by Brutus; he recounts that "tough times [*dura tempora*]" wrested him from "the groves of Academe."‡ He now makes up for lost time, or at least tries to.

Vocabularies and sensibilities of textual culture saturate both epistolary book-rolls. For instance, Horace writes to an orator friend, urging him to stay vigilant in his philosophical pursuits and to call for "book-rolls along with candlelight [*librum cum lumine*]" so that he might read every morning before entering the forensic fray; teases a poet who keeps thieving verses from book-rolls in the Palatine library; whines about wanting to stay holed up in his farmhouse to read; nervously messengers some sealed volumes to Augustus; and encourages a poet friend who wants to know how to keep his patron happy to abandon his poems without a fuss any time his patron invites him out.§ One letter in the assemblage is addressed not to a person but to a personified book-roll: "Toward Vertumnus and Janus,** book-roll [*liber*],†† you seem to be looking, / so that you might sell yourself [*prostes*], tarted up by the pumice of the Sosii [*Sosiorum pumice mundus*]. / You hate the keys and seals so agreeable to the modest;‡‡ / you moan about being shown to so few [*paucis*] and you praise publicity [*communia*]: / you were not brought up that way. Away, then, down to

---

*Horace, *Epistulae*, 1.1.12.

†Horace, *Epistulae*, 1.7, 1.19, 1.20.

‡Horace, *Epistulae*, 2.2.45–46.

§Horace, *Epistulae*, 1.2.35, 1.3.14ff, 1.7.12, 1.13, 1.18.

**These are the areas of Rome where book-roll stalls were stationed.

††For a treatment of the book-roll as a pretty slave-boy eager to be set loose (*liber* with a short 'i', as we see here, means "book-roll," where *liber* with a long 'i' means "freed thing") to find a new household, see Pearcy, "The Personification of the Text and Augustan Poetics in *Epistles* 1.20," 458. Horace carries this slave-boy language (if, indeed, that's what it is) into *Epistulae*, 2.2. As Ovid plays around with in his exile poems, *liber* with a long 'i' can also mean "child" (though it more frequently shows up in the plural as *liberi*, children), which is what Socrates called a little book-roll that lacks the protection of a "father" in the *Phaedrus*.

‡‡Horace's other book-rolls stay shut up in secure cases.

that place you itch to go. / Not once I send you out [*emisso*] can you return. 'What, wretched me, have I done? / What did I want?' you will say, when someone tears into you [*te laeserit*], and you find / yourself forced into a confined space, when your lover [*amator*], having had plenty, grows languid."*

The Sosii brothers, book-roll-hawking literary agents or booksellers, have outfitted Horace's work with the sheen of surface appeal, which suits their purposes more than his, and now it wants not to roll around in his small social circle but to strut its stuff on the streets. Horace, however, has not prepared it for the pawing it will encounter there. The brothers' *pumex* has overpowered Horace's *lima;* now, (the) many want to fondle the text, whether they can handle it or not. Doubtless the smooth book-roll will hook someone, but how long before the "lover" loses interest and, having rolled the *liber* up tightly, tosses it aside with a yawn? The book-roll will not end its journey there, however; it will continue to be "dear" to Rome until the fading and wrinkling, which beset both fleshy and fibrous *corpora,* combine with all the stains from the caressing hands of the masses to render it a raggedy old thing. Then, it will sit silently as bookworms graze upon it, or it will flee to Utica or be sent as a captive to Ilerda, that is, get shipped to the far reaches of the empire. Horace will laugh as the bookroll, now babbling in senility, helps boys at the far reaches of Roman influence learn their ABCs.

His contemptuous cackle represents one way of surrendering authorial control. Mostly, though, Horace expresses befuddlement at how a poet can possibly get any sort of purchase in Rome, when everyone to whom he might appeal has different and often fast-fading literary enthusiasms. Horace had complained to Maecenas that the people have misattributed his fondness for the few to snobbery; instead, he claims, and not too diplomatically, that the crowd is "a multi-headed monster" that he does not know how to handle.† Later, Horace uses a cooking metaphor to express his frustration: "it seems to me pretty close to having three dinner guests who disagree," since what pleases one diner the other two find acrid and repulsive. Catering to an extensive multiplicity of tastes seems beyond his or anyone's skill.‡

This is an acute rhetorical anxiety, of course, and one by which poets who compose badly are untroubled: they "take joy in their scribbling and worship themselves and, / if you are quiet" when they ask for a critical opinion, "they praise whatever they have written, the blissful creatures."§ On the other hand,

*Horace, *Epistulae*, 1.20.1–8.
†Horace, *Epistulae*, 2.2.76.
‡Horace, *Epistulae*, 2.2.61–64.
§Horace, *Epistulae*, 2.2.106–108.

"he who desires to make a legitimate poem [*legitimum ... poema*], / when he picks up his wax tablets [*tabulis*] also picks up the character of an honest censor [*censoris ... honesti*]; / he will dare, if words fall short in splendor or / lack weight or are deemed unworthy of their position, / to move them [*movere*] from their place, although, unwilling to go, / they linger on within the precincts of Vesta."* Is all this trouble worth the struggle? "I should prefer to seem a giddy and sluggish writer," Horace discloses, "if only my bad things [*mala*] delighted me or at least duped me, / than to be wise and snarling."† He then relates a tale of a distinguished gentleman who acted faultlessly in all areas of his life but exhibited one peculiarity: it was his occasional pleasure to sit in an empty theater, where, he believed, he was enjoying the finest dramatic performances ever put forth. After some family members intervened, shaking him out of it and giving him drugs to fully "restore" him to his senses, he chided them for depriving him of his one true pleasure and the "most gratifying error of my mind."‡ Horace disdains delusion and again embraces wisdom, along with an old habit: silently talking to himself about moral matters and committing his "chats" to *chartae*.§ He cannot, will not, dupe himself.

He will, though, call in heavy reinforcements to lift his sagging morale. Addressed to Maecenas, 1.19 is one big petulant pout about the reception of *Odes* 1–3, which had been published in 23 B.C.E., three years prior. Several responses irk Horace. One is the poetic productions of a slew of imitators. They want to copy his *corpus* so much that they would guzzle exsanguinating concoctions were Horace to grow pale, just so they could resemble him: "O imitators, servile herd, often does your big fuss [*tumultus*] move my / bile, often my sense of humor!"** Partly melancholic, partly amused, Horace proceeds to credit himself—as he does in *Odes* 3.30—with being the first to step on alien land "with precise or concise foot [*pressus pede*]"—that is, to place shapely Latin feet into lyric meters that had been the Greeks' territory.†† He had led "a swarm" behind him.‡‡ That Horace brought forth "novelties" (*immemorata*) that are "read by the eyes and held in the hands of the well-born [*ingenuis*]" boosts his spirits.§§ The two touchstones

---

*Horace, *Epistulae*, 2.2.109–114.
†Horace, *Epistulae*, 2.2.126–128.
‡Horace, *Epistulae*, 2.2.128–140.
§Horace, *Epistulae*, 2.2.145ff.
**Horace, *Epistulae*, 1.19.19–20.
††Horace, *Epistulae*, 1.19.22.
‡‡Horace, *Epistulae*, 1.19.23. *Pressi* is one adjective Cicero used to describe the "thin" kind of speech that results from filing away at what was very minimal material to begin with.
§§Horace, *Epistulae*, 1.19.33–34.

of this brief self-congratulation, novelty and textuality, become bedrocks in *Epistulae* 2.1.

The second reader-response irritant induces tears instead of sighs: the *ingratus lector*, quite different from the *ingenuus* one.* Those types praise and love him at home but carp at him as soon as they step over the threshold into public life. Horace attributes this changeability to public expectations about poetic presence—and presents—in public. Ungracious readers are not content with the delights his book-rolls provide and want him "to hunt for the votes of the public, who blow this way and that, / at the cost of meals and gifts of well-worn clothing."† It is public appeals to their power to choose—which is another translation of *lecto,* read—that such readers want. Horace, however, refuses to act like a desperate politico. Moreover, he does not seek out "noble writers" with whom he can pontificate or kiss up to *grammatici* who lecture publicly about poetry.‡ All this keeping himself to himself makes the public suspicious. If, for example, he says, "To a tightly-packed theater / I am ashamed to recite my unworthy writings and attribute weight to trifles," they say, "Laugh it up; for the ears of Jove you keep your writings / aside: for you believe that you alone dispense the honey of poetry, / you alone are pretty."§ The ungracious readers take or, rather, mistake Horace's bashfulness for a holier-than-thou hold-out of his sweet honey for Augustus. In response, Horace momentarily considers sticking his nose in the air like the snob he is but decides he would get clawed and so calls for a truce instead. The retired gladiator from 1.1 wants to stay that way.

Perhaps expectedly by this point, Horace enters the fray again, issuing another book-roll of *Odes* before writing up the two long "letters" that form the second book-roll of the *Epistulae.* He begins his address to Augustus by subtly linking his poetic work with Augustus's political labors—Augustus "ornaments" the customary ways of *res Italia* and "emends" them with laws—and acknowledging it would be "an offense [*peccem*]" against the public good if he were to occupy Augustus "with a long chat [*longo sermone*]."** This mingling of poetic and political missions foreshadows the content of the letter. On the matter of Roman poetry's development—which turns out to be the main topic of the letter—Horace says that if, as many suppose, it parallels Greece's in that the earliest writers are or are to be considered the best, then the discussion can end right there. He assumes, though, that Augustus wants to hear more, and, for his part, Horace certainly has a stake.

*Horace, *Epistulae,* 1.19.41.
†Horace, *Epistulae,* 1.19.37–38.
‡Horace, *Epistulae,* 1.19.39–41.
§Horace, *Epistulae,* 1.19.41–45.
**Horace, *Epistulae,* 2.1.3–4.

The undue deference to and preference for older poetry comes mostly from the people, Horace charges, who can be "correct" in certain poetic judgments but "blunder [*peccat*]" in thinking poetry is like wine.* Those among them who deem ancient poetry unrefined join Horace and "Jove" in that assessment. Horace has much fondness for the poems of Livius, for example, but cannot believe anyone could deem that old Roman poet "to seem to have been emended and pretty and not far off from perfect [*emendata videri / pulchraque et exactis minimum distantia*]." Only some of the words attain "decorum," and those few attainments "unjustly carry off and sell the whole poem."† Ancient poetry deserves honor but not endless goodwill and immunity from criticism; if the Greeks had resisted novelty, what now would be old?‡ And what would the public have to read and wear out by constant handling (*legeret tereretque*), each to his own, if not for a profusion of new material?§ In the peaceful lull following the Persian War, Horace recounts, Greece took to playing and, with a flirt here and a flit there, took up temporary enthusiasm for all sorts of cultural pursuits. In contrast, in its former times of peace, Romans used to conduct themselves with decorum, tending to their business, respecting their elders, and guiding the young and impressionable; however, now everyone is seized with an unseemly zeal for "writing [*scribendi*]."** Horace himself, who again "affirms" that he writes no verses, as he claimed in *Sermones,* requests his pen, sheets, and scroll case first thing every morning.†† Ignorance of a skill often discourages its practice—in navigation, medicine, and carpentry, for example—but the "learned and unlearned [*indocti doctique*]" both scribble poems.‡‡ Horace has a good reason for his poetic defense of good poetry: poems matter because they are not useless. Poetry has a pedagogic function, including among its merits the power to "correct" roughness, envy, and anger in those who read it, thereby emending common character flaws.§§

Augustan *pax* has ushered in a wobbly poetic age, though, if the experience of Athens is any guide, the poeticizing craze will soon give way to a mania for something else. Meanwhile, standards are needed. Horace returns to tracing Roman poetry's genealogy back through the Greeks, kicking off this effort by noting the irony that "Greece, made captive, captured her savage victor, and

*Horace, *Epistulae,* 2.1.63, 34.
†Horace, *Epistulae,* 2.1.71–75.
‡Horace, *Epistulae,* 2.1.78.
§Horace, *Epistulae,* 2.1.92.
**Horace, *Epistulae,* 2.1.109.
††Horace, *Epistulae,* 2.1.113.
‡‡Horace, *Epistulae,* 2.1.117.
§§Horace, *Epistulae,* 2.1.118–138.

brought the arts / into untamed Latium."* Greek influence on Latin poetry first strongly asserted itself after the Punic wars, when certain Latin-writing poets took a shine to Sophocles and Aeschylus. Goaded on by natural spunk and sharpness, each poet produced results with which he was "happy," but, "unknowing, he deem[ed] blotting [*lituram,* erasure] demeaning [*turpem*] and fear[ed] it."† Though writing in a different genre of poetry from Lucilius, these early Roman tragic poets shared in Lucilius's lack of love for the *lima* (file).

Though Horace claims to be impressed by the artistry of poets of his time who write for the stage, he professes horror at the rowdy behavior of the theater audience, making such a spectacle of themselves that Democritus, the so-called laughing philosopher, would watch *them* and not the play were he around. Playwrights might as well tell their tales to a "deaf donkey."‡ For that reason, Horace turns to poets who "prefer to entrust themselves to readers, / rather than deal with the snobbishness of arrogant spectators."§ And Augustus should mind them also, if he "wishes to fill with book-rolls [*libris*] that gift worthy of Apollo," the library on the Palatine, since any "spur" from him will be a great motivator.** Such stimulus, however, would produce yet more poets to whose various sensitivities Augustus would be exposed, if only through association: "we are wounded / if a friend has dared to criticize a single verse; / we roll back [*revolvimus*] to places already recited, even when not requested; / we lament that our labors go unnoticed / along with the fine texture [*tenui ... filo*] of our poetic productions; / we hope it will come to this very situation, that, as soon as / you learn we are forming [*pingere*] songs / you will summon us, and drive away our poverty, and compel us to write."†† It is Augustus's approval and the magnitude of his achievements, rather than, for instance, the threat of punishment, that compel poets to write. He gives their artistic suffering a dignity it otherwise sorely lacks.

Augustus must be choosy, though, if he wants to avoid the mistake mighty Alexander committed when he forbade all but the best visual artists to render his physical likeness but entrusted the form of his reputation to a beloved but second-rate verbal artist, for whose "uncultivated" and "poorly born" verses Alexander paid dearly, literally and figuratively.‡‡ A powerful man's personal affection for a poet can be disastrous. Horace encourages Augustus in his support of

---

*Horace, *Epistulae,* 2.1.156–157.
†Horace, *Epistulae,* 2.1.165, 167.
‡Horace, *Epistulae,* 2.1.199–200.
§Horace, *Epistulae,* 2.1.214–215.
**Horace, *Epistulae,* 2.1.216–217.
††Horace, *Epistulae,* 2.1.221–228.
‡‡Horace, *Epistulae,* 2.1.232–244.

Vergil and Varius, the epic poets, and regrets that his own "chats crawl upon the ground" rather than soar on epic wing.* Yet, he knows his own strength and, besides: "I'm not caught up in any duty that could weigh me down, nor desirous to / have my face deformed by placement in wax / nor to be graced by verses poorly [*prave*] made, / lest I am expected to blush at the sloppy [*pingui*] gift once it is given, and, / with my very own writer, laid out in a closed scroll case, / be carried into that block that sells incense and perfumes / and pepper and whatever else is wrapped in useless sheets [*chartis ineptis*]."† Wax keepsakes of poets' visages—whose resemblance to traditional death masks Horace plays up—were one part of the cult of personality that certain poets encouraged or merely had to contend with, as were tributes by lesser poets. Horace here describes a funeral march of sorts: a poor eulogy read in his honor and his *imago* crammed into a scroll case, carried through the streets, and deposited among other marketplace items.

Throughout this poem, Horace parallels his interests with those of Augustus, even making the dodging of awful poets who want to praise them a shared concern. Rather than refer to his *lima* and the refinement its use brings about, Horace instead focuses on past poets who did not compose carefully and, in one case, caused embarrassment for a person of eminence. Moreover, he appeals to Augustus's most recently commissioned library, whose contents reflect on Augustus. If Rome truly has arrived "at fortune's summit," then it requires works commensurate with its lofty status. Romans should not produce or settle for uncouth and substandard productions.‡ In his final published work, the *Ars Poetica*, which is sometimes classified as the third book-roll of the *Epistulae*, Horace ostensibly instructs two scions of an aristocratic family on poetic propriety but all the while addresses Rome on the bad habits it must emend if Latin literature is ever to overtake what came before it.

Write Does Not Make Right

Ars Poetica, weighing in at only 476 lines, only seems slight. Its power and punch proceed from its abiding concern with appropriateness, including an emphasis on the embarrassment—provoked by reader responses ranging from snoring to annoyance to derisive laughter—that looms for writers who circulate unfit poems. The prospect of shame can be a mighty motivator of caution. Horace explicitly addresses the Pisos, two well-born young men seemingly caught up in the scribbling craze that makes Horace cringe. He might be getting a dig in at their prissy

---

*Horace, *Epistulae*, 2.1.250–1.
†Horace, *Epistulae*, 2.1.264–270.
‡Horace, *Epistulae*, 2.1.32.

pose of entitlement at 379–384: people without the body or skill for military training or athletic hobbies have sense enough not to make public spectacles of themselves, but ignorance of and inability in *ars poetica* do not stop aristocratic Romans from "daring to form verses," thinking themselves all the while totally and utterly free from error.* Ellen Oliensis highlights the social tensions behind Horace's "rhetoric of authority" in the *Ars*: Horace's poetic mastery yet comparatively lowborn status clashes with the Pisos's poetic incompetence yet highborn status.† As a whole, the poem seems offered in a wryly instructional spirit, with discouragements and restrictions doing much of the didactic and rhetorical work.

Horace's advice on *corpus* care and correction fits within his larger emphasis on avoiding error. Early on, he volunteers that most of "us" writers are deceived by *specie recti* (a semblance of the correct or appropriate): "working to be brief, / I become obscure; aiming for smoothness [*levia*], / some fall short in nerve and verve; one promising grandeur is swollen [*turget*]; / another creeps across the ground, too cautious and afraid of a storm."‡ In sum, any "flight from a fault leads to an error," if attempted without art.§ Horace's sense of proper poetic registers aligns with Cicero's articulation of kinds of speaking from across his rhetorical works, especially the language of verticality and falling. Then, using a musical analogy, Horace acknowledges that sometimes the string does not yield the sound that a hand and heart intend, and he reckons that gracious readers will excuse a few offenses so long as errors are not so plentiful that they distract and detract from the rest of the poem.** The poet who continually flubs either greatly offends or becomes a joke, his few good lines provoking laughter and surprise.†† Horace even reveals his own displeasure when he notices a place in Homer where the bard seems to have snoozed for a moment, but he concedes that drowsiness can sneak into long works.‡‡ Short poems have no such excuse.

As he does in other works, Horace tilts the advantage toward Greek approaches to poetry so as to first injure and then energize his readers' national pride. Nascent poets should "roll out [*versate*]" Greek exempla by night and by day, because "to the Greeks the Muse gave *ingenium*, to the Greeks the ability to speak with well-rounded mouth [*ore rotundo*], / greedy for nothing except

---

*See, e.g., Horace, *Epistulae*, 2.1.109–117.
†Oliensis, *Horace and the Rhetoric of Authority*, 198–199, 211–215.
‡Horace, *Ars Poetica*, 25–28.
§Horace, *Ars Poetica*, 30.
**Horace, *Ars Poetica*, 347–353.
††Horace, *Ars Poetica*, 357–358.
‡‡Horace, *Ars Poetica*, 358–360.

glory."* Romans, on the other hand, love to number-crunch and accumulate wealth, so "how can we hope to form poems / worthy to be coated with cedar oil and stored in smoothed out cypress," that is, to be treated as objects worthy of preservation?† The difference between Greeks and Romans is one of attitude, not aptitude. "Our poets have left nothing unattempted," even roaming behind the paths broken by the Greeks, yet something other than "care for money [*cura peculi*]" holds them back from dominance: a lack of care for the *corpus*.‡ "The strength and fame of Latium's arms would not be more powerful / than its tongue, if only each and every one of its poets was not offended / by the labor of the file and delay [*limae labor et mora*]. You, O blood of Pompilius, condemn any poem that / many days and many blots [*litura*] have not restrained and / not corrected ten times to the pared fingernail [*praesectum ad unguem*]."§ Horace proposes a compositional ethics of the slow, deeming the "delay" of "many days" an integral part of the poetic art. In *Sermones* 1.4, Horace thanks the gods "for making him scanty of speech," able to hold back and issue words few and far between.** Tied to that restraint is scraping and scrapping with the metaphorical file, leaving behind erasure holes (*litura*) of dissatisfaction. On those writers who, as Oliensis puts it, "will not condescend to labor over their creations, like the lowly artisan who sweats to give his statues the requisite finish," Horace attempts an attitude adjustment.††

Earlier (lines 32–35), Horace had introduced a craftsman adept at forming fingernails (*unguis*) and imitating soft hair in bronze but who was displeased with his final product because he could not put together (*ponere*) a whole body. "Now I myself, if I should care to compose [*componere*] something, / should no more want to be that way than to live with a nose bent out of shape, / but being admired for my black eyes and black hair."‡‡ To form a sound body should be a sculptor's and a wordsmith's first priority, only after which should each and every articulation be filed down, even a given *corpus*'s all ten fingernails. No detail is too small for editorial attentions. Horace uses the phrase "to the fingernail [*ad unguem*]" on only one other occasion in his oeuvre, to describe someone in Maecenas's circle called Fonteius Capito an *ad unguem / factus homo*.§§

*Horace, *Ars Poetica*, 268–269, 323–324.

†Horace, *Ars Poetica*, 331–332.

‡Horace, *Ars Poetica*, 330.

§Horace, *Ars Poetica*, 285–294.

**Horace, *Sermones*, 1.4.18.

††Oliensis, *Horace and the Rhetoric of Authority*, 209.

‡‡Horace, *Ars Poetica*, 35–37.

§§Horace, *Sermones*, 1.5.32–33.

Armand J. D'Angour writes that *ad unguem* functions "as a metaphor that implies a high level of finish and a comprehensive perfection. In [a] similar vein, *ad unguem factus homo* depicts a wholly admirable individual in particulars and in toto: a gentleman to his fingertips."* Capito displays "physical or intellectual refinement (or both)," and Horace's application of this index of cultivation to poetics functions similarly to point to an aesthetic attentiveness to the form and content of the whole *corpus,* right down to the fingernails.†

Horace does not clip the discussion of fingernails there. Wrongly convinced that "miserable *ars*" and strait-laced soundmindedness would exclude them from the poetic mount of Helicon, "a good part [of poets] do not care [*curat*] to cut their fingernails [*unguis*] / or their beards, seeking out deserted places, avoiding the baths."‡ As poets attempt to affect the look and smell of a genius far beyond the niceties of *ars,* basic hygienic measures fall out of favor; Agathon's razors are certainly nowhere to be seen. Horace has seen and smelled this problem before. In *Epistulae* 1.19, he cites the old adage that "no poems can please for long, or live, / that are written by water drinkers," and he complains jokingly that ever since he proclaimed that only the forum—that is, oratory—is for sober people, "poets have not ceased / to compete in wine by night, and to stink of it by day," as if sloshing Bacchic beverages will lead to pleasing poems with staying power.§ "What?" laughs Horace, "if someone, with a grim and wild look and bare feet / and a thinly woven toga, copied Cato, / would he thereby represent the virtue and habits of Cato?"** Roman poets seem to want to cut corners by mimicking external signals of poetic preeminence that are more proverbial—the poet out of his wits due to unmanageable talent or a great deal of wine—than actual. Horace also uses hair- and nail-cutting to make a personal poetic plea in the first poem of the *Epistulae.* In a moment of frustration, he vents that Maecenas cares more when Horace gets a shoddy haircut or "cuts his nails oddly [*prave sectum unguem*]" than when Horace's "whole order of life" seems out of sorts, Horace's unsound body causing more upset than his unsound mind.††

Mess, muddle, and mediocrity will not do for the Pisos. Horace alerts them to the high expectations poets face, especially compared to orators: "a legal consultant or middling [*mediocris*] prosecutor / may not boast the eloquent vigor / of Messalla, or know as much of as Cascellius Aulus, / yet still have value: neither

---

*D'Angour, "*Ad Unguem,*" 417–418.

†D'Angour, "*Ad Unguem,*" 413.

‡Horace, *Ars Poetica,* 295–298.

§Horace may be alluding to lines from a comedy of Cratinus, the contempory of Aristophanes treated in chapter 1. See Cratinus, *Testimonia and Fragments,* fragment xliii.

**Horace, *Epistulae,* 1.19.2–3, 10–11, 12–14.

††Horace, *Epistulae,* 1.1.94–104.

men, nor gods, nor bookshops [*columnae*] / permit poets to be mediocre [*mediocribus*]."* If a poem falls short of the top, it might as well fall to the bottom.† So that neophyte poets might prevent that sad sagging and sliding downward, Horace offers this advice: "if at some point you write something, let it fall into the judging ears [*iudicus auris*] of Maecius and of your father and of mine, too, and, having put the page [*membrana*] indoors, keep it shut up for nine years. You can blot out [*delere*, also "cut out"] what do not put out [*non edideris*]; a voice sent out [*vox missa*] does not know how to return."‡ Horace previously named *mora* (delay) an essential supplement to working hard with the file, though he did not specify the duration of this critical distance. Holding back a poem gives its author opportunity to keep altering it; Horace tellingly emphasizes erasure over other editorial options such as altering or adding. He also signals the poem's material immaturity, as it has not yet advanced to the papyrus stage. In comparing the vagaries of released book-rolls with spoken words, Horace highlights the wandering ways of words set loose. Because words, written or spoken, are all but blind and directionless, poets do well to prepare for this one-way trip by seeking the critical judgments of trusted friends beforehand.

Punning on *emendas* (a form of both *emendo*, "to emend," and *emo*, "to sell"), Horace warns against offering presents to whoever agrees to assess one's poems, since such an enticement will draw flatterers who will fawn over the poem in all manner of over-the-top and exclamatory ways.§ Horace encourages the Pisos to seek out his trusty critic Quintilius and describes what an editing session with him is like. After Quintilius points out what needs correction: "If you could not do better / after two or three frustrated attempts, his verdict would be to cut it out entirely [*delere*] / and to return the badly shaped verses to the lathe [*tornatos*]. / If you preferred to defend your defect rather than change it, / he would waste not one more word or bit of useless work, / to keep you from loving yourself and yours alone and without rival. / A good and prudent man will condemn lifeless verses, / blame the harsh, a black mark smearing the disheveled [*incomptis*] with a sweep of the pen [*calamo*], cut away dizzying / ornament, force light onto what is too little clear, / find fault with ambiguous phrasings, will note what should be changed, / will become an Aristarchus."** Horace provides a detailed view of the editorial process at the stage when trusted friends

*Horace, *Ars Poetica*, 369–373.
†Horace, *Ars Poetica*, 378.
‡Horace, *Ars Poetica*, 385–390.
§Horace, *Ars Poetica*, 419.
**Horace, *Ars Poetica*, 439–450. Aristarchus was a Hellenistic (second-century B.C.E. Alexandrian) critic of Homer. His name comes to mean any critic who is notoriously hard to please.

are called in for the harshest judgment they can muster. A "good and prudent" critic will not hold back for fear of offending his friend over a little thing, since little things can lead to serious problems, such as being received with derision and malcontent.* If the Pisos, and the many poets and readers throughout Rome, would absorb the tenets of Horace's *ars,* Latin literature could move from faking it to making it.

Horace preferred to leave the world to Augustus and to legislate the word, but he did hail their respective work as emendation with a civic orientation. A *censor* of uncorrected poems, Horace took the greatest offense at insensitive glibness and affected escapes from the bathing and shaving of *ars.* His corrective tool of choice was the file, though he never represented himself using it within his poems. Instead, it was an object he brandished while he made pertinent points about modern-day poetics. In the *Sermones* and the *Epistulae,* he holds the *lima* high for Roman readers to see, hoping they will warm to it and come to deem the rough verses produced by past poetic greats like Lucilius as unbefitting the times. In the *Ars Poetica,* he wags it admonishingly before poets put off by the demands of editing and by the inherent imperfection its use would suggest exists in their poetic output. Throughout his *corpus,* Horace shows a marked philosophical bent, even stressing that "writing rightly [*scribendi recte*]" arises from "being wise [*sapere*]" and directing aspiring poets to seek out the "Socratic sheets" for instruction on wisdom.† In accordance with this approach to poetics, the scrape of the file is not a quick superficial treatment that attracts readers who like shiny objects but rather a deliberate, diligent refinement of material not meant for everyone. Though Horace wrote in an awkward and ill-defined political time, his repeated emphasis on the file does not hint at fear and trembling at the risk of falling out of line with the order of things. Instead, he linked the less hesitant use of the file with the finer control of self-expression, which had long been a concern of those who cared about words, and the greater glory of Rome. By forging that latter connection, Horace did not cave to but rather worked within civic circumstances—a change of guard, continued Roman expansion, a massive new library—to establish a secure place for his book-rolls.

*Horace, *Ars Poetica,* 450–453.
†Horace, *Ars Poetica,* 309.

CHAPTER FIVE

OVID'S EXILIC *EXPOLITIO*

A sliding variation on the wayward themes of deviation and violation marks the limits of poetic license: flaw, defect, flub, blunder, slip-up, error, mistake, fault, offense, and crime suggest a range of dangers for the uninhibited poet. Horace had defiantly asserted that even if his "too free [*liberius*]" verses resulted in exile, he would write from there, but he never had occasion to fulfill that pledge.* Sixteen years after Horace's death, however, Publius Ovidius Naso had ample opportunity to reflect on the nature of poetic license and its loss when he was expelled suddenly by Augustus from Rome to Tomis, now the resort town of Constanţa, Romania, on the Black Sea. Born in Sulmo in 43 B.C.E., the year Cicero's head and hand(s) were severed and displayed on the speaking rostra in the Roman forum by order of Marcus Antonius, Ovid was spared the grisly sight of dismembered eloquence.† He was not, however, ultimately spared a similarly wrenching end. By traditional accounts, Ovid came of age when the time-honored forms and fora of public speech had been closed or at least had lost their civic charge. Yet, his writings from exile contain snapshots of ongoing, influential *eloquentia* in Rome. It was in Ovid's interest to depict a Rome where public persuasion was not dead, of course, but he mentions major speeches in the courthouse and on the Senate steps, delivered to a "full forum."‡

Ovid himself had received the finest rhetorical education his family's money and status could secure. Seneca the Elder, his contemporary, highlighted Ovid's schooling, tellingly emphasizing Ovid's inability to keep his *licentia* in check

---

*Horace, *Sermones*, 1.4.103, 2.1.59.

†See Plutarch, *Life of Cicero*, §48–49, and Seneca the Elder, *Suasoriae*, 6.17 (quoting from a lost book-roll of Livy). See also Richlin, "Cicero's Head," and Butler, *The Hand of Cicero*. For a comparison of the respective exilic writings of Cicero and Ovid, see Claassen, *Displaced Persons*.

‡*Facundia* (fluent speech) mentioned at *Tristia* 1.9, 3.5.29; *Epistulae Ex Ponto* 1.3.11, 1.2, 1.9, 1.6, 1.7, 2.2, 2.5.69, 3.5. Ovid also mentions private audiences with Augustus (that Ovid hopes his friends are seeking out on his behalf). "Full forum [*pleno foro*]" at *Epistulae Ex Ponto* 3.5.8.

even as a student.* Ovid's own account of his rhetorical training operates as part of his ongoing effort during exile to characterize himself as a playful poet with neither the *corpus* nor the *mens* for onerous, laborious, ambitious public life.[†] Politics are not and have never been his game, he claims. In the final poem of the fourth book-roll of his *Tristia* (usually translated as *Sorrows,* but its adjectival form, *tristis,* can mean "sullen" or "harsh"), Ovid details his youth and young manhood, a process of growing into his role as the younger son of the current generation of a long-established noble family.

Through the care of their father, Ovid and his brother went to Rome at a tender age. From the start of their education, his exactly one-year-older brother "tended toward *eloquentia,* born geared up for the wordy forum [*ad eloquentium ... tendebat ... fortia verbosi natus ad arma fori*]."[‡] Ovid, in contrast, found that, already, even as a boy (*iam puero,* 19), the Muse dragged him to do her work. Often, his father would call poetry a "useless" pursuit and remind his son that even Homer left behind "no wealth," discounting, of course, the opulence of Homer's literary gifts. "Moved by his [father's] words," Ovid utterly foreswore Helicon and "tried to write words loose from measure. But spontaneous poetry would come in befitting meter, and whatever I tried to write was verse."[§] Ovid and his brother had just attained purple-bordered togas when the latter died, only twenty years of age. Alone, Ovid advanced along the *cursus honororum* only as far as triumvirs before opting not to enter the Senate house and professing not to have been made out for public life, using the aforementioned excuses. All the while the Muses were persuading him to embrace the way of life he had always loved.** He then describes the close-knit circle of poetic greats he both esteemed and joined, including Horace, and remarks upon his almost instant renown.[††] Until 8 c.e., Ovid was writing and publishing regularly, widely, and without hassle. His sudden ejection from Rome occasioned the *corpora* whose care (or supposed lack thereof) I make my concern in this chapter.

In three parts, I emphasize the editorial dimension of what Stephen Harrison has called Ovid's "self-conscious rhetoric of poetic decline" in his exilic works.[‡‡] First, again and again in both *Tristia* and *Epistulae Ex Ponto,* Ovid begs

*Seneca the Elder, *Controversiae* 2.2.8–12 and 9.5.17 (*licentia* at 2.2.12). Much more recently, Richard Lanham has enthusiastically embraced Ovid as a *homo rhetoricus,* and George Kennedy has afforded him ample space. See Lanham, *The Motives of Eloquence,* and Kennedy, *The Art of Rhetoric in the Roman World,* 405–419.

†Ovid, *Tristia,* 4.10, cf. *onus,* 36; *labori,* 37; *ambitionis,* 38.

‡Ovid, *Tristia,* 4.10.17–18.

§Ovid, *Tristia,* 4.10.19, 21, 21–22, 23–26.

**Ovid, *Tristia,* 4.10.39.

††Ovid, *Tristia,* 4.10.56.

‡‡Harrison, "Ovid and Genre," 85.

the reader's pardon for the roughness of his verses.* In the temporally prior
Tristia, he frames the matter largely as one of unsuitability: smooth verses
would not befit his circumstances. He is a repentant exile in a savage, unsophisticated place. In the later *Epistulae Ex Ponto,* he uses the frame of inability: he is
too exhausted and depleted to edit. Second, throughout the five book-rolls of the
Tristia, Ovid performs explicit editorial work not only on them but also on the
Metamorphoses, attempting to transform that text and critical judgments about
it from afar.† Though Ovid reports that he was working on the *Fasti* as well as
the *Metamorphoses* when he learned of his banishment, he claims an incomplete
state for the text all about changes because it offers him more personally relevant rhetorical options given the change in what he calls *mea tempora* (my
times/my temples; the Latin seems purposefully ambiguous, as I explain later).
Third, the four book-rolls of the *Epistulae Ex Ponto* feature a recurring lament
for the lost sociality of poetic creation, correction, and reception. In the *Tristia,*
too, Ovid complains that he lacks a comprehending, appreciating audience to
whom he can air his works in progress. The goad of the ear—both the judging
ear of friendly critics and the eager ear of a finished poem's readers—is gone.
Ovid emphasizes his sad singularity in both exilic collections, but only in the
Epistulae does he call out to his previous social circle by name. He intimates that
the blame for the offending verses is not his alone: he gave people, specified
people, what they wanted to hear.‡ But rather than stress their partial responsibility, he tries to persuade his faraway friends to look out for him in any way
they can. The strain of repetition Ovid interweaves with this editorial one is his
frequent boast of wide, deep, and abiding influence. Being recalled in his own
time was not his only rhetorical aspiration.

The contemporary readers of Ovid's exilic output seem to have found such
repetition monotonous.§ What link those recurring strains are the iterations of
attention Ovid affords to the correction of his writings. Because of his distance
from Rome, his self-defense is thoroughly textual, but, more than that, its very
textuality plays a large role, since Ovid disavows the smoothness of textual
cultus in an effort to capture goodwill. Bookishness abounds; Ovid even declares
that sorrow gnaws his heart as bookworms do book-rolls.** To an extent

---

*I do not treat Ovid's other exilic work, *Ibis,* which bears a Callimachean imprint; see
Hawkins, *Iambic Poetics in the Roman Empire,* 32–86.

†As has been acknowledged by Hinds, "Booking the Return Trip," Farrell, "The Ovidian
Corpus," and Martelli, *Ovid's Revisions,* 152–164.

‡Cicero had done that with Brutus in *Orator,* §35, using the language of *crimen, culpa,*
and *error.*

§See, e.g., Ovid, *Epistulae Ex Ponto,* 3.7, 3.9, and 4.15.

**Ovid, *Epistulae Ex Ponto,* 1.1.72–74.

unmatched by any previous writer, Ovid displays his editorial body, continually importing to readers' minds the image of a man trying to correct his mistakes. Asomatic poetry would not serve Ovid's desperate need to keep his body present *in absentia,* but he does express worry that readers will mistake his depictions of his increasingly sensitive and finicky body for mere "daintiness [*delicias*]."* Nevertheless, in that same poem he goes on to describe his *corpus* as slender (*gracili corpore*) and his exilic limbs piteously shriveled for lack of vigor and paler than new wax (*parvus in exiles sucus mihi pervenit artus, / membraque sunt cera pallidiora nova*), which, of course, is written upon.† Despite his "sad" state, Ovid doubles and puns with the bodily vocabulary of textual culture: his exilic *corpus*—his text, himself—is *exilis* (slight, thin, shriveled). The language of thinness stretches back to the *leptos* (thin, peeled) verse of Aristophanes's Euripides and of Callimachus, but it was particularly prominent in the Attic debates of Cicero's time. Cicero had deemed the speech of the neo-Atticists *tenuis* and *exilis.*

Expolitio (thoroughly polishing, finishing off) is another style word suggestive of editing. For Cicero, *expolitio* indexes activities of time and care that produce thorough polish, in evidence on the textual or actual body. He pairs it with qualities such as brightness, neatness, smoothness, and compactness. Earlier in the century, the *auctor ad Herennium* had described *expolitio* as "supporting and adorning a speech" and "outfitting and enhancing argumentation," providing a seven-part mini-speech for demonstration.‡ The *auctor* urges readers to learn how to execute *expolitio* because it will help them treat even "a simple matter in a multiple way."§ After Ovid's time, Quintilian includes *expolitio* in his inventory of tropes in his *Institutio Oratoria,* where it refers not to concision but to copiousness (*copia*), namely to the excessive (*ex-*) working of a point of argument: *expolitio* speaks to "the repetition of proofs and accumulation out of abundance."** Ovid tropes with editing throughout his exilic writings, turning it this way and that so that the ostensibly harsh (*tristis*) circumstances of his compositions will be inescapably on show. Though the repetition may wear on the nerves of readers, it may also wear down their resistance to doing the bidding of a desperate *relegatus.* But there is another aspect, too. What gives editing rhetorical status is that it pertains to a writer's respect for what his readers find attractive,

*Ovid, *Epistulae Ex Ponto,* 1.10.16.
†Ovid, *Epistulae Ex Ponto,* 1.10.21, 27–28.
‡*Rhetorica ad Herennium* 4.56–58.
§*Rhetorica ad Herennium* 4.56.
**Quintilian uses the Greek *epexergasia* (8.3.88). Both Alcidamas and Isocrates use variants of *exergasia.*

normative, or repulsive. That Ovid claims to notice errors and yet not to correct them is a confrontational stance, even if, especially if, he has thoroughly edited his verses. Attending to Ovid's exilic *expolitio* gives additional depth and texture to our understanding of what Luigi Galasso calls Ovid's "rhetoric of repetitiveness" in the exilic works.* Whereas scholars used to attribute Ovid's repetitiveness to his waning poetic energies, more recent scholars have argued to the contrary that there is rhetorical intent and poetic control behind Ovid's reiterations.† *Expolitio* recommends itself in particular as an Ovidian trope because, on the one hand, it straddles the domains of style and argumentation, and, on the other hand, it trains attention on how Ovid repeatedly deployed lamentations about his lack of thorough polish as an argument.

Ovid's professedly *exilis* exilic poetry was occasioned, of course, by his exile. According to Ovid, who provides the only surviving side of his case, Augustus banished him for "two crimes, a poem and a mistake [*duo crimina, carmen et error*]."‡ Much to the exquisite agony of millennia of readers, Ovid does not reveal the *error,* describing it only as one committed by his eyes and not his tongue, not willful, and not told to anyone else.§ He blames the mistake on his timidity rather than on audacity.** The *carmen* in question is the romping *ménage a trios* that is the tripartite *Ars Amatoria;* in its full form, it rolled around Rome for at least eight years before its author faced criminal charges. Issued well after Augustus's stringent social reforms regarding marriage, child production, and adultery, the book-rolls purport to contain lessons on making love, an artful process dependent upon constant manipulation and grounded in rhetorical activity.†† These lessons on luring and securing desirable persons are taught by a *praeceptor amoris,* professor of love, or Professor Love. Book-roll one begins with the poetic *ego*—that is, the "I" within the poem—introducing itself as Professor Love (*ego sum praeceptor Amoris*), and book-rolls two and three close with the Professor Love requesting that reader-pupils credit Naso as their teacher (*NASO MAGISTER ERAT*).‡‡ In openly identifying Professor Love with himself, Ovid

---

*Galasso, "*Epistulae Ex Ponto,*" 205.

†Besides Galasso, see Williams, *Banished Voices,* and Williams, "Ovid's Exile Poetry."

‡Ovid, *Tristia,* 2.207.

§Eyes and accident: *Tristia* 2.103–108 (it seems he witnessed something unsavory and did not report it), 3.1.52, 3.549–550. Silence: *Tristia* 2.208, 3.5.47–48, 3.6.11.12, 4.10.99–100; *Epistulae Ex Ponto* 2.3.87–88. Plea that his transgression be considered an error and not a wicked deed (*errorem . . . non scelus*): *Tristia* 4.10.90.

**Timidity appears at *Epistulae Ex Ponto* 2.3.88.

††Ovid, *Ars Amatoria* 1.459–462. Both the *Lex Iulia de adulteris coercendis* and the *Lex Iulia de maritandis ordinibus* were issued in 18 B.C.E.

‡‡Ovid, *Ars Amatoria,* 1.17; 2.744 and 3.812.

lost any protection the *persona* might have offered his person had the two been disambiguated.*

By peddling bold advice on a salacious series of sexual topics and even positions, Ovid may have stuck his nose in Augustus's highly sensitive political business. Yet, even if writing naughty poems is a crime, there remains to account for a strange delay between Augustus's reforms, Ovid's flaunting of them (if indeed that is what he does), and Augustus's choice to relegate him. Ovid twice wonders about that delay, pointing out that he had come before Augustus several times after "publishing [*edideram*]" the "writing in which he blundered [*scripto peccavimus*]," and, "I remember, you approved of my life and my ways."† "A not new fault [*non nova culpa*]," Ovid sorrowfully observes, "is made to suffer a new punishment."‡ It seems, then, that Ovid's mysterious *error*, whatever it was, offered Augustus's cause to put Ovid's earlier book-rolls under close scrutiny. An advisor of Augustus seems to have taken on that responsibility with zeal. "Ah! How uncivilized [*fera*] and too cruel the enemy who read my playthings [*delicias meas*] to you," picking out only the naughty parts, Ovid wails.§ As Peter Green points out, "a sexual scandal could—can—always be relied upon to distract public attention away from more serious political and economic problems."** Of the two crimes, the *carmen* was easier than the *error* to identify publicly by Augustus, and to correct.

Ovid divulges that he was condemned by Augustus's own "harsh words [*tristibus verbis*]," rather than through a senatorial decree or special court.†† Those procedural details would have been falsifiable for at least some readers and may call the legality of Ovid's expulsion into question. Ovid decries learning about his relegation when he was not present in Rome and therefore unable to make his case with speed and urgency.‡‡ His self-defensive plea in the second book-roll of his *Tristia* is too little, too late: "trust me, my ways differ from my poems – / my life is modest, my Muse a joker – / and the better part of my work is a fabrication or fiction; / it's more permissive than its composer. / Nor is a book-roll an index of character, but rather respectable pleasure; it offers many things apt to stroke the ears."§§ Just as his writings from exile explore the ethical and

---

*For a political reading of Ovid's erotic poetry, see Davis, *Ovid and Augustus*.

†Ovid, *Tristia*, 2.529–532, 89–92.

‡Ovid, *Tristia*, 2.540.

§Ovid, *Tristia*, 2.77–78. In Latin, a "reading" is always a "choosing," since *lego* can mean either.

**Green, *The Poems of Exile*, xxiv.

††Ovid, *Tristia*, 2.131–4.

‡‡Ovid, *Epistulae Ex Ponto*, 2.3.83–90.

§§Ovid, *Tristia*, 2.353–358. Ovid also calls his Muse *lascivia* (*Tristia* 2.313) and again *iocata* at *Tristia* 3.2.6 and 5.1.20.

aesthetic dimensions of the vocabulary of poetic mistakes with which I opened this chapter, they also engage the legalistic side of rhetorical redress.*

Given Ovid's admitted disinclination for arguing about and orating on non-fictive legal and political matters, his "misfortune," as George Kennedy notes somberly, "was that he was given a case to plead."† Ovid warns his first "little book-roll [*parve liber*]" sent from Tomis to Rome not to defend itself if attacked by "biting words," since his ca(u)se is not good for much of a legal defense.‡ He cannot resist, though, later shaming a Roman rascal who uses his "eloquent mouth" to defame him: "against an easy ca(u)se anyone can be eloquent, / and the smallest amount of strength suffices to smash what is already shattered."§ Ovid also calls upon the *facundia* (fluent speech) of his élite friends, attempting to put them into service as his *advocati*.** Further, that Ovid calls the "shabby" little book-rolls he sends to Rome to make his case his "children" might be the textual equivalent of the courtroom commonplace of bringing one's bedraggled kids before the jury to tug on their heartstrings.†† A significant juncture of the poetic and legalistic comes in the word *iudex*, since an evaluator of a legal case and a critic of poetry are both called a "judge."‡‡ Near the end of *Tristia*, Ovid all but rests his case when he declares that "Thalia," the Muse of comic and light verse, "has been conquered and enclosed by the law."§§ The choked constriction of his poetic *licentia* seems assured; he continues to write, however. Those legalistic types of what Jo-Marie Claassen calls "exilic appeal" make up one limb of the rhetorical posture Ovid assumes to advance his ca(u)se.***

Ovid's exilic *expolitio* does not indicate a slackening of his formerly taut poetics, but rather the skilled working through of his relegation in writing. All writing is difficult: Ovid describes his early work as the product "of care and vigilant labor."††† The exilic page thickens its resistance, though; especially for one exiled for his writings. Ovid repeatedly dramatizes the difficulties faced by his *exilis corpus*—meaning his writings and himself—and the language of his lament is frequently the language of textual culture, especially editing.

---

*See McGowan, *Ovid in Exile*, especially 41ff on the abundant legal language in Ovid: "Roman literature is saturated to the core with terms of the law, and many words in the Latin language often carry a legal significance outside any immediate legal context" (41).

†Ovid, *Tristia*, 4.10. Kennedy, *The Art of Rhetoric in the Roman World*, 405.

‡Ovid, *Tristia*, 1.1.1, 25–26.

§Ovid, *Tristia*, 3.11.20 (*ora diserta*).

**Ovid, *Tristia*, 1.9.57ff, and *Epistulae ex Ponto*, 1.2.67ff.

††Consider, e.g., Cicero, *Orator*, §131; Quintilian 6.1.30.

‡‡Ovid, *Tristia*, 1.1.37, 2.80, 2.98.

§§Ovid, *Tristia*, 5.9.31.

***Claassen, *Displaced Persons*, 117.

†††Ovid, *Tristia*, 2.11, 1.1.108.

A Sad Mind in a Sad Body?

Tristia begins with Ovid talking to his little book-roll (*parvus liber*) and preparing it for its journey to Rome. Unlike certain other Roman poets, Ovid apparently denies his creature the treatments and trappings of textual *cultus*.* To sashay into town looking smooth would seem shameless and impenitent, so the little book-roll instead walks the long road without a berry-dyed cover page, a coat of papyrus-preserving cedar oil, and sturdy white horns (*candida cornua*): it is utterly defenseless. Nor will its "dark brows [*frontes*]" have been "polished with brittle pumice [*fragili ... poliantur pumice*]," meaning the book-roll's fibrous "hair [*hirsutus, comis*]" will hang in its eyes like the vagabond it is. A final indignity: its whole body will be splotched with *litura*, blots.† Though he has denied his little book-roll all his former textual traits and identifiers, Ovid informs it that everyone will know it from its *color*: "you want to dissemble, but you are obviously mine."‡ In ancient Roman rhetorical training, to apply *color* to a topic is to tint it with perspective, and Ovid's somber point of view, darkening every poem, points to his authorship. Just as his book-roll lacks the purple tinge of berry juice and the golden hue of cedar oil, so has his style shed all its vibrancy. Or so Ovid claims. The *color* could just as well refer to the insuppressible and distinctly Ovidian poetic abilities that enable his dissembling protestations, which any attentive reader back in Rome would recognize.

As it trudges through Rome in search of a guide, Ovid's third exilic book-roll voices its own concerns.§ "Inspect me," it invites, "and you will see nothing here except *triste*," advertising upfront that its contents are sad/harsh and part of Ovid's exilic collection rather than the forbidden *Ars*. "Appropriate to its times [*temporibus conveniente*]," it is neither golden from cedar oil nor smooth from pumice (*pumice levis*), blushing (*erubui*, that is, turning red—yet more *color*) at the mere thought of being "more chic [*cultior*]" than its creator.** Like its sibling, *Tristia* 1, *Tristia* 3 bears a sad suffusion of blots (*suffusas ... lituras*), but more shocking still is promised evidence of impure Latin, a result of the "barbarous land [*barbara terra*]" where it was written.

---

*Ovid, *Tristia*, 1.1.1–14. E.g., Catullus 1.1 and Horace, *Epistulae*, 1.20.

†Horace insists on an editorial stage of *litura* at *Ars Poetica* 293. As I show, Ovid used to make *litura* at the suggestion of Atticus's friendly file (*Epistulae* 2.4.18). See Hinds, "Booking the Return Trip," and Williams, "Representations of the Book-Roll in Latin Poetry," 187–189, for Ovid's use of this word in his *Heroides* (letters from literary heroines to their deadbeat lovers).

‡Ovid, *Tristia*, 1.1.61–62.

§Ovid, *Tristia*, 3.1.1–20.

**Near the end of this poem, the book-roll's letters begin to tremble and it becomes pale as wax (yet another *color*) as it imagines the prospect of facing Augustus.

The book-roll's "hair" could use detangling. Ovid has already described his personified little book-roll as "hairy," when, two poems over, he calls his cheeks "hairy."* Their bodies display the overgrowth of mourning, a sanctioned type of scruffiness, readers may deduce. His is not the beard of the unkempt poetic madman so hateful to Horace in the *Ars Poetica,* however. Referring to Ovid's designation of the verses of the third-second century B.C.E. Roman poet Ennius as *hirsutius* (more hairy), Gareth Williams points out that *hirsutus* "also carries the literary connotation of stylistic coarseness," and one unbefitting the current polish Rome has achieved.† Ovid's verses, he would have readers believe, are also untouched by the razor, an editorial tool dear to the overly refined Agathon, treated in chapter 1. The (cultivated) shabbiness of his *corpora* accords with their *tristis* situation.‡ Of all the off-putting characteristics of the native people of Tomis, Ovid seems most off-put by their untrimmed mangles of abundant locks.§ A representative remark: "their mouths are concealed uncouthly by their long hair [*oraque sunt longis horrida texta comis*]."** Their exit-way of speech—that most civilizing possession—is shaggily blocked. This strand of *corpus* care braids together Ovid's book-rolls, himself, his verses, and the native people. They bear aesthetic similarities.

Ovid pulls not only his *locus* but also his *tempus* into his argumentation. Both a catalyst for rhetorical action and a criterion of its appraisal, time or time-liness holds a place in ancient rhetoric as *kairos* in ancient Greek and *tempus* in Latin.†† For example, in *De Oratore,* Cicero's Crassus declares that no one kind of speech is congruent with every case, audience, person, and *tempus.*‡‡ Quintil-ian would write a few decades after Ovid's death that an orator needs to know what is fitting given his *locus, persona,* and *tempus.*§§ It is a mark of rhetorical sensitivity, then, that Ovid adjusts his speech to his immediate time and place, which he asks readers to recognize. As *Tristia* rolls on, he dwells on the con-cinnity between the content and the circumstances of his writing. "If any faults [*vitiosa,* vices] should show up, in my *libelli,* and they will, / take their time [*suo tempore*] for an excuse, reader. / I am an *exul,* it is my consolation, not fame, that

---

*Hirsutus at *Tristia* 1.1.12, *hirta* at 1.3.90.

†Ovid, *Tristia,* 2.259. Williams, "Representations of the Book-Roll in Latin Poetry," 186. Horace uses it that way, too, in *Epistulae* 1.3.

‡Ovid, *Tristia,* 5.12.36, *digna sui domini tempore, digna loco.*

§Hirsutos at *Epistulae* 1.5.76, *hirsutis* at 3.5.6.

**Ovid, *Tristia,* 5.7.50; a nice chiasmus.

††Whereas ancient Greek has *chronos* and *kairos* to differentiate time from the timely time, Latin has only *tempus* (Quintilian 3.4.26–26).

‡‡Cicero, *De Oratore,* 3.4.210; see also Cicero, *Orator,* §71.

§§Quintilian 4.1.52, 9.3.102, 11.1.4.

I seek."* Ovid expresses gratitude that the Muse did not abandon him, joined with him in crime (*iuncti criminis*) as she is: writing sends him into a Bacchantic frenzy, during which he forgets his present and pressing ca(u)se.† As soon as the flow of writing ceases, though, the unscrubbed verses call out for editorial attention, once more snapping Ovid back to full awareness of his sad state. "This laboring care [*cura*] is for whom now? / Will the Sauromatae and Getae read my writings?" he asks sarcastically, implying that the natives cannot read Latin and, besides, shabby things suit their aesthetic.‡ Ovid asks this question, of course, of his Roman readers. Though even the most unabashed adoration from them would reach him in a much-reduced affective form, even thinking he could possibly secure it in the first place makes editing seem less ridiculously vainglorious.

Toward the end of the *Tristia,* Ovid claims to have no doubt that there will be not a few "barbarisms" in his little book-rolls, "but not the man but the place [*loci*] is culpable."§ Using alibi language, he acknowledges early on that "as you carry out my instructions, book-roll, you will likely be blamed [*culpabere*] / for being beneath the high praise of my *ingenium.* / But it is the duty of a judge to seek out both the issue and the circumstances [*tempora*] of the issue. / If they ask about the time [*tempore*], you will be safe."** The time and place of its composition let it off the hook, ensuring its release and further circulation. "Any fair judge," though, "will marvel" at their very creation "and read the writings—such that they are—with goodwill."†† Ovid uses nearly the same formulation in his proposed preface to his collection: "Whoever reads these items—if anyone does— consider even before that / the time [*tempora*] and place [*loco*] in which they were composed. One will be fair to writings he knows to be / from the *tempus* of an exile and a barbarian place: / and amidst so many adversities, he will be amazed that any poem at all / could be produced by my sad hand."‡‡ He ends the poem by asking again that readers "deem the little book-roll, such that it is, worthy of kindness / and excused by the condition of my lot."§§ Mitigating circumstances, he pleads, excuse any poetic crimes in his exilic works.

On occasion, Ovid vividly presents his exilic writings as rough drafts, and he carries the spirit of these depictions throughout the work.*** Though he may

---

*Ovid, *Tristia,* 4.1.1–3.
†Ovid, *Tristia,* 4.1.23, 41, 39–40.
‡Ovid, *Tristia,* 4.1.92–93.
§Ovid, *Tristia,* 5.7.59–60.
**Ovid, *Tristia,* 1.1.35–39.
††Ovid, *Tristia,* 1.1.45–46.
‡‡Ovid, *Tristia,* 3.14.27–32.
§§Ovid, *Tristia,* 3.14.52.
***See, e.g., Ovid, *Tristia,* 1.1 and 3.1.

be trying to elicit sympathy by describing them as grubby wanderers, I have argued instead that Ovid deploys those raggedy representations to showcase his acute rhetorical sensitivity to his situation, that is, both to his sad legal status as *relegatus* and to his harsh location ("as my *status* is pitiful [*flebilis*], so is my poem pitiful [*flebile*]").* His little book-rolls claim not to want to draw attention to themselves, but of course they do; overtures to appropriateness imply an assumed audience. That Ovid builds into his writings lots of room for improvement means that their contents are not yet finished, that *he* is not yet finished. Just like that of the *Metamorphoses,* to which I turn momentarily, their incompletion models the ongoing nature of his rhetorical redress.

As he comes to the horrible realization that his pleas fall on deaf ears, however, Ovid's attitude toward editing undergoes a change in frame. It first appears in the final book-roll of *Tristia,* as inability creeps in with unsuitability: "My *ingenium* has been ground down by the long suffering of bad things, / and no part of my old vigor remains. / If ever, as now, having taken up a wax tablet, / I want to force words into feet, / I write no poems, or only the kind you currently see, / worthy of his master's times [*tempore*], worthy of his place [*loco*]."† Since the early days of his exile, the *materia* of his ca(u)se has seemed too heavy for him to bear in light verse, but now he crumples, especially under the value-adding weight of editing.‡ As every passing day brings Ovid nearer to dying far from home, he professes to wonder why he should keep his Naso to the grindstone.

Ovid claims that leisure (*otium*), that condition for which he was born, "has corrupted his *corpus.*" He and his verses cannot stay in shape when they are stuck, as they are, "sluggishly in place [*inerte situ*]."§ A "forced, unwilling hand" grips the writing tools, even though "it does not at all please my mind to bother with such cares [*curas*], / nor does the Muse come when called to the hard [*duros*] Getae. / Yet, as you can see, I struggle with drawing out verse: / but it can be no softer than my fate. / When I read it over [*relego*], I am ashamed to have written it, / because I see many things / that even I, who made it, would erase [*lini*] with worthy judgment [*iudice digna*]. / But, however, I do not emend [*emendo*]. This labor is greater than the one to write [*scribere*], / and my exhausted mind cannot bear to suffer anything hard [*durum*]. / Am I, really, to start using the file more bitingly [*lima mordacius*], / and submit to the voice of judgment [*iudicium vocem*] every single word?"**

---

*Ovid, *Tristia,* 5.1.5.
†Ovid, *Tristia,* 5.12.31–36.
‡Ovid, *Tristia,* 1.5.56.
§Ovid, *Epistulae,* 1.5.5, 8.
**Ovid, *Epistulae,* 1.5.10–20.

The poem makes its own sad case, exhibiting itself as evidence of Ovid's decline.* Writing is tough enough on his system but erasure and emendation too much for his worn-down mind to endure. (Notice that the native people and editing share the adjective *durus*.) He scoffs at the notion that he should *more* deeply sink his file's teeth into his weak little words and call out each word by name to evaluate it. The promise of fruit is "the most justifiable cause for labors," but "to this time [*tempus*], my work [*opus*], and you venture to recollect everything, / has not been productive—and if only it had not been destructive! / Why, therefore, do I write, you may well wonder? And I wonder myself, / and with you I often ask what I want out of it."† It is not that he has become that old cliché, the insane poet (*sanos negat esse poetas*), with rhyme but without reason; rather, the overpowering forces of habit and familiarity pull him into his poetic process, just as a wounded gladiator rejects fighting only to find himself back in the sands again.‡ This easing, Ovid claims, is precisely his poeticizing aim: "nothing is more useful / than these arts, which have no use."§ As he explained in *Tristia* 4.1, writing gives him moments of precious oblivion. But, again, whereas composition comes easily, any intensive labor seems groundless: "why should I polish [*poliam*] my poems with fussy care [*sollicita cura*]? / Should I fear that the Getan people will not approve?"** A little labor suffices to make him the best poet in the whole uncivilized region, and though such a "theater" ought to be enough for his *infelix Musa*, Ovid wonders how he might—if he can—stretch himself to Rome and prove reports of his death premature.†† As his work rolls along the road to Rome, it might find favor with pockets of readers, but "that fact certainly yields its author nothing whatsoever": who cares to be praised by anyone but Romans? Ovid wonders, though, whether his "middling writings [*scriptis mediocribus*]" will stand up to the scrutiny of polished people.‡‡

One poem begins with an upfront recognition of Roman readers' disgruntlement with his repetitions, and Ovid expresses relief that readers seem to have missed his many other blunders.§§ Though each "author praises his own work," Ovid sees all the rough spots in his writings: "why, therefore, if I see my delinquency, do I go on blundering, and suffer the crime to stay in my writings, you

*Ovid, *Epistulae*, 1.5.5, 15.

†Ovid, *Epistulae*, 1.5.25–30.

‡Ovid, *Epistulae*, 1.5.31, 37–38. This analogy resembles Horace's in the first poem of his own *Epistulae*.

§Ovid, *Epistulae*, 1.5.53–54.

**Ovid, *Epistulae*, 1.5.61–63.

††Ovid, *Epistulae*, 1.5.85–86.

‡‡Ovid, *Epistulae*, 1.5.78, 83.

§§Ovid, *Epistulae*, 3.9, 5 (*vitium*), 6 (*peccat*).

ask?"* Everyone can sense a malady, but not everyone possesses the "art" of healing. Yet, Ovid quickly dispenses with this platitudinous medical analogy and purports to reveal the sad truth: "often, when wanting to change [*mutare*] some word, I just leave it, / as my strength cannot stand up to my judgment. Often . . . it irks me / to correct [*corrigere*, to smooth out] and endure the onus of long labor. / The very labor of writing relieves and lessons the laboriousness, / and the growing ⌊*crescens*⌋† work builds steam in my chest. / And as to correct [*corrigere*] is as much less arduous / as great Homer was greater than Aristarchus, / so it wears down the mind with the slow chill of cares [*curarum*], / as a racer restrains an enthusiastic horse with the reins. [. . .] And I seem to myself scarcely sane, I who makes poems, / and cares [*curem*] to correct [*corrigere*] them among the feral Getae."‡

Inability again fuses with suitability. Ovid stresses that his unvarying circumstances motivate his lack of variety (*unus sensus*), and, just as when cheerful he wrote cheerfully, now that he is sorrowful he writes sorrowfully: "each time [*tempus*] has a type of work [*operi*] appropriate to it [*conveniens*]."§ Repetitive he might be, but he does not always write to the same person. Learned readers might grow weary of reading the same petitions again and again, but Ovid's "Muse is a true index of my no few bad experiences, / and has all the weight of an incorruptible witness [*testis*]."** Besides, Ovid concludes, he has directed his care not toward producing a book-roll for fame's sake but toward selecting letters that most displayed his dutiful pose toward others. Having collected them, he joined them *sine ordine* (without order).†† Here is yet another editorial explanation—an intervention, really, like the others—that accounts for some facet of his texts Ovid suspects readers find distracting.

Several times in the *Epistulae Ex Ponto*, Ovid worries openly that his brutal depictions of his exilic environs present a land far too rough to be believed.‡‡ One could say the same of his constant disavowals of *corpus* care, and indeed, as I have shown, the book-rolls claim to be bound up—internally and externally— with the harshness of Tomis. (And if the one cannot be believed, then . . .) Throughout the course of his exilic *corpora*, Ovid works to maintain a rhetorical

---

*Ovid, *Epistulae*, 3.9.13–14.
†This is the same word Ovid uses to describe the unedited *Metamorphoses*.
‡Ovid, *Epistulae*, 3.9.17–26, 31–32.
§Ovid, *Epistulae*, 3.9.34–36; see also *Epistulae Ex Ponto*, 4.15.33–34.
**Ovid, *Epistulae*, 3.9.45–50.
††Ovid, *Epistulae*, 3.9.54, 53. If not Ovid (unlikely) then someone imposed order at some stage, since the poems have almost a symmetrical ring composition. See Martelli, *Ovid's Revisions*, 118–229.
‡‡Ovid, *Epistulae*, 3.9.50, 4.9.69–88, 4.10.35–36; also *Tristia*, 3.10.35–36.

stance appropriate to his altered and then stationary circumstances. In the first few book-rolls of *Tristia,* he presents his lack of editing as a sound-minded choice not to expend energy on textual or poetic refinements unbefitting his *relegatus* status vis-à-vis Rome or beyond the linguistic and aesthetic grasp of his hirsute new neighbors in Tomis. This responsiveness to *tempus* and *locus* shows Ovid to be in top rhetorical form. Increasingly, Ovid offers a new perspective on his refusals to refine, confessing to see his unintentional errors but to find their removal either irksome or impossible. His recurring protestations against *corpus* care function in nearly every poem as part of the exilic *expolitio* through which he again and again works through his limited rhetorical options. In the very last poem of the exilic collection, he first rears up against someone back home who is tearing into his verses—whether literally or figuratively is unclear and rather beside the point. First boasting of the invulnerability of poetic *ingenium* and the invincibility of a poet's fame, Ovid closes the poem by begging that this person-ification of envy cease ripping him apart: "what good is it to you to slip the steel into my dead limbs [*extinctos artus*]?"* Since Ovid's limbs (*artus*) and his artful skill (*ars, artis*) in joining them have already died, one expects that this decom-position cannot harm him, but Ovid feels every wound keenly.

Self Correction

Though Ovid may well be a hostile witness, he testifies in the second book-roll of the *Tristia* that work was progressing on the *Fasti,* a poem about the Roman national calendar and of which half survives, and on the *Metamorphoses* when Augustus's lightning bolt struck him out of the blue. Ovid narrates, avoiding the language of publishing: "I wrote [*scripsi*] six little book-rolls [*libellos*] of the *Fasti* and as many again, / and each roll [*volumen*] covers a month, / and it was written [*scriptum*] recently under your name, Caesar, / and dedicated to you, the work interrupted [*rupit opus*] by my lot.†. . further and I have spoken about [*dictaque*]—although it failed to receive the final hand [*manus ultima*]— / bodies turned into new faces [*facies corpora versa novas*]."‡

The "final hand" refers to those last finishing touches that are manually administered with a metaphorical editorial implement, such as the file (*lima*). Both the *Fasti* and the *Metamorphoses* want for completion, but Ovid emphasizes the inchoate state of the latter throughout the *Tristia,* while he mentions the

---

*Ovid, *Epistulae,* 4.16.51.
†Ovid, *Tristia,* 2.549–552.
‡Ovid, *Tristia,* 2.555–556.

former only here.* Ovid continually insists that the *Metamorphoses* was *sine fine* (without finish), either lacking an ending or lacking final editorial enhancements.† Peter Knox doubts Ovid left the *Metamorphoses* in a shabby state: "the composition of this masterpiece was surely the preoccupation of the years immediately preceding his exile."‡ Leaving aside the bothersome issue of Ovid's sincerity, Ovid's classification of the *Metamorphoses* as a work in progress opens up particular rhetorical angles.

In the introductory poem to the first book-roll of *Tristia* (and thus of the whole *corpus*), Ovid relies on a pun to anthropomorphize the volume—a *parvus liber* is a small book-roll, but a *parvus liber* is a small child—and continually goads and directs it in the imperative mood as he readies it for Rome.§ The last encounter the book-roll should make when it arrives "home" (that is, at Ovid's house) and joins its "brothers" (*fratres*) in the round book-roll cases (*scrinia curva*) is with the "three by five volumes about changing forms [*mutatae formae*], / poems recently snatched [*rapta*] from my funeral," that is, the *Metamorphoses*.** Ovid commands his exilic book-roll to "tell" those volumes that "the face [*vultum*, the about-face, really] of my fortune can be regarded among those changed bodies [*mutata corpora*]."†† Ovid seems to be attempting to insert his own tale of transformation into his book-rolls about change.

A few poems later, Ovid again couches the incompletion of the *Metamorphoses* in *corpus*-care terms. He asks that sympathetic readers alter "the face of his image [*imagine vultus*]" on whatever objects they possess (or to which they have access)—busts exhibited in libraries and portraits on book-roll covers are likely what he means—taking away the bacchic ivy draped around "my temples [*temporibus ... meis*]."‡‡ If such readers wish to behold a "better likeness [*maior imago*]," Ovid bids them to read his poems: "these I enjoin you to read, such as they are, these poems speaking of the changed forms of humans [*mutates*

---

*Ovid, *Tristia*, 1.1.116–121, 1.7.12–40, 2.62, 3.14.19–24, 4.10.63. For more on the various layers of Ovid's construction of the *Fasti*, see Fantham, "Ovid, Germanicus, and the Composition of the *Fasti*".

†Ovid, *Tristia*, 2.63.

‡Knox, "A Poet's Life," 6.

§Considered metrically, it is a visual pun but not an aural one, as the 'i' has a different length. Horace's book-roll (*liber*) in *Epistulae* 1.20 seems to be presented as a freed slave, but Ovid's *liber* here seems to pun on its similarity to "child." Ovid openly calls his book-rolls his children and himself their parent throughout the *Tristia*. See Davisson, "Parents and Children in Ovid's Poems from Exile."

**Ovid, *Tristia*, 1.1.107, 106, 117–118.

††Ovid, *Tristia*, 1.1.119–120.

§§Ovid, *Tristia*, 1.7.1, 3.

hominum dicentia formas], / the work interrupted by the unlucky flight of their master."* Ovid previously described the *Fasti* as *rupit opus*; then, as here, *opus* pertains both to Ovid's poetic labor and to its product, the text. He then confesses to having thrown the "deserving little book-rolls [*meritos libellos*]" on the fire as he prepared to leave the city, "either because I had come to detest the Muses, on account of my crime, / or because the poem itself was still growing and undeveloped [*crescens et rude*, rough]."† Unlike Vergil, Ovid was able to destroy that which had yet to receive its finishing touches.‡

He then accounts for their survival: "since they were not altogether snuffed out, but still exist— / many copies had been written out, I reckon— / I now pray that they may live on and delight the unlazy leisure of the reading public / and remind them of me. / They are not able, however, to be read patiently by any, / if unaware that they have gone without the final hand [*summam manum*]. / The work [*opus*] was taken away in the middle of its hammering [*incudibus*] / and the final file [*ultima lima*] was denied to my writings [*scriptis*]."§ Ovid induces readers to reframe what seems to be a magisterial poem as a gangly rough draft instead. His editorial tools—unjustly denied to this work—include the *lima,* a tool mentioned often by Cicero and Horace, and the hammer of a smith. If Ovid can lead readers to marvel at what the *Metamorphoses* could have been had he only been able to edit it properly, then he can put them in a sympathetic mood toward more than just that *corpus.*

In the next lines, Ovid discloses that he wants not only sympathetic indulgence but also editorial assistance. As well as taking up the incomplete *corpus,* he wants the reader to "take these six lines also, to be placed at the head [*frons*] of the first book-roll / if you approve: / 'You who touch [*tangis*] these volumes bereft of their parent, / to them at least let a place be granted in your city. / And your favor will be all the greater, since these were not published [*non edita*] by him, / but snatched [*rapta*] as if from their master's funeral. / Therefore, whatever faults [*vitii*] this rough [*rude*] poem will have, / they would have been emended [*emendaturus*], if it had been permitted.'"** Once placed *in primi fronte libelli,* these lines will be a literal pre(-)face. This textual facelift changes the look of flaws by casting the dark pall of exile over the whole *Metamorphoses.* Ovid highlights the tangibility of his incomplete efforts, again uses the text-as-abandoned-child figuration, and emphasizes that he did not authorize the text's circulation (*non edita*) or get the time to edit it before it was pulled from him.

*Ovid, *Tristia,* 1.7.11, 12–14.
†Ovid, *Tristia,* 1.7.19, 21–22.
‡Cicero, *Pro Archia,* §30; Horace, *Ars Poetica,* 285–294. *See* n26.
§Ovid, *Tristia,* 1.7.23–29.
**Ovid, *Tristia,* 1.7.33–40.

Thinking materially, Joseph Farrell points out that the "alteration of the poem thus depends on possession of a physical copy of the text. It is as if Ovid, having burned his autograph, were unable to alter his own poem, while anyone else who may have obtained one of the other versions in circulation might revise it *ad libitum.*"* Ovid must persuade readers to do his editorial bidding in Rome. Stephen Hinds argues that this poem is "about how the *Metamorphoses* can be redeployed, how it can be rewritten, to reflect the circumstances of Ovid's exile, and thus, ultimately, help him book his trip home."† Ovid continues, though, to reflect on the incompletion of the *Metamorphoses* in later book-rolls, both in the lines from *Tristia* 2 cited earlier and also in 3, 4, and 5.

In the third book-roll, the *Metamorphoses* morphs into one of several works that requires a stern hand, both to whip them into shape and to protect them. Ovid addresses an unnamed benefactor (most likely his literary agent, Brutus) who is refining, readying, assembling (*conficio*) Ovid's poems, all except that "*Ars* that ruined its artificer."‡ *Conficio*, similar to *expolitio*, means "finishing off," but it also can mean "killing," thus aptly capturing the precarity of Ovid's literary legacy. Calling his little book-rolls his body and emphasizing (again) their orphan status, Ovid urges:

> so far as you're able, keep my *corpus* in the city. / Flight [*fuga*] was decreed to me, flight was not decreed to my little book-rolls [*libellis*], / which did not merit their master's punishment. [10] / Often a father is exiled, deposited on a far border somewhere, yet / those things born of the exile are allowed to be in the city. / In the fashion of Pallas my poems were created by me without a mother; / these are my offspring, my progeny. / These I commend to you, of which, the more stripped of their parent they are, [15] / the greater burden [*sarcina maior*] they will be to you, their guardian [*tutori*]. / Three of my children [*nati*] have caught my contagion: / make the rest of the crowd§ publicly your care [*curae*]. / There are also three by five volumes [*volumina*] on changing forms [*mutatae formae*], / songs snatched [*rapta*] from the funeral of their master. [20] / That work, if only I had not perished first, / might have enjoyed a more secure name [*certius nomen*] from my finishing hand [*summa manu*]: / but now, uncorrected [*incorrectum*], it has come into the people's mouths, / if, that is to say, anything at all of mine is on the mouth of the people.**

*Farrell, "The Ovidian *Corpus*," 141.
†Hinds, "Booking the Return Trip," 437.
‡Ovid, *Tristia,* 3.14.5–6.
§In Cicero, *Brutus,* §123, Brutus refers to Cicero's output as a "crowd of volumes."
**Ovid, *Tristia,* 3.14.8–24.

Ovid's book-rolls sprang Athena-like from his head, but, unlike the goddess of war and wisdom, his children are not fully formed. The less parental attention his book-rolls have received, the more they need a guiding and guarding hand. *Sarcina* refers to the burdensome nature of tidying and bundling the literary output of a destroyed man, but the word specifically pertains to the difficulty of carrying a child; in *Tristia* 1.1.126, Ovid tells his little book-roll that it will be a *sarcina laturo magna* (a big burden to be borne), and here are the labor pains. The addressee of this poem is asked to carry unfinished works to term. Athena was not the only divinity born of the body of Zeus: Zeus stitched fetal Dionysos into his thigh after accidently killing Semele, Dionysos's mortal mother. Ovid's poems, like Dionysos, will be "twice-born."

Ovid asks, therefore, not only for legal guardianship but also for surrogacy, a risky proposition under the circumstances. (*Sarcina* also means "sorrow" or "trouble" and as such is a synonym for *tristia*.)* The *Ars* may be beyond help, but the others need care. First among them is the *Metamorphoses,* which, Ovid repeats, was "snatched" from his funeral before he was able to smooth them out lovingly with his finishing touches. Accordingly, they have an "uncertain name"—this could be a pun, since their title is "Changes"—and in an uncorrected state are being read and talked about by the people, if at all. The incompleteness of the massive, fifteen-book-rolled *corpus* offers Ovid an excuse to continue preparing it to meet with readers and adding new tales of transformation. He has suggested that his own tale be inserted, attempted to add a preface, and asked his literary executor to help his still-growing works reach maturity.

Ovid requests in the very first poem of *Tristia* that his own *mutatio* be included among the changed forms.† An intriguing inversion leaps out when one compares the opening two lines of the *Metamorphoses* (as we have it) with the two lines in which he describes the *Metamorphoses* in *Tristia* 2. The *Metamorphoses* opens with: "My soul bears up to speak about forms changed into new / bodies . . . [*In nova fert animus mutatas dicere formas / corpora*]."‡ In *Tristia* 2, Ovid reverses the order, and around the transformative action of a verb with poetic-textual resonance, no less: bodies are "turned [*versa*]," not into new "forms [*formas*]" but into new "faces [*facies*]."§ Ovid may have three faces in mind: the *frons* (front, forehead, face) of the *Metamorphoses* itself, since he has asked the reader to insert a pre(-)face); that of his exilic textual *corpus;* and his own. The latter two faces closely resemble each other. Both bear hair, which is

---

*In Horace, *Epistulae,* 1.13, where a donkey-like creature transports Horace's book-rolls to Augustus, Horace describes the load with this same word.
†Ovid, *Tristia,* 1.1.119–120.
‡Ovid, *Metamorphoses,* 1.1–2.
§Ovid, *Tristia,* 2.555–556.

against their custom, and the book-rolls and their author slowly come to resemble a swan.* "Already my temples [*mea tempora*] imitate a swan's plumage, / and white old age bleaches my black hair," Ovid reports, and a few poems later he opens his fifth exilic book-roll by deeming it a swansong.[†] The sound and sense of the book-roll mimics the sight of its author. Ovid's swanification itself resembles another famous anthropoavian transformation in Roman poetry, not in his *Metamorphoses* but in Horace's *Odes*.[‡] As the reader unfurls the final poem of the second book-roll of the *Odes*, Horace himself takes a turn:

> Neither ordinary nor delicate wing will lift me / through the liquid air, / a two-form poet, nor will I remain on the earth /any longer, and, too great for envy, / I will quit its cities. / I, blood of poor /parents, will not, I, whom you call to you, / delightful Maecenas, will not die, / nor be contained by the waves of the Styx. / Already now rough skin coats my legs, /and I turn white on all the parts above, and pushing out /through my fingers and shoulders are smooth feathers. / Already better known than Icarus of Daedalus, / I, singing and winged, will survey the shores of the sighing Bosphorus, / and the Gaetulan Syrtes, / and the Hyperborean plains. / The Colchian and the Dacian, who feign not to fear / a Marsian cohort, and at the far reaches / the Geloni, they will all know me, and the skilled / Iberian will learn of me and the Rhonian drinker. / Let be absent from my bodiless funeral dirges, / and lowly distress, and lamentation; / hold back your hollering and / dismiss the hollow honor of a tomb.[§]

Ovid, too, has left the earth's cities, being now in a place that is the very antithesis of the Roman *urbs* and its urbanity and hence clanking with all manner of foreign peoples. Ovid writes often of his book-rolls' peregrinations, not just to and around Rome but all over the sprawling empire. That poets issue "winged words" has been fluttering in the air since Homer, but flapping alongside the winged words in this Horatian ode and in many of Ovid's works is doomed Icarus.** In the middle of book-roll eight of the *Metamorphoses*, bystanders watch Icarus flail through the air and into the sea, his wing-wax melted from getting too near the sun and the whole ingenious device now entangled with his

---

**Hirsutus appears at *Tristia*, 1.1.12, *hirta* at 1.3.90.

†Ovid, *Tristia*, 4.8.1–2, 5.1.11.

‡See also Vergil, *Eclogue*, 9.35–36: *nam neque adhuc Vario videor nec dicere Cinna / digna, sed argutos inter strepere anser olores.*

§Horace, *Odes*, 2.20.

**Ovid wishes he had wings in *Tristia* 3.8; see also *Tristia* 1.1.88–90 for an Icarus reference.

limbs and dragging him under. Ovid is a Daedalus to his poems, which are both pieces of his engineering and his children, and an Icarus in his own sad tale.

Ovid, *mutata* and *versa* (changed and turned), is rightly agitated. When he thinks of his *mutata*, his "*manus demens* [mad hand], furious at itself and my pursuit, / sends my poems into the blazing hearth. / And so, since not many of them survive, / you should read them, whoever you are, with ready goodwill."* As he did with his *Metamorphoses,* out of anger with his situation and displeasure with their incompletion, so he does with most of his exilic works. The "final hand" offers a poem either editorial care or utter destruction. Near the end of the *Tristia,* Ovid again mentions the corrective flame. Just as when he was young, his "Muse cannot be held back from composing poems. / I write and then destroy the written little book-rolls in the fire: / a small ash heap is the final product of my pursuit. / I am not able and yet I long to lead out no more verses: / and so my labor is placed on the fire, / and not unless part crawls out of the flame by chance or cunning / will my *ingenium* reach you. / If only likewise my *Ars,* which ruined a teacher who feared nothing of the kind, / had been turned [*versa*] to cinders."† On show is the heat of Ovid's anger that he did not burn the poem that has caused all subsequent editorial/funeral pyres, though of course he had no inkling of its catastrophic potential at the time. He also manages to sneak in another note to the reader to treat any verses that reach Rome with kindness, since they represent a dying breed. The threat of scarcity always drives up value.

In the *Tristia,* Ovid repeatedly characterizes his fifteen book-rolls on change as still changing, as not yet rendered static by the stiffening preservative of polish and cedar oil. By *sine fine* (without finish), he means not only that they lack polish but also that they lack an ending, for his ending is their ending. His ending is also their new beginning, if readers insert the preface he provides them. The *Metamorphoses* in common circulation today begins not with a sorrowful preface but with an announcement of scope: the text will treat of changes from the hurly-burly churning of chaos and leading *ad mea tempora* (to my own times).‡ Variations on *ad mea tempora* spring up all over the *Tristia,* and the phrase refers sometimes to "my times" and other times to "my temples."§ *Tempus,* just like the Greek *kairos,* most often refers to time, but it can refer to a vital part of the body, that is, a part of the body most sensitive to penetrative weapons, such as the neck or the head. Ovid's white hair springs from his temples

---

*Ovid, *Tristia,* 4.1.99, 101–107.

†Ovid, *Tristia,* 5.12.59–68.

‡Ovid, *Metamorphoses,* 1.4.

§Ovid, *Tristia,* 1.1.4: *temporibus huius*; 1.7.4: *temporibus meis*; 4.1.105: *mea tempora*; 4.8.1: *mea tempora.* Hinds, "Booking the Return Trip," f.n. 24, 434, notes this doubling but considers only 1.1.4 and 1.7.4 and does not go into *kairos.*

and his times. People expelled from their homelands often age prematurely. However striking and irreversible the transformation of Ovid's literal *corpus,* his literary *corpora* continue to flux.

Ovid's persistent appraisal of his *Metamorphoses* as unfinished demonstrates the power of the connection between his fibrous *corpus* and his fleshy one: both will undergo more change because of his exile. Though he invites readers to help him edit the *Metamorphoses* by adding a preface and perhaps too an epilogue about his own swanification, any alterations Ovid makes to his exilic writings he makes alone, as he continually reminds his readers.

Poetic Sodality and Solidarity

The sociality once produced by and enabling poetic composition, editorial preparation, and textual circulation—and now lost to Ovid—structures much of the *Epistulae.* A current convention of academic writing receives pride of place in either the acknowledgment segment of a book or the first or last footnote of an article, some form or other of "thanks to [insert friendly critics here] for providing excellent feedback on an earlier version and straightening me out on the few key points, though of course all remaining errors are solely my responsibility." If Ovid was not the first writer to suffer the entailments of that arrangement, then he was certainly the most notorious one. Though what is both a practical and textual convention for us was not yet so clearly one in antiquity, I have shown in previous chapters that ancient writers relied on trusted others to look over a text before putting it out (*edo*) in public. For example, at least thirty years before Horace advocated editing with friends in the *Ars Poetica,* Cicero relied on the collaboratively editorial aspect of poetics to dispense advice about deed-doing and decision making in his philosophical treatise *De Officiis:* one should approach our plans as poets do their verse, submitting them to the scrutiny of trusted friends so that all mistakes can be caught and corrected.* The interactive nature of poetic editing must have been proverbial to Romans, since Cicero never deployed analogies grounded in unfamiliar territory.

Yet, only Ovid was made to assume full responsibility for his friend-aided poetic crime. The convention of collaborative editing proved irresistible to him as a commonplace, since he could play up two important implications. Its being lost to him, he edited alone and without the goad of the ear, so readers should cut him some slack. Further, if those esteemed people with whom he formally swapped verses or to whom he disclosed his own were truly his friends, they would share his burden by speaking up for him or at least by protecting his poetic

*Cicero, *De Officiis,* 1.147.21ff.

legacy. *Corpus* care for the relegated Ovid came to include the sheltering care others could give to his unprotected body of work.

Ovid depicted nearly all the editing of his postrelegation writings as undertaken alone and as more burdensome than his increasingly "*gracilis corpus* [skinny body]" can handle.* In one poem of exception, Ovid asks the literary benefactor who bundles up his writings—except the *Ars* but seemingly including Ovid's exilic writings up to that point—as a sort of definitive collection of sorts (or maybe even an uncomfortably premature retrospective) to insert an explanatory prologue:

> Place in the front of my little book-rolls [*libellis*] this I don't know what, / which comes to you having been sent from a different world. / Whoever reads them—if anyone reads them—let him think through beforehand at what time [*tempore*] and in what place [*loco*] they were composed. / He will be fair to writings, once he knows them to be / from an exilic time and barbaric place: / and, further, given all the adversities, he will be amazed any song at all / was pulled from me and sustained by my sad hand. / All sorts of bad things have broken my genius, whose / *fons*, even before, was never very generative and the channel it cut small. / But whatever was, with no one keeping it active, it has disappeared, / and it is long dead, dried up in place. / Here there is no abundance of book-rolls, through which I might be challenged and helped along: / for book-rolls there is the noise of bows and arms. / No one here in this land, if I were to recite my songs, / has intelligent ears I could make use of: / there is no place set apart. The guard on the wall / holds back the hostile Getae, as does the closed gate. / Often when I am trying to find a word, or a name, or a place, / there is no one I can seek out for certainty. / Often when I am trying to say something—shameful to admit!—/ words fail me and I seem to have surrendered my powers of speech. / Thracian and Scythian mouths surround me with sound, / and I seem to be able to write in Getic measures. / Believe me, I fear that you will read Sintic and Pontic words mixed in with Latin / in my writings. / Therefore, deem the little book-roll [*libellum*], such as it is, worthy of kindness, / and excused by the condition of my lot.†

Within this editorial supplement, for whose placement he relies on a loyal friend, Ovid nestles the narrative of his solitary composition circumstances. Imagine a

---

*_gracili corpore_ at *Epistulae* 1.5.52 (contrasted to his strong *mens*) and 1.10.21.

†Ovid, *Tristia*, 3.14.25–52. Compare it with *Tristia*, 1.1.35–48. Ovid showcases precisely what reader reactions he hopes to provoke by representing the rough circumstances of exilic poetic creation and referring again and again to the poems' lack of editing. It is an explicit rhetorical strategy.

bookish person like himself not having access to roll after roll of reading material. Also, no one can act as his sounding board, since there are no *intellecturis auribus* within earshot. Lacking the linguistic flow that opens up when one composes with helpful and learned friends, Ovid dries up, becoming nearly speechless. His writing, meanwhile, becomes choppy, as non-Latin words slice in like the barbarians they are. Of all these difficulties readers of his exilic verses must be informed or reminded, and no doubt they will be aghast at Ovid's sad situation and all the more impressed with his being able to eke out anything at all.

Again Ovid pines for "ears comprehending of Latin words" and grumbles that he must both address and critique himself.* Auto-criticism in exile has not been Ovid's strong suit; in frustration, he typically turns to ash anything that needs more work than he can give. Ovid drops straggling hints, though, that his exilic works are, despite all their author's infelicities, being enjoyed by Roman readers.† For example, toward the end of *Tristia*, Ovid writes in recognition of a letter from a well-wisher who encourages him to keep up his efforts. Ovid wonders if this friend's attempt at persuasion (*suades*) stems from the current success his earlier exilic works are enjoying in Rome.‡ Ovid professes to be torn. Though wishing to oblige this request, he again mentions being woefully without book-roll or ear (*non liber, non aurem*) and shivers to think he might be losing his Latin and learning the harsh language of the even harsher locals.§ Writing well grows more and more difficult.

Adding to his pains, it seems that few of Ovid's companions want to have anything to do with him, let alone spin long paper trails across the empire for some Augustan crony to discover. In the penultimate poem of *Tristia*, Ovid chides a (former?) friend for not sending any consolatory letters to him, for not making any contact at all after the sad news broke. Ovid presents this unnamed associate with a communication analogy: just as we used to stay up all night talking, "so now should our letters bring back and forth our silent voices, / and our paper and our hands [*charta manusque*] should carry out the function of our tongues."** Throughout the *Epistulae Ex Ponto*, Ovid presents his letters as replacements for his tongue and for his physical presence.†† And *corpus* care appears in various ways, as well. For instance, Ovid pleads with a callously

---

*Ovid, *Tristia*, 4.1.90–92.

†See William, "Representations of the Book-Roll in Latin Poetry," 182–184, on the richness of *infelix* as a literary adjective in Ovid's exilic *corpora*.

‡Ovid, *Tristia*, 5.12.43.

§Ovid, *Tristia*, 5.12.53–8. See also *Tristia*, 5.7.53–64, *inter alia*.

**Ovid, *Tristia*, 5.13.27–30.

††Ovid, *Epistulae*, 1.2.6 (*epistula . . . loquar tecum*); 1.7.1 (*littera pro verbis*); 2.6.1 (*qui praesens voce solebat*); 2.6.3–4 (exile's letters are his tongue); 4.9.11–12.

unresponsive addressee: "Correct this, I pray! And if you correct this one thing, / there will be no blemish on an exceptional body [*corpore*]."*

The ears in *Tristia* are synecdochic for all the editorial bodies in Rome that would hear him out when his verses were rough and snatch him up when his verses were finished, and few poems reveal their respective addressees. The ears in the *Epistulae Ex Ponto,* however, are specific, and Ovid names names. He openly concedes in the opening poem of his *Epistulae* that though his correspondents back home do not want to be revealed by name in these forthcoming letters, they cannot prevent it. He shirks responsibility with a characteristically poetic smirk: even *he* cannot prevent it, since it is his Muse that refuses to abdicate her duty to call upon them all by name and thank them for their various past kindnesses to him.† The *Epistulae Ex Ponto* are open letters, public letters, written for the public eye and not just for whomever Ovid plainly names. Ovid is all the time sending private prose letters, too.‡

In these public letters, Ovid rein forces the bonds of friendship. He writes to a whole range of contacts, from the children of the man who first encouraged him to publish his poems—like Maximus, whose head Ovid kissed when Maximus was a baby and who now resembles his father in eloquence—to associates he has not known for long but whom he understands to be deeply troubled by his situation.§ Luigi Galasso compares Ovid's technique to that of a blackmailer (Ovid *is* using the blackmailer's medium), but Ovid divulges the potentially damaging "secret" of their acquaintance with him before extracting what he wants.** Though he obliquely hints that his critics in Rome never discouraged him from publishing anything—that is, they are at least partly responsible for his *Ars* ever seeing the light of day—in two instances he is careful to isolate those naughty book-rolls. In one letter to the aforementioned Maximus and another to Maximus's brother, Messalinus, Ovid recalls their approval of all his works, all *except* the *Ars.*†† It does not serve Ovid's case to taint anyone by association with that work; he needs all his associates free to argue his case.

At the beginning of the *Epistulae,* Ovid wistfully recalls all the talking he used to do with his family and friends.‡‡ It is precisely their speech that he calls

*Ovid, *Tristia,* 5.13.13–14.
†Ovid, *Epistulae,* 1.1.17–20.
‡Ovid, *Epistulae,* 4.2.5–6.
§Salanus, in *Epistulae* 2.5, is well known around Rome for his eloquence, and Ovid describes him with words similar to those Horace uses self-reflexively at the end of *Odes* 1.1.
**Galasso, "*Epistulae Ex Ponto,*" 200.
††Ovid, *Epistulae* (*exceptis domino qui nocuere suo,* 1.2.133–136; *Artibus exceptis,* 2.2.103–104).
‡‡Ovid, *Epistulae,* 1.2.49–50.

upon, since his too-distant voice has failed to keep his case on the docket.* Though hoping to be proved wrong, he calls himself *dilecto Nasone* (the formerly beloved Naso), and underlying his constant appeals to memory is the hope that the emotions behind fond remembrance might be activated for present purposes.† Every letter has a tie-in to Ovid's past poeticizing, but I isolate four recipients and four letters: Atticus, Macer, Severus, and Tuticanus.‡ These four letters recommend themselves because they contain entreaties not for the addressees to try to move Caesar to move Ovid but for them simply to remember their dear friend of old. The letters do this memory work by linking past communicative intimacy either to past collaborative editing (Atticus, Tuticanus) or to the all-abiding bond of poetic solidarity (Macer, Severus, Tuticanus). Poets, particularly, must stick together and support one another, since harsh times can strike with little warning.

Atticus is to Ovid what Cicero's friend Atticus was to him: a trusted critic and champion of his work. Though Ovid does not want to doubt the steadfastness of his friend's support, he cannot help but wonder whether Atticus "remains mindful of your unlucky friend, / or has your care weakened and deserted its post?"§ For his part, Ovid unceasingly engages his friend in his thoughts, even remembering certain facial expressions. Back in the day, they mixed bouts of joking with their serious talk, the too-short day struggling to hold their long verbal exchanges. They even managed to stuff some editorial activities into their word-packed agenda: "poems only just made [*factum modo*] often came to your ears [*ad auris*] / and a new Muse was subjected to your judgment [*iudicio*]. / Those that you praised I deemed to have pleased the public already. / This was the sweet reward of my recent cares [*curae recentis*]. / My book-roll having been scraped by the file [*lima rasus*] of a friend, / not just once were erasures [*litura*] made due to your advice."** Atticus was that most treasured thing to a writer of Ovid's ilk: a predictor of public reception. His approval was "sweet" and his editorial elbow grease less savory but nonetheless essential.

Ovid longingly recalls how inseparable they were, seen side by side all over Rome. Surely even if Atticus swilled great gulps from the river Lethe, he would not forget; Ovid's fate cannot be as dark (*non candida*) as all that.†† Even so, he ends the poem: "So that, however, this faith of which I have spoken cannot be

---

*Even his wife (*Epistulae* 3.1) and new son-in-law (*Epistulae* 4.8) are asked to do persuasive work on his behalf.

†Ovid, *Epistulae*, 1.8.1.

‡Ovid, *Epistulae*, 2.4, 2.10, 4.2, 4.12.

§Ovid, *Epistulae*, 2.4.3–4.

**Ovid, *Epistulae*, 2.4.13–18.

††Ovid, *Epistulae*, 2.4.30.

false / and my credulity stupid, look out for / and guard [*tutare*] your old companion with constant fidelity, / as it suits and as much as I will not be burdensome" (31–34). If everyone back in Rome did not know of their closeness—and, as they were seen together in the forum, in the city's strolling places, and at the theater, who would not know?—everyone does now. Atticus should not betray an intimacy so close that Ovid let him hear, hold, and wear down his newest poetic additions. That Ovid uses the same verb of defense (*tutor*) here as he did in *Tristia* with regard to the guardianship of his book-roll babies suggests that to protect him is to protect them. Ovid fully invests himself in the survival of his textual *corpus.*

Though it is unclear whether Atticus is a poet—his knack for knowing what will please readers and his skill with the file suggest so—there is no doubt about Macer. Ovid characterizes their relationship as one of long years; if Macer does not recognize the imprint of Ovid's signet ring in the letter's waxy sealant or Ovid's distinctive handwriting once he breaks the seal, then it is only because Macer no longer cares for him (*cura mei*).* They are joined not only by a long acquaintance but also by family (Ovid's current wife is related to Macer somehow) and poetic pursuit, though Macer has been wiser in his choices. Ovid credits him with writing on whatever details of the Trojan war Homer left out, thereby giving that great theme the "final hand [*summa manu*]."† In essence, Macer has perfected Homer, no mean feat. Apparently, Macer has been sending his verses to Ovid in exile, allowing his stationary friend to travel to assorted locales and even to spy on the occasional nymph. Thinking back to his days in Rome, Ovid recounts their uncountable words, which even the long days of summer could not contain (Ovid clearly had a lot of time to talk), and hints at their conspiratorial giggling about doing particular though unspecified poetic deeds. Such memories place Macer amid the Black Sea's population, and Ovid hopes Macer will use his memories to place Ovid back in Rome, to dwell in his "remembering heart."‡

That Severus is a poet of high standing flusters Ovid (so he says) so much that he has up to this point delayed mentioning his fellow poet and thus dedicating to him that very thing that Severus has in fertile abundance: verses. Ovid, meanwhile, struggles to flow against the clogging "silt of misfortune." If even Homer had been cruelly deposited here he would have fared no better.§ What Ovid especially misses is the goad of the ear: "a hearer stirs up zeal, and virtuosity

*Ovid, *Epistulae,* 2.10.8.
†Ovid, *Epistulae,* 2.10.14.
‡Ovid, *Epistulae,* 2.10.52.
§Ovid, *Epistulae,* 4.2.19, 21–22. See Ovid, *Tristia,* 1.1.47–48: were Homer here, no doubt his *ingenium* would fall away, too.

grows with praise, / and *gloria* sports an immense spur."* Being alone and uninterested in loafing about, playing games, or drinking himself stupid, he tries to
cultivate the infertile soil anew.† While he scratches away with his writing tools,
Ovid asks Severus to send on "some work of his own recent care [*aliquod curae
mitte recentis opus*]."‡

Tuticanus, whose name Ovid cannot gracefully squeeze into his meter, has
for that reason not yet received a letter. In recompense for this waiting time,
Ovid pours on the affect(at)ion, fondly recalling how he and Tuticanus had been
friends since nearly boyhood and calling their bond fraternal. When Ovid was
first getting hold of the reins of poetry with "tender hands [*tenera manu*]," Tuticanus acted as "a good exhorter and leader and companion," and "often I corrected [*correxi*] my little book-rolls based on your censure [*censore*], / often,
based on your admonishments [*admonitu*], I made erasures."§ Tuticanus, meanwhile, produced faultless sheets worthy of Homer. In showcasing only his own
faults, Ovid emphasizes his reliance on his friend for aid and flatters Tuticanus's
comparative perfection. From a green early age to a late white-haired one, they
shared this "continuity" and "concord" of poetic and interpersonal interest, and
"unless this moves you [*te moveant*], then I will think your heart to be made of
hard [*duro*] iron / or encased by unconquerable steel."** Has Tuticanus shut
himself up from Ovid's entreaties? Ovid thinks not, imagining his friend asking: "what it is you seek?" Yet, in his wretched state, Ovid does not know what
he wants or what is most useful or advantageous, since *prudentia*, an invalu-
able rhetorical asset, has left him completely.†† Ovid advises Tuticanus, therefore, to make inquiries on his behalf as to what can be done to ameliorate his
sad situation.‡‡

Those four letters are representative of Ovid's letter-writing *persona,* varying ratios of pushy and pathetic, and of his particular reliance on what he hopes
is poetic solidarity. Fairly early on in the *Epistulae,* Ovid exclaims woefully that
amicitia (friendship) has degraded herself into a *meretrix* (prostitute), turning
tricks for favor and gain.§§ That indictment of friendship's honor speaks to Ovid's
mounting frustrations that none of his former companions have stepped in to
help him, figuring there is only trouble to be had from doing so, though that

---

*Ovid, *Epistulae,* 4.2.35–36. A partial echo of *Tristia,* 4.12.37–38.
†Ovid, *Epistulae,* 4.2.39, 44.
‡Ovid, *Epistulae,* 4.2.50.
§Ovid, *Epistulae,* 4.12.24, 23, 25–26.
**Ovid, *Epistulae,* 4.12.29, 31–32.
††Ovid, *Epistulae,* 4.12.47.
‡‡Ovid, *Epistulae,* 4.12.45–50.
§§Ovid, *Epistulae,* 2.3.19–20.

would not deter a true friend. As all his *Epistulae* are collated and circulated around Rome, readers (apparently) grow weary of the repetitive pleading.* Ovid intends, though, for each letter to function as its own persuasive piece, even at the expense of the variegated artfulness of the whole collection.

With every attempt to write him off, however big (*relegatio*) or small (not answering a letter), Ovid redoubles his efforts, discomforting though he says they are. His exilic book-rolls circulate around Rome, calling on and calling out his former friends and keeping his name and perhaps his ca(u)se alive. That he responds to reactions from readers other than his formerly close circle of élite friends means his work is being copied, circulated, and evaluated more broadly. Being recalled to Rome was a pressing short-term rhetorical objective, but Ovid also had a mind toward the larger and longer scheme of things. Tucked in amid the various forms of Ovid's exilic *expolitio* are bold assertions of wide textual spread and influence in his own time *and* after.† One pronouncement with a lovely mix of tenderness and sassiness occurs in a poem Ovid addressed to the quickly prepared *littera* (letters) he personified and sent off to his daughter by marriage, Perilla.‡ Perilla loves her book-rolls and writes her own verse. When he could, Ovid acted as a critic, teacher, and encourager of her productions.§ Afraid his exile has turned her against poetry, he puts on a brave face, asserting the freedom of his mind from Caesar's jurisdiction and binding his fame and name to the worldwide spread of mighty Rome.** If Augustus cannot keep Ovid's textual *corpora* out of Rome, then Augustus has no chance of controlling the poet's travel to and reception within other regions—and times. Ovid's distinctive *licentia* lives on.

---

*Ovid, *Epistulae*, 3.7, 3.9, 4.15.

†Ovid, *Tristia*, 1.6.35; 2.7 (public wanted to know him); 2.119–120 (the *doctus* of Rome know him); 3.3 (Ovid's death, his epitaph); 3.7.43–54 (Caesar cannot chain his mind or control his fame); 4.10; 5.7.30; 5.9.6; 5.14 (his letters to his wife a *monumenta libellis*). *Epistulae*: 2.6.33–34; 3.2.27–36; 4.8.43–54; 4.10.7–8; 4.16.3–4 and 45–46. The end of the *Metamorphoses* boasts the most striking example.

‡Ovid, *Tristia*, 3.7.2.

§Ovid, *Tristia*, 3.7.4, 23–26.

**Ovid, *Tristia*, 3.7.48, 52–54.

CHAPTER SIX

THE CARES OF QUINTILIAN

Twice, Quintilian was rushed. The *magnum opus* commonly known as the *Institutio Oratoria* (*Education/Formation of the Orator*), which spans twelve book-rolls and the course of an orator's life, went out into Rome before Quintilian was, he says, truly ready to write it or to release it.* In the preface to the first book-roll, Quintilian describes the composition conditions: friends prompted him, the challenge of analyzing and synthesizing so much material thrilled him, and the unauthorized circulation of notes taken at his lectures irked him. "Two book-rolls on the art of rhetoric are circulating under my name, although neither published [*editi*] nor prepared for that. One is a two days' lecture taken down by the boys who were present; the other is many days' worth, and as much as my good pupils were able to take down in their notes, but they showed far too much love for me and temerity in putting them forth as a publication [*editionis*], however honorably. So, in the present book-roll, although some content remains the same, much has changed, many things have been added, and everything is more turned out and, as much as I am able, worked out."† Appointed in the early 70s C.E. by the emperor Vespasian to an imperial chair in rhetoric, the first position of its kind in all of the ancient world, Quintilian found his opinions on rhetoric and oratory in high demand. A few enterprising students decided to exploit their proximity, perhaps for pay.

At least in part, Quintilian wrote the *Institutio* in the early-to-mid 90s to correct the record. He could not recall "his" lecture notes from Rome's bookstalls, but he could rely on the quality and comprehensiveness of the *Institutio* to put the earlier texts out of demand. Clearly, Quintilian intended for it to circulate publicly at some stage. The question is: when? In the general preface

---

*George Kennedy takes Quintilian's word for it, blaming the "haste" Quintilian mentions here for any areas of the text Kennedy perceives to be hiccups (see, e.g., *Quintilian*, 501).

†Quintilian I.preface.7–8. Quintilian officially dedicates the work to his friend Marcellus Vitorius. For a prospectus on The Quintilian Project, which endeavors to create "a rhetorical edition" of Quintilian, see Boyle, "Low Fidelity in High Definition," 128.

addressed to a bookseller named Trypho, which opens the entire published work, Quintilian describes the publication conditions. He reflects upon time. He acknowledges Trypho's "daily" urgings "to send out [*emittere*]" his "book-rolls [*libros*]." He explains that the composition has taken two years, most of which he spent not with the *stilus* but with "innumerable authors and authorities," reading and readying.* That he has spent time with the *lima* (editorial file) is the subtle conclusion he sets up with the subsequent sentence, where he admits to wanting to heed Horace's advice from the *Ars Poetica* that writers wait nine years before sending forth any piece of writing: Horace's formulation is "*labor limae et mora* [the labor of the file and delay]."† But Quintilian believes Trypho's tenacious tale that there is an eager demand for the work that is worth satisfying with immediate publication. In the end, Quintilian releases his book-rolls to Trypho, comparing the *corpus* to a ship setting sail and calling upon the "faith and diligence" of Trypho to ensure they go out in "the most correct form [*emendatissimi*]." Given that many ancient writers complain about error-ridden copies, this is a necessary rather than a finicky request. As Peter White observes, "in their concern for profit, [booksellers] were apt to dispense with the step of proofing and correcting copies against the master text."‡ Quintilian's fellow Spaniard the epigrammatic poet Martial also entrusted his work to Trypho, apparently a big name in the lively book-roll acquisitions market at the end of the first century c.e.§

To use an idiom he liked, Quintilian followed in the footsteps of everyone from Plato to Cicero when he called upon the body and its divisions and variations to structure his project.** He adopted *corpus*-based critical language early to evaluate his own task. He judged "nude" handbooks of rhetoric that excessively anatomize the art to "slurp out the juice of ingenuity and leave the bones [*ossa*], which, while they should exist and be bound each to each by their

---

*Quintilian 1.preface.1.

†Horace, *Ars Poetica,* 285–294. Amusingly, Quintilian later mentions that the poet Cinna took nine years to write *Smyrna* and Isocrates took ten to write his *Panegyricus,* and Quintilian points out that orators do not have that kind of time (10.4.4).

‡White, "Bookshops in the Literary Culture of Rome," 278. For complaints about errors, White, 278, n. 30.

§Martial, *Epigrams,* 13.3. In an earlier poem, and likely teasingly, Martial named Quintilian "the foremost guide of rambling [*vaga*] youth," that is, of young men who would wander in their words or ways if not for his instruction (*Epigrams* 2.90). Martial's poetry contains many references to editing and filing. J. Miro Seo argues that Martial's use of textual language is allusive but also part of his effort to mark his works as "material commodities available for purchase or theft." Seo, "Plagiarism and Poetic Identity in Martial," 567.

**See footsteps (*vestigia*) at 1.preface.3 and 10.2.10, for example.

ligaments [*nervis*], still require a body [*corpore*]."* He meant for his own account to be shapely, strong, solid. Still, he thought it might, in places, prove "dry and arid" to the "delicate ears" of particular people.† Too aware of the scope of his challenge to hope for completeness, Quintilian aimed for generative, suggestive copiousness (*copia*).‡ He demonstrated his ability to survey and weigh an ungainly amount of texts and traditions. He made the managerial magisterial. As Erik Gunderson explains, Quintilian's work "archives these other theories of rhetoric as part of its own performance of rhetorical-*cum*-theatrical mastery."§ The *Institutio* enacts its central lesson: from boyhood forward, an orator starts from a place of great abundance and then grinds down—but not too far down—to what is worth keeping.

Body language appears thickly in every book-roll, and a case could be made that most instances pertain to what Sheila Dickison and Judith Hallett have called "the Latin TLC": *tempus* (time), *labor* (work), *cura* (care).** Some of Quintilian's body language is explicitly or metaphorically textual, however, and it is upon those instances that I focus. In particular, I argue that the file (*lima*) contributes to the definition and realization of the *orator perfectus* at every step. Whereas Cicero's terminology for the "types of speech" absorbed writing and editing—seen in words such as "filed" and "polished"—Quintilian's entire instructional method bears an editorial tinge. Rhetorical exercise and experience function editorially, eliminating the awkward, the ugly, and the excessive on the oratorical *corpus,* be it the orator's actual body, his spoken one, or his textual one. I consider the first two sorts of bodies only when they are clearly building toward the third. Since Quintilian was operating in a historical context wherein it was not rare for excellent orators to publish their speeches and his training regimen prepared an orator for what he would be expected to do once his voice secured a place in public life, it follows that Quintilian should cast editorial vocabulary back into all phases of an orator's formation.

For Quintilian, one purpose of rhetorical training is to render art second nature, to make easier that which is difficult. Quintilian calls this process of

---

*Quintilian 1.preface.24.

†Quintilian 3.1.3.

‡*Copia* at Quintilian 3.1.22. He also explains, "if I say all that might be said on each subject, the work would never be finished [*finis*]" (1.preface.25).

§Gunderson, "The Rhetoric of Rhetorical Theory," 111. Elsewhere, Gunderson refers to the *Institutio* as an "encyclopedic survey of the departments of oratory" in which Quintilian "collects, sorts, and comments upon centuries of Greek and Roman thought on oratory" (Gunderson, "Discovering the Body in Roman Oratory," 172).

**Dickison and Hallett, *A Roman Women Reader,* xi. They use "the Latin TLC" in their acknowledgments to thank friends for their scholarly sociality, an ancient practice, as I have shown.

habituation *hexis* (Greek, lit. "having") and sometimes renders it in Latin as *facilitas* (ease).* Thinking editorially is one strain of habituation. Nowhere is that connection more clear than in his pairing of *facilitas* with *copia* (abundance). According to James J. Murphy, Quintilian set out "to change the psyche of the student, to make him 'rhetorical,' not merely by having him learn a set of rules, but also by having him exercise a wide variety of language uses so that ultimately he has familiarity with a large number of options."† *Copia* enables *facilitas,* the thinking goes, because the more speeches one has heard, read, studied, and delivered, the more easily one can produce fitting speech. That virtuous cycle cannot be left to whirl unattended, however; Quintilian's emphasis throughout the *Institutio* is on the careful elimination of excess. The more easily his words come, the more suspiciously the orator must visit them with the editorial file.

As Cicero did, Quintilian aims to stop eloquence from changing beyond recognition. Its constitution, its health, and its appearance receive his close scrutiny. Before composing the *Institutio,* Quintilian wrote *De Causis Corruptae Eloquentiae* (*On the Cause of Corrupted Eloquence*), the title clearly investigative and the work itself perhaps conclusive; it does not survive. Quintilian pulls a vocabulary of corruption throughout the *Institutio,* however.‡ That he would spend two years preparing a detailed work about the *orator perfectus* suggests he did not think eloquence was beyond the point of no return: the *Institutio* is an instruction manual aimed at the maintenance of uncorrupted eloquence, not a de-extinction plan. In his estimation, corruption streams from those schools of rhetoric that have broken with practicality and reality. Issuing from such schools are two very different types of bodies, both unfit for oratorical duties (*officia oratoris*): a puny one that he calls Attic and a pretty one that he calls *virilitate excisa,* or castrated, and that is clearly the exoticized Eastern body Cicero and other writers from the first century B.C.E. had called Asian.§ Similarly to Cicero, Quintilian deems those types excessive or reductive, depending upon the angle at which he comes at them, but it is the context-independent obsessiveness of those who pursue those forms that strikes him as most unbecoming an orator. The orator he forms is the picture of masculine hardiness, nimble yet not mincing and trained and tested in how to respond to actual, difficult, public circumstances, rather than fashioned to fuss over fake cases. No matter his named area of focus in a particular book-roll, Quintilian views it through this bodily, gendered, critical language. The two corrupt extremes afford him a spacious middle

*Quintilian 10.1.1, 10.5.1.
†Murphy, "A Quintilian Anniversary and Its Meaning," 109.
‡See Brink, "Quintilian's *De Causis Corruptae Eloquentiae* and Tacitus' *Dialogus de Oratoribus.*"
§Quintilian 5.12.17.

in which to situate his perfect orator.* Moreover, that they arise from excessive management in the pursuit of a particular "look" allows him to keep certain implements from eloquence's toolkit, the file (*lima*) foremost, without seeming overelaborate.

To those who would deprive the orator even of that, Quintilian is similarly absolutist: "I am not unaware that there are those who would exclude all care [*curam omnem*] pertaining to *compositio* and contend that rough talk, however it happens to flow, is at one moment more natural and at another more manly [*virilem*]. If by this they mean that only that is natural which originated first from nature and remained in a state prior to *cultus*, this overturns the whole art of oratory."† *Cultus* enjoys a range of original referents and lexical descendants. Typically, it refers to that which has been cultivated and cultured through some process or another of development and augmentation. That Quintilian and his contemporaries struggled over the meaning, value, and function of *cultus* is clear enough from this passage: "Let no one from among the corrupted call me inimical to those who speak with *cultus*. I do not deny it to be a virtue, but I do not assign it to them."‡ The larger passage pertains to *ornatus*—"ornament" is the usual, unsatisfactory translation, and I will continue to translate the word as "enhancement"—and Quintilian's attempts to delineate a masculine strain. Cultivating an "attractive virility" is the challenge.§

A usable definition for *cultus* when it appears in literal or figurative corporeal contexts, as it often does in Quintilian, is *corporis cura et ornamentum* (the care and enhancement of the body).** That definition also includes the other improvement-related word Quintilian uses, *cura* (care). The *cultus* of oratory is like the *cultus* of masculinity: ancient men are uneasy when talking about either, but they consider certain elements of care to be basic grooming undertaken out of a polite recognition of the existence of others. Respecting the senses and sensibilities of those with whom one shares space is a kind of sociality rather than vanity, if held within certain patrolled limits. As Gunderson notes, "those who cross the lines that are invisibly or visibly laid down thereby reveal themselves impotent and illegitimate," namely dried up neo-Atticists, plush eunuchs, or painted women.††

Ovid's troublesome (for him) *Ars Amatoria* contains the fullest extant ancient account of grooming for men and for women, including attention to hair care,

---

*See, e.g., Quintilian 12.10.80.

†Quintilian 9.4.3.

‡Quintilian 8.3.7.

§Gunderson, "Discovering the Body in Roman Oratory," 177.

**Thesaurus eroticus linguae Latinae, s.v. cultus.

††Gunderson, "Discovering the Body in Roman Oratory," 187.

manicures (literally *cura* of the hands), and perfuming.* Quintilian's work mentions many of the same treatments and implements, sometimes applied metaphorically to verbal or textual bodies, sometimes to fleshy ones. Hair-related verbal treatments, for instance, range from depilatories to curling irons, of which Quintilian does not approve.† Fingernails, integral to Horace's design of the poetic body, appear also, but only so Quintilian can make this point: "Eloquence is to be approached with more spirit, she who, if her whole body is strong, will not regard polishing her nails [*ungues polire*] and putting back her hair as relevant to her care [*curam*]."‡ Robust oratory does not need to be perfect to any of its tips. Quintilian does, though, privilege the rubbing out, scratching out, or polishing out of the unattractive and extraneous on "her" body as a whole. Quintilian's entire rhetorical project can be understood through a hermeneutics of *cura* (care). The *cura*-based lexical family is the progenitor of "curative" and "curation," both of which apply to Quintilian's labors: he sees what ails various oratorical *corpora* and means to cure them through his curation of rhetoric's traditions and orations. Once Rome has rhetoric's theoretical, practical, and critical history pressed into a pedagogically oriented *opus,* there will be no excuse for the sort of ignorance responsible for the forms of corrupted eloquence he identifies.

The uncorrupted, uncorruptable *vir bonus* is Quintilian's most familiar formulation. It features in his very definition of the orator: "I seek to develop the perfect orator, who cannot exist unless he is a good man [*vir bonus*]."§ Originating with Cato Maior, the *vir bonus* is an archaic, no-nonsense Roman conception. Yet neither the noun *vir* nor the adjective *bonus* is simple; indeed, in combination they form either a paradox or a pleonasm. That strange ambiguity arises from the range of meanings of *bonus.* In chapter 1, I showed that Aristophanes

---

*While recommending men keep their nails neatly trimmed and their head, facial, and nose hair tidy (*Ars Amatoria* 1.518–520), he cautions them "not to take pleasure in curling your hair with the iron or in scraping your legs with biting pumice [*nec tua mordaci pumice crura teras*]" (1.505–6). Such *corpus* care befits lascivious girls and men who seek men (523–524) but not a cultivated and impenetrable aristocrat. Ovid addresses women and hair removal at 3.193–194.

†E.g., depilatories at 2.5.12 and 8.preface.19; curling irons at 2.5.12. Quintilian also does not approve of orators who grow philosopher beards to affect wisdom (12.3.12).

‡Quintilian 8.preface.22. Quintilian obviously admires Horace's *Ars Poetica,* quoting from it on several occasions (e.g., 8.3.60). Because *eloquentia* is a feminine noun and is referred to with feminine pronouns, it is difficult to tell when an ancient writer is personifying eloquence. It seems here that Quintilian is.

§See, e.g., 1.preface.9; "*vir bonus dicendi peritus* [good man skilled in speaking]" at 12.11.9. For a formulation of the *vir bonus* consideration as "the Q Question," see Lanham, *The Electronic Word,* 154–194. Arthur Walzer has argued that Quintilian's *vir bonus* is the Stoic wise man. See Walzer, "Quintilian's 'Vir Bonus' and the Stoic Wise Man."

had fun with Agathon's name, teasing out the registers of *agathos:* morally wholesome, technically sound, good-looking, and good-but-not-great. *Bonus* is analogous to *agathos.** Joy Connolly aptly describes the complexities arising from a rhetoric-centric application of the iffy types of *bonus* to *vir:* "Rhetoric and its object, eloquence, are constituted in and made possible by things that the Romans (and other cultures, ancient and modern) defined as not-manly: the artful manipulation of words, the willingness to deceive, the equation of power with persuasion rather than action, verbal ornament, theatricality, emotional demonstrativeness."† When *bonus* leans toward good looks or the merely satisfactory "good enough," then *vir* risks detachment from its referent. As is commonly noted, *vir* occupies the base of the abstract noun *virtus* (strength, excellence, goodness), such that the *bonus* of moral goodness paired with *vir* accentuates this quality of uprightness to the point of redundancy. Managing that tension between *vir bonus* as incongruous and *vir bonus* as superfluous, Quintilian explains what it means to look and sound Roman (emphasis on the "–man") in public and in publication, the latter of which is unavoidably artificial because of the medium alone. Plenty can talk, but few go through the trouble of publishing textually what they have said, and they must be able to stand up to judgments that would cause lesser men to wither.

Quintilian little remarks upon his time in Rome. The year after Quintilian's return to Rome in 68, after having completed his rhetorical education there as a young man, was particularly turbulent. Galba, Quintilian's seventy-year-old fellow Spaniard, who was hailed as Caesar and whom Quintilian accompanied, was the first of four emperors to hold power in 69 alone. This so-called year of the four emperors saw civil war and the deaths of tens of thousands of Romans. Galba was assassinated in the Forum by those loyal to Otho, who committed suicide after he and soldiers loyal to him lost a battle against the troops of Vitellius, who died fighting another faction of the army that had thrown its support behind Vespasian.‡ Vespasian ruled for the next decade. As George Kennedy pithily puts it, "somehow Quintilian survived and turned to teaching."§ Vespasian committed himself to education as a force for stabilization in this wobbly era. Jumping several years ahead to Domitian's time as emperor, Quintilian tells of his retirement from pleading and teaching, but he does not mention the

---

*Erik Gunderson notes the "class valences" of *bonus,* according to which, with the force of a noun, it is translated as "gentleman." See Gunderson, "The Rhetoric of Rhetorical Theory," 116.

†Connolly, "Virile Tongues," 84.

‡For an overview of those bloody two years, see Boatwright, Gargola, and Talbert, *The Romans,* 335–337.

§Kennedy, *The Art of Rhetoric in the Roman World,* 488.

political situation of the time, which was grisly.* According to the account of Suetonius, Domitian's virtues (including correction-driven attentiveness to contemporary *mores*) degenerated into vices (including paranoia), and he killed writers across genres, in one case crucifying the copyists of a historian he had executed. He also killed many senators, some of whom were of consular rank. He even devised new tortures for extracting information.† While researching and writing the *Institutio,* Quintilian received an invitation from Domitian to tutor his grandnephews in rhetoric. Quintilian praised Domitian's as "eminent in eloquence, among other things."‡ Scholars sometimes consider that appraisal fawning, but one must suffer from a sad poverty of sympathy not to understand why Quintilian would want to stay in Domitian's good graces, especially if Quintilian had quit public life for his own safety in the first place. And, anyway, Domitian had not started off so bad. Though he was not very scholarly and left the writing of all his letters, speeches, and edicts to others, he had begun his *imperium* by "taking care [*curasset*] to repair, at the greatest of costs, the libraries [*bibliothecas*] that had been consumed by fire, seeking copies [*exemplaribus*] from everywhere and anywhere and sending to Alexandria those who could copy and correct them [*describerent emendarentque*]."§ Beating deep beneath the suspicion and cruelty was an archivist's heart.

Training

As all handbook writers do, Quintilian begins by explaining how his project differs from those of his predecessors and competitors. "Nearly all others who have handed down the art of oratory in writing have set out this way: as if all the other kinds of learning had been perfected [*perfectis*] and they had only to put the final hand on eloquence [*summam in eloquentia manum*]," he surveys.** Quintilian begins at the very beginning, across domains. The arc of his project extends from the start of an orator's education to the end of an orator's public career, bending from the historical beginnings of rhetoric to its current form, from *inventio* to *actio,* from *exordium* to *peroratio,* and from composing a clause to publishing a speech-text. His account is foundational, definitive, maybe even final. The idiom of applying the *summa manus,* which he uses to describe the aim of his predecessors and competitors, often appears in editorial contexts. In the previous chapter, for instance, I noted that Ovid claimed that his *Metamorphoses*

---

*Quintilian 2.13.12.
†Suetonius, *Domitian,* §10.
‡Quintilian 4.preface.
§Suetonius, *Domitian,* §20.
**Quintilian 1.preface.4.

had gone without "the final hand [*manus ultima*]."* Other handbook writers, then, treat readers as nearly finished products of oratorical education received elsewhere who seek only a bit of burnish to achieve a luster that will set them apart. Quintilian writes for a much broader readership, but he shares with these other handbook writers a focus on the perfect: he means to explicate the formation of the *orator perfectus* in its entirety.†

The *orator perfectus* is not a Platonic phantom, unlike Cicero's eponymous orator in *Orator*, but some people have natural advantages that make their approximation to or attainment of that unparalleled status more likely. Still, even the most advantageous of natures needs "lots of writing, reading, speaking, and continuous exercise [*scribendi, legendi, dicendi multa et continua exercitatione*]."‡ For that reason, the first task of a pedagogue is to discern the nature of his charges.§ A good teacher quickly and accurately gauges talents and tendencies, which differ from person to person as much as body types do. Quintilian offers an athletic analogy: "Just as one skilled in matters of the *palaestra*, when he comes into a gymnasium full of boys, after testing body and mind in every way, can discern for what class of contest they should be trained, so a teacher of eloquence, once he has knowingly observed what talent—be it for the compressed and filed [*presso limatoque*] kind of speaking, or sharp, weighty, sweet, rough, sparkling, or witty—promises each the most reward, will fit himself to an individual, so that in each area, where a given boy is eminent, he will be pushed forward."** Quintilian joins Cicero in naming Isocrates as gifted at discerning which students need the file to reduce their profusion and which have the opposite need.†† Rhetoricians hoping to shape future orators rather than historians,

---

*Ovid, *Tristia*, 2.255.

†Quintilian 1.preface.9. Quintilian does acknowledge certain eloquent Roman women, but he is no warrior for equality of the sexes. Nonetheless, he joins Cicero in recognizing Cornelia (c. 191–100 B.C.E.), daughter of the general Scipio Africanis, wife of Tiberius Sempronius Gracchus, and mother of Tiberius and Gaius Gracchus, who had received a first-rate education and took great care over that of her sons. The eloquent advisory letters she wrote to her sons evidently circulated beyond them to yet greater readerships (e.g., Cicero, *Brutus*, §104, §211; Quintilian 1.1.6–7). Quintilian also praises Hortensia, daughter of Cicero's rival, Hortensius. Famously and not without scandal, she spoke publicly in front of the Second Triumvirate when it levied upon women of her class a sizable tax in 43 B.C.E. Quintilian adds that her speech was still read in his time—that is, more than one hundred years postdelivery—"and not only on account of her sex" (1.1.6). She was successful in getting the tax reduced, and a version of her speech is preserved in the *Civil Wars* of Appian.

‡Quintilian 1.preface.27.

§Quintilian 1.3.1.

**Quintilian 2.8.3–4.

††Cicero, *De Oratore*, 3.36; Quintilian 1.8.11.

for instance, should prefer those who are "plump" of spirit. Training slims down wild abundance and tones down exuberance. So, too, as Quintilian puts it, over years of experience, "reason will file away [*limabit*] a great deal, and something too will be rubbed away [*deteretur*] by mere use itself, so long as there is something from which cutting [*excidi*] and chiseling [*exsculpti*] away is possible."* The orator who is thickly and richly layered will rub against the various obstacles and challenges of public life and take on a shine from the friction. Of orators who are thin to begin with there will be nothing left.

Quintilian believes "the future orator [*futurus orator*]" should be trained with others in a school, since such an environment encourages not only sociality and lifelong friendships among students but also a culture of competition, emulation, and correction.† He who is educated socially learns early that an orator "lives in extreme publicity and in the middle of the light of *res publica*." Conversely, he who is educated privately "grows pale in his solitary life in the shadows."‡ When the latter finally emerges, he is blinded by the light and totally unaware of how his talents match up to others.

The most well known set of preparatory exercises are the *progymnasmata*, a term clearly borrowed from athletics. They are usually counted as fourteen, ranging from vivid description (*ekphrasis*) to invective (*psogos*), and all prepared an aspiring orator to address facets of real rhetorical situations he might face. *Progymnasmata* also socialized élite young men to think of themselves as culturally entitled to speak in public and to speak up for others who were not permitted to speak. Through the *progymnasma* of character-making (*ēthopoeia*), for instance, they learned to craft language that sounded like that of those who could not speak in a particular public setting (a mother) or at all (a murdered person).§ Training in *declamatio* (declamation) became a staple of the school curriculum in the first century B.C.E. and was distinguished by two types of practice speeches: *suasoriae* (mock deliberative speeches) and *controversiae* (mock judicial speeches). The causal relationship between declamation and decline—of eloquence, of authentic opportunities to affect public life—was in Quintilian's

---

*Quintilian 2.4.7. At 10.5.22, in the context of writing, Quintilian reiterates that a good teacher *inanem loquacitatem recidet*. Cutting back seems the most important thing for a fully developed or developing orator to learn to do well.

†Quintilian 1.2.18–29. *Futurus orator* is an interesting formulation. It seems to mean "the person who wants to be an orator in the future," but it could also mean "an orator possible only in some future time."

‡Quintilian 1.2.18, repeated at 10.5.17.

§See Bloomer, "Schooling in Persona"; Fleming, "Quintilian, *Progymnasmata*, and Rhetorical Education Today."

time and remains a lively area of discussion and debate.* Rejecting the assertions of ancient and contemporary writers who would dismiss declamation,
Gunderson has suggested that "in their declamation we . . . see Romans coming
to be, and not a dying rhetoric passing away."† Far from dismissing declamation
himself, Quintilian argues that *realistic* declamation exercises benefit not only
emerging orators but also established ones.‡ They are fun but useful, too. Quintilian recommends that students visit the courts from time to time to hear real
cases, real eloquence, and real failure. Such visits are vital for students laboring
"about fictitious matters [*in rebus falsis*]" whose fancifulness threatens to carry
students into the clouds.§

Teachers vary in quality, but Quintilian deems three particular qualities
corruptive: silence, dryness, and highly imaginative ignorance. The silent teacher
offers no critical guidance, which is essential where corrections are concerned.
That sort of teacher will set back some students, but the more naturally talented
ones may fare all right. A dry teacher, the second type, has and encourages in
students ungenerative, desiccating preferences that Quintilian identifies with
an Attic tendency. This sort of teacher stunts the development of all of his students: "Their leanness [*macies*] is considered a sign of health and their feebleness
[*infirmitas*] of judgment, and while they think it is enough to be without vice,
in avoiding vices in that way, they are without virtues."** In a later book-roll,
Quintilian writes that "a dried-up and overly cared-for and contracted [*siccum
et sollicitium et contractum*] way of speaking is unpleasing in the youth, since
it suggests an affectation of *severitas*" that does not befit their inexperience.††
The third type of teacher, the ignorant teacher, has no clue what the world of
competitive speech is like and does not recognize when his classroom becomes
dangerously artificial. This classroom will tend toward the Asianist form, since
the teacher will presume that more is more. The danger of abundant artifice
extends beyond the risk that the student will embarrass himself in real rhetorical situations. One of the values of declamatory exercises is that they teach
one to speak for others, which requires a declaimer to think and feel as those
others might. These exercises build sympathy and community. Outlandish, far-
out declamation scenarios encourage creativity and cleverness at the expense of

---

*For an overview of the points of contention, see Gunderson, *Declamation, Paternity,
and Roman Identity*, 1–28.
†Gunderson, *Declamation, Paternity, and Roman Identity*, 25.
‡Quintilian 10.5.14.
§Quintilian 12.1.15–16.
**Quintilian 2.4.9.
††Quintilian 11.1.32.

connection.* Quintilian's issues with these three types of teachers are not petty differences of opinion.

To select exempla for reading, criticism, and imitation is a primary pedagogical task, one that should be undertaken with caution. If students read old material (Cato, the Gracchi) too early or exclusively, then they are at risk of developing "a harsh and bloodless style"; and if they read material currently in vogue, then they are at risk of developing affection for a "very sweet [*praedulcis*]" kind of speech that even boys can learn to produce.† The best items to evaluate are those whose composition is "smooth and squared-off but possessing a manly vigor nonetheless."‡ The worst preferences for a pedagogue to impose on his students arise from captivation with the results of plucking or pumicing stray hairs, applying curling irons to already luscious locks, and dipping into paint pots.§

Quintilian also asks that pedagogues not be sarcastic in their criticism or effusive in their praise, since both faults temper a student's willingness to work hard.** A student should be the center of attention only when he has produced something "more thoroughly filed than usual [*elimaverint*]," and even then a pedagogue needs to encourage discussion of how it could be better still.†† Those who are trained by teachers who encourage abundance and then its careful regulation and reduction may face criticism for being "choosy and measured."‡‡ Quintilian does not think that uncontrollably flowing or squeezed-dry speech has a claim to true eloquence, but "nonetheless it must be acknowledged that learning does take something away, just as the file [*limam*] takes something away from rough things and the whetstone from blunt things and years from wine, but it takes away defects, and though there will be less, due to the thorough polishing of literary study, it will be better."§§ Proper rhetorical training is an additive whose ultimate worth lies in subtraction. The primary function of a pedagogue and of rhetoric itself is to refine and refinish, repeatedly, at all steps. "Anxiety about finding, judging, and comparing [*quaerendi, iudicandi, comparandi anxietas*]" rhetorical materials belongs to that time "when we are learning [*dum discimus*]," not "when we are speaking [*dum dicimus*]."*** Throughout the

---

*Quintilian 6.2.36.

†Quintilian 2.5.21–22. He returns to this topic in the tenth book-roll.

‡Quintilian 2.5.9–10.

§Quintilian 2.5.12.

**Quintilian 2.2.7 (sarcasm), 2.2.10 (applause).

††Quintilian 1.7.5.

‡‡Quintilian 2.12.6.

§§Quintilian 2.12.8.

***Quintilian 8.preface.29.

Institutio, Quintilian distinguishes those who sublimate anxiety into appropriate care from those who never learn to handle their anxiety in productive ways. The wear and tear of preparing for and participating in the very public world of oratory, which Quintilian credits with filing down excess, reduces certain orators to trembling balls of nerves, a point to which I return later.

Composing, Styling, Delivering

Gorgias may have been the first to render *logos* a body—and a teensy one, at that.* Plato's Socrates may have been the first to flesh out the comparison: a speech should be "put together [*sunestanai*] like a living thing [*zōion*] that has a body [*sōma*] of its own, so as to be neither headless [*akephalon*] nor footless [*apoun*], but to have both a middle [*mesa*] and ends [*akra*], drawn together [*gegrammena*] appropriately [*prepont'*] in terms of one another and the whole."† Knowing how a speech ought to fit together is essential not only for synthesis but also for analysis; otherwise, one "hacks at joints, like a bad butcher."‡ Hellenistic handbook writers may have stretched the somatic analogy yet further, especially with regard to types of style. Romans, though, ran corporeality through all five *partes* of rhetoric, starting with the inventional step of gathering textual *corpora* as a sculptor gathers models.§ Through the assistance of writing, speech parts and wholes become bodies that make all the right moves or that lack grace and a fine bearing. Quintilian added further definition and detail. This section briefly attends to a few representative examples in the contexts of arrangement, style, and delivery.

Quintilian compares the structure of a speech to the human body.** Since those who practice a corrupt sort of eloquence tend to heap together words or clauses they have been wanting to use without any thought to art (from *ars,* joining), Quintilian makes it a point to emphasize that a speech should be a cohesive "body [*corpus*]" rather than a pile of "limbs [*membra*]."†† He proceeds through the typical *partes* of a speech, from *prooemium* to *peroratio.* The *prooemium* he envisions as the face of the speech. Since "neither our words nor our looks should promise too much," a *prooemium* should seem "cared for but not clever [*accurate non callide*]."‡‡ It is the most important part of the speech for an

---

*Gorgias, *Helen,* §8

†Plato, *Phaedrus,* 264c.

‡Plato, *Phaedrus,* 265e.

§Cicero describes doing precisely this in the opening of the second book-roll of his *De Inventione* (2.1–10).

**Quintilian 7.10.7.

††Quintilian 7.10.14–17.

‡‡Quintilian 4.1.60; 4.1.58.

orator not to maul with a memory lapse or stall of extemporaneous flow, since either results in a "face" crisscrossed with scars.* The *prooemium* should be the size it needs to be to sit atop the rest of the speech comfortably and proportionately, just like a head (*caput*).† If an orator is able, on the spot and from the start, to enfold content from their opponent's speech, then, "even though the rest has been written up and worked out [*scripta atque elaborata*], the whole of the speech will seem extemporaneous, since nothing in the beginning gave off a sense of having been prepared."‡ The *prooemium* makes the first impression, and it lingers in the assessment of the rest of the speech's body.

Quintilian explains that all orators agree that *elocutionis ratio* is the most difficult, since style demands a great deal of "work and care [*labor et cura*]."§ Corrupted speech fails because of problems not with invention or arrangement but with *elocutio*: words shuffled together in an unrestrained fashioned or so carefully placed as to be nearly discrete units rob themselves of their potency.** Quintilian takes recourse in the language of the body's internal structures, configurations, and circulation. The *res* (subject matter) is the "sinew [*nervis*]" of the case or cause, and the orator builds upon and around this central nervous system.†† In the words of George Kennedy, "to regard style as something independent of subject is to corrupt it."‡‡ In the words of Quintilian, "healthy bodies, with both a good circulation and firmed-up by exercise, acquire this very thing [that is, decorum] from that which also gives them strength, for they give off a color, and a tightness, and a brawniness; but if to this one adds womanly depilatories and paints, the forms themselves are disfigured by that very labor."§§ Here again a body-based comparison pits the athletic against the cosmetic, a hard-won masculinity against an easy femininity. Uncorrupted style is internal to and integrated with subject matter (like muscles); corrupted style is either superficial, slapped and slathered on top of it (like make-up), or dehydrating, pulling out anything juicy (like a seaweed wrap).

Though delivery has not occupied me in this book, given my textual focus, the proper management of the physiology of the self during delivery is, of course, a signal of rhetorical competence. That is far from all it is, however.

---

*Quintilian 4.1.61.
†Quintilian 4.1.62.
‡Quintilian 4.1.54.
§Quintilian 8.preface.13. Since I discussed the *genera dicendi* and rhythm at length in chapter 3, I will not give more attention to them here. For his views on style, see Quintilian 8, but the treatment extends through 11.
**Quintilian 8.preface.17.
††Quintilian 8.preface.18.
‡‡Kennedy, *Quintilian*, 89.
§§Quintilian 8.preface.19.

Gunderson stresses that "the orator's body is a public object, the object of close public scrutiny. Care must be taken to make sure that appearances are kept up. . . . Accordingly, he ought to look good. But in looking good, he should look like a good man: this is our *vir bonus* again. He must look neither disheveled nor like a dandy."* An orator's "look" refers not only to (mostly) static elements, such as his dress and hair, but also to that which morphs moment to moment: his facial expressions, vocal modulations, gestures, and ambulatory movements. Hands and fingers were of particular interest to Romans; they seem, themselves, to speak. One of the conversationalists in Cicero's *De Oratore* refers to the peerless eloquence of Crassus's index finger.[†] Similarly, some people today may recognize the so-called Kennedy or (Bill) Clinton thumb. Quintilian names more than a dozen hand gestures across only a few subsections, parsing the gestures according to the part of speech in which they best fit.[‡] He also addresses the eyebrows, the nostrils, and the neck.[§] Even imaginary practice, where an orator transports himself into a scene and rehearses his words and gestures entirely in his head, gets attention.** To be put to full effect, details such as those need to be incorporated into the rest of what an orator is learning: certain subject matter demands particular speech types that in turn recommend specific kinds of delivery. Determining the most appropriate alignments requires judgment, and an orator's critical capacities are nourished through exercises and examples that allow him to think through the choices a given orator made. "Nature did not make eloquence so dry and poor that there should be only one way to say something well."[††] That is why an orator must undertake a program of intaking and overtaking, encountering *exempla* but exceeding them, too.

Listening, Reading, Surpassing

Quintilian posits that many have wondered whether "writing or reading or speaking [*scribendo . . . an legendo an dicendo*]" best builds oratorical ease (*facilitas*). He smirks at the cute presumption, as if it were one and done.[‡‡] The three "are so intertwined and interdependent that if one of them is missing, work undertaken on the others is in vain."[§§] A shared aim is building verbal opulence (*ops*) and copiousness (*copia*). Some orators think plentitude arises from stocking

---

*Gunderson, "Discovering the Body in Roman Oratory," 177.
[†]Cicero, *De Oratore*, 2.45.188; Quintilian 11.3.94.
[‡]Quintilian 11.3.85–111.
[§]Quintilian 11.3.78 (eyebrows); 11.3.80 (nostrils); 11.3.82–83 (neck).
**Quintilian 10.7.26.
[††]Quintilian 10.5.5.
[‡‡]Quintilian 10.1.1.
[§§]Quintilian 10.1.2.

an inventory of synonyms—*thesaurus* does mean treasure—but Quintilian thinks that sort of amassing "assembles together a crowd, from which to grab whatever is near, without discrimination."* The orator should not hoard words as if they are things unto themselves; rather, an orator should carefully listen and read (a sort of listening from afar) to learn how to do things with words.†

Visiting speaking venues to listen permits the orator to experience eloquence-in-motion. There will always be a certain "danger [*periculum*]" in the air that makes listening to even mediocre orators exciting. Present, too, will be social pressures to approve or disapprove: independence of judgment tends to be "wrenched [*extorquet*]" by the clamor.‡ Reading takes the orator away from that environment. "Reading is freeing [*libera*]" because the orator can—should—do two things that are impossible during a live speech: ruminate over certain passages until they disintegrate in his mouth, and be open about his preferences without fear of immediate and public shows of disapproval.§ Because "the virtues of oratory are frequently hidden by industry," the orator should read a book-roll *in toto;* an orator may in the *prooemium,* for instance, claim to skip over a particular issue and then bring it back again in some other place.**

The question of who to read is one Quintilian finds dizzying. His short answer is only "the best [*optimus*]," but he knows the best is a contested category.†† To name who is worth reading would be an endless and probably thankless task, and Quintilian points to Cicero's struggles with plentitude in *Brutus.*‡‡ He also mentions an "*ordo* [line-up, ordering]" from the Hellenistic period.§§ Fragmentary evidence suggests that Callimachus, whom we met in chapter 2, devoted a division of his extensive *Pinakes* (*Lists*) to oratory. He was aiming to be extensive rather than exclusive, however. As Neil O'Sullivan has shown, "canon" comes from an ancient Greek word, but the ancients had no word for "authoritative, select list." What they did have were "lists of authors regarded by their compilers as representing the best in a particular genre" and that were "polemically motivated."*** In every designation of superiority lies a snub. Quintilian feels that the orator who is really striving to be the best can draw something useful out of anything he reads.†††

*Quintilian 10.1.7.
†Quintilian 10.1.15; 10.2.27.
‡Quintilian 10.1.16–17.
§Quintilian 10.1.19.
**Quintilian 10.1.20.
††Quintilian 10.1.20.
‡‡Quintilian 10.1.38.
§§Quintilian 10.1.54.
***O'Sullivan, "Caecilius, the 'Canons' of Writers, and the Origins of Atticism," 32, 35.
†††Quintilian 10.1.57.

When the orator is ready to begin modeling (*imitatio*) the writing of others, the biggest question is: old (*veteris*) or recent (*recens*)? "For some," Quintilian points out, "think that only the old ones should be read and they judge that there is nothing in them except natural eloquence and manliness; while others prefer the lasciviousness and daintiness of recent examples, in which everything is composed to delight the pleasure of the unskilled multitude."* He answers generally that "all eloquence has something in common; we must imitate that underlying commonality."† He answers specifically by spanning from Homer through Demetrius and into the Stoics on the Greek side and from Vergil through Julius Secundus, who features in Tacitus's *Dialogus de Oratoribus,* on the Roman side. Along the way, Quintilian even weighs in on poetic competitions, such as that between Horace and Lucilius.‡ The key to choosing whom to imitate is simple: the orator should recognize his own strength (*vis*) and seek out orators and writers whose strengths match his own, thereby building upon what he knows he does well.§ Then he can expand his skills.** Pointing out the strengths and weaknesses of his charges is the first duty Quintilian named for pedagogues back in the earliest book-roll, as he himself recalls here. Pedagogues excel at "adding to, emending, and changing" the tendencies of their students—Quintilian uses similar verbs in his section on *emendatio*—but the orator needs to come to know himself, accepting what he does well and what he does not, what can be improved and what cannot.†† But, still, an orator must reach beyond himself, since cases and causes will not conform to him.

The step beyond *imitatio* (modeling) is *aemulatio* (rivaling). Once the orator figures out what the greats do, he should figure out how to outdo them. Quintilian encourages gentle, generative fault-finding: Homer nods, Demosthenes nods, Cicero plods.‡‡ In keeping with his usual advice, Quintilian declares that the *orator perfectus* will be he who can add his own to those of his models, while also recognizing what in them is redundant and wandering.§§

---

*Quintilian 10.1.43.

†Quintilian 10.2.22.

‡Quintilian 10.1.94.

§Quintilian 10.2.18. Quintilian thinks no one can beat Cicero: "Indeed, as for me, it would be enough if I were able to follow him in all things" (10.2.25).

**Quintilian 10.1.58–59.

††Quintilian 10.2.20.

‡‡Quintilian 10.1.24–26; 12.1.14ff (Cicero's faults), 12.1.21–27 (*Cicero non perfectus, Demosthenes non perfectus*), 12.10.12ff (Cicero's faults, Atticism debate).

§§Quintilian 10.2.28.

Writing, Thinking, Extemporizing

Quintilian's orator needs a plentiful supply of midnight oil. He will burn so much of it that only a robust respiratory system will be able to swallow all the smoke.* *Lucubratio,* that is, work undertaken by lamplight, offers deep silence and solitude, which no one doubts best contribute to quality writing.[†] "Vigilance, endurance, struggle, paleness" is to be the orator's mantra.[‡] This exhausting work undertaken in darkness and this reference to paleness recall the types of orators Quintilian reckoned would not hold up to the intensities of real oratorical practice.[§] Throughout the twelve book-rolls of the *Institutio,* Quintilian describes various scenes of orators getting their words in order. He imagines some orators, contemptuous of method, staring at the ceiling for days, waiting for inspiration to strike.[**] He sees others "seeking out single words and then weighing and measuring what has been found."[††] He pictures Plato poring over his wax tablets, writing out the first clause of the first line of his *Republic* in multiple ways so as to find the best rhythm.[‡‡] That particular scene proved irresistible to several ancient writers. For instance, in his *On Composition,* written in the final third of the first century B.C.E., Dionysius of Halicarnassus described Plato's editorial attachment to his dialogues as follows: "Plato did not cease, even when eighty years old, to comb and curl his dialogues and braid the plaits together in every way. Likely every word-lover knows the stories of Plato's love of labor [*tēs philoponias*], especially that of the wax tablet they said was found after his death, with the beginning of the *Republic* ("I went down yesterday to the Piraeus together with Glaucon the son of Ariston") in elaborately varying [*poikilōs*] orders."[§§] That dandy description of Plato demonstrates that even a philosopher, and one who wrote nearly exclusively about a philosopher who never wrote anything, can take great care in styling his words with his *stilus,* or at least that is the fantasy he inspires. The Plato of Quintilian is far less fastidious than that of Dionysius, but, in general, the line between struggle and despair, motivation and anxiety, care and flair is thin enough that the orator needs to heed it constantly—but not nervously.

---

*Quintilian 11.3.23.

[†]Quintilian 10.3.25, 27, 22. For more on lucubration, see Ker, "Nocturnal Writers in Imperial Rome."

[‡]Quintilian 7.10.14 (*Vigilandum, durandum, enitendum, pallendum est*).

[§]Quintilian 1.2.18.

[**]Quintilian 2.11.4; 10.3.15.

[††]Quintilian 8.preface.27.

[‡‡]Quintilian 8.6.64.

[§§]Dionysius of Halicarnassus, *On Composition,* §25. See also Diogenes Laertius, *Lives* 3.37.

In agreement with Cicero, Quintilian thinks that writing is vital to training in an orator's early years, to preparation for cases and causes thereafter, and to textual publication eventually. Writing—that an orator does himself and that he reads—is absorbed into all five traditional *partes* of rhetoric, hardly surprising given the core roles of *imitatio, emulatio,* and *judicium* in rhetorical education. But Quintilian devotes exclusive attention to the *stilus* and *lima.** Like every other affordance of rhetoric, they are devices for developing what Greek writers call *hexis,* a word Quintilian renders as *facilitas* (facility, ease). Methods for developing a facility with writing include exercises of translation, turning, and transferring: Greek to Latin, Latin to yet other Latin, poetry to prose.[†] One could work with the words of *auctores maximi,* such as those itemized in the first half of this tenth book-roll, or with one's own wax, *à la* Plato, making lots of forms from the same material.[‡] If one is very daring, one could even try verse, as Cicero did. Perhaps that is a step too far, but Quintilian points out its value: "if all of our material derived from litigation, our flash would necessarily wear away, and our limbs [*articulus*] harden, and the point of our ingenuity dulled by daily fights."[§] The orator should take the occasional frolic in the grotto of the Muses, if only to get it out of their systems there in a place set apart from the forum.

When it comes time for an orator to pick it up, the *stilus* should be "slow while diligent" with its pointed end, while its paddled end should focus on any part of a speech giving off a sort of "suspicious ease [*suspectam facilitatem*]," which could arise from ignorance or overconfidence that could get checked by others.[**] The two corrupted forms are, again, at extremes. At one pole are those who work themselves up so much in an effort to be perfect from the get-go that they give up and go silent; at the other pole are those who create a gnarled forest (*silva*) of words that they must hack through to locate the path of their own discourse.[††] The "more correct" way, Quintilian advises, is the way of care (*cura*), whereby the orator "forms the work from the beginning such that it will be engraved with a chisel, not constructed all over again," as he emends.[‡‡] If affect and heat enter, disrupting the plan, the orator can give way. Sometimes.[§§] When he does, however, he may want to be alone, that is, without an *amanuensis,* the taking on of which has become popular. Quintilian quotes the poet Persius, who

*Quintilian 10.3.
[†]Quintilian 10.5.2, 10.5.4
[‡]Quintilian 10.5.9.
[§]Quintilian 10.5.16.
[**]Quintilian 10.3.5, 10.3.7.
[††]Quintilian 10.3.12, 10.3.17.
[‡‡]Quintilian 10.3.18.
[§§]Quintilian 10.3.18.

labels a "too light kind of speaking [*leviter dicendi genus*]" as one that "thumps not the desk nor smacks of bitten nails."* Horace described his own compositional habits in similarly percussive terms. But the orator cannot dictate when lip-deep in cuticle and may not want his desk poundings observed. If he does not let his *amanuensis* go in such circumstances, then he will suppress his process, resulting in language Quintilian is sure will not sound or read well, since it features "neither the precision of the writer nor the impetuosity of the speaker."[†]

Whether one (or one's *amanuensis*) writes on wax or parchment (*membrana*, literally "skin"), one should leave room for adding things later, while rereading and correcting.[‡] The subsequent section pertains exclusively to *emendatio*, which Quintilian lauds as "the part of our study with the greatest utility by a long shot [*pars studiorum longe utilissima*]."[§] Given his emphasis throughout the *Institutio* on thoughtful reduction and compression, a reader will hardly be surprised at Quintilian's enthusiasm for emendation and its trifold workings: "to add, to take away, and to change [*adiicere, detrahere, mutare*]."** Adding and removing are easy, but "to compress what is swollen, to elevate what is too close to the ground, to tie back luxuriance, to order what is irregular, to bring together the loose, to hold together the scattered, is a two-fold operation. For we have both to condemn what had pleased us and find what had escaped us."[††] The key to performing that work is *tempus*. Putting time between when one has written and when one emends makes it more likely that the words will seem "new and not yours [*nova atque aliena*]"; otherwise, a writer treats his words with "the sort of adoration afforded a newborn baby."[‡‡] This process of literal alienation loosens bonds of affection. The orator can take that emotional distance too far, however, ripping into the draft upon return like a sadistic plastic surgeon, "cutting away even at that which is well put together [*integra*]." What emerges is "crisscrossed with scars, and exsanguinated, and made worse by care [*cura*]."[§§] Quintilian believes orators who treat their words so brutally need to work harder to align their expectations and their abilities: "something must please us, or in the very least suffice, so that our work is polished by the file [*opus poliat lima*], not rubbed out

---

*Quintilian 10.3.21.

[†]Quintilian 10.3.20. The roles of *amanuenses* in producing vast heaps of writing are not well studied, a point to which I return briefly in my Conclusion.

[‡]Quintilian 10.3.32.

[§]Quintilian 10.4.1.

**Quintilian 10.4.1.

[††]Quintilian 10.4.1.

[‡‡]Quintilian 10.4.2; 10.3.7: *Omnia enim nostra, dum nascuntur, placent; alioqui nec scriberentur.*

[§§]Quintilian 10.4.3.

entirely."* The orator can also take temporal distance too far. Often, what an orator writes is necessary "for present use"; above all, an orator must be of "help [*auxilium*]."† The Callimachean poet Cinna edited his *Smyrna* for nine years, the rhetorician Isocrates edited his *Panegyricus* for ten years, but the *emendatio* of the orator must "have an endpoint [*finem habeat*]" that suits the task at hand.‡

When one cannot write—when doing other tasks or even lying in bed—one can think through a speech, a process Quintilian calls *cogitatio*.§ Since the memory tends to fall into ruts carved by lines of written speeches, he privileges thinking out over writing out a speech.** When there is no time to think, one has to extemporize. The ultimate test of whether *stilus* and *lima* are working as they should is the orator's response to extemporaneity. Careful writing practice ought to lead to the impressive improvisational control of one's linguistic limbs (*membra*) during sudden changes in oratorical situations or sudden necessities. A sudden situation that must be addressed immediately is like a smooth wax tablet, waiting to hold the orator's first impressions but not permitting of a turn of the *stilus*. If the orator has trained himself to be a fluent writer, then he should be able to speak extemporaneously with few bumps.

An orator does not have to prefer to improvise but does have to be able to do it; if not, he should be a writer.†† Speaking eloquently is intrinsically pleasurable, to the speaker and to the audience, and it brings reputation and praise to the speaker, especially when it seems to rise from a moment, urgent and unexpurgated.‡‡ But the foremost benefit of extemporaneous eloquence is its extrinsic use. If the orator cannot save "an innocent citizen" or even his own friends or intimates unless he can ask for delay and quiet in which he might scribble and prepare, then he is not an orator.§§ To write well requires silence and solitude. Even though the writing may serve a very public purpose, the process of producing it is antisocial. Unlike Isocrates, Cicero, Ovid, and Pliny, Quintilian does not write about collaborative editing; the aforementioned *amanuensis* is, in Quintilian's limited imagination, anyway, a bureaucratic functionary and not a Tiro-like confidant. Extemporaneous speaking is entirely different: the presence of others "excites [*excitatur*]."*** Quintilian's use of multiple verbs with an

*Quintilian 10.3.15, 10.4.4.
†Quintilian 10.4.3, 10.4.4.
‡Quintilian 10.4.4, 10.4.3.
§*Quintilian 10.6.1.*
**Quintilian 12.9.20; 12.19.16–17.
††Quintilian 10.7.4.
‡‡Quintilian 10.7.17. Quintilian bests Alcidamas, from chapter 1.
§§Quintilian 10.7.2.
***Quintilian 10.7.16.

ex- prefix highlights that time pressures pull out from the orator what habit has made part of him. Ideally, the orator will combine the labors of his house (*domus*) with the gifts of the moment (*tempus*).*

Publishing

For the orator, in the space between thinking through or writing out words and presenting them to others, the *ardor* of stimulation cools and the arduousness of production slips from memory. Detachment from the circumstances of creation makes it far easier for the orator to delete or delay all but what truly accords with various registers of propriety. The transition or, perhaps more accurate, the translation of speeches to speech-texts is complicated by double or even multiple receptions; as I show in the next chapter, on occasion Pliny would show speech notes to a friend to mark up, deliver the improved speech, prepare it for textual publication, send it to trusted friends to look over, recite it to any associates he could entice to listen, edit it again, and then release it. I opened this chapter with Quintilian's expressed wish to his publisher Trypho for time in which to "weigh carefully [*perpenderem*]" what he had written, as Horace had instructed poets to do in *Ars Poetica*. Quintilian creates the impression that clamoring readers won out over solitary *labor limae,* but a reference further within the work indicates that Quintilian did not publish on harried terms. Quintilian was a reputable orator in his own right and admits to having "sent out" only one speech.† He qualifies that humble number with "to this point [*in hoc tempus*]," hinting that more speech-texts may be forthcoming, and he attributes the release of that one speech to his "juvenile desire for glory." Many other speeches of his circulate, but he contests how much they are "his": "for those others that circulate under my name, having been corrupted by the negligence of notaries who captured them for profit, have only the smallest part of me in them."‡ Quintilian has become an industry unto himself.

Publishing speeches was, according to Quintilian's chronology of oratorical activity, the work of a senior orator looking toward his legacy and the instruction of the rising generation, which may explain why he had published only one speech so far, and rashly, at that. While composing the *Institutio,* Quintilian had just retired from pleading and teaching, so he himself was entering the period of life when publishing speeches for those purposes was appropriate. At the end of the tenth book-roll, Quintilian accounts for how some speech-texts come to circulate, using as examples Servius Sulpicius—who had studied rhetoric along

---

*Quintilian 10.6.5–6.
†Quintilian 7.2.24.
‡Quintilian 7.2.24.

with Cicero and whose death from illness while on an embassy to Marcus Antonius was the theme of the Ninth Philippic—and Cicero. The word Quintilian
uses to refer to these items is *commentarii,* defined in a modern lexicon as "the
title of a book on any subject which is written without care."* Cicero uses that
word six times in *Brutus* to refer to archival records he examines.† He does not
use it at all in *Orator,* wherein, as I detailed in chapter 3, he mentions the written
works of only Isocrates, Demosthenes, and himself. Quintilian explains that some
speeches "have been spread all around in book-rolls [*in libros digesti*]," gesturing
to those of Sulpicius. Quintilian then calls the three extant speech-texts of Sulpicius *commentarii,* albeit ones marked "by exactitude, as they seem to me to have
been composed by him especially as a memento for posterity."‡ The *commentarii*
of Cicero, on the other hand, "fully fitted to the time at hand, were afterwards
collected [*contraxit*] by Tiro; in offering this excuse, I do not dismiss them, but
instead esteem them as all the more admirable."§ Quintilian points to Cicero's
commentarii for evidence of a common way of preparing speeches when one
has a heavy docket of cases or causes: "writing out the most necessary parts and
especially the beginnings, covering the other parts with thinking brought from
home, and meeting extemporaneously anything that emerges suddenly."** It
seems that *libri* refer to speeches in full and finished form, *commentarii* to
speeches with some parts fully written out and the rest in heading or outline
form, and that *commentarii* resemble *libri* when they are "*exacti* [exact, precise],"
as Sulpicius's were. *Libri* must not be a physical designation, since it would be
odd for Cicero's collected *corpus* of speech-texts, however abbreviated, not to
amount to a *libri.* Quintilian's classifications, then, do not settle debates about
what, precisely, circulated, especially when we recall that he called one version
of Cicero's *Pro Milone* a "little speech [*oracticula*]," and he quotes from the complete version throughout the *Institutio.*††

Quintilian marks speech publication as the final step in an orator's journey
by addressing the matter in the final book-roll, the twelfth.‡‡ The primary questions are: how much of the delivered speech is to be represented in the speech-
text, and how much extra content or polish can the speech-text feature? Some

---

*Lewis and Short, *A Latin Dictionary,* s.v. *commentarius,* ii, m. (sc. *liber*).

†E.g., Cicero, *Brutus,* §55, §60. In *De Oratore* 1.5, Cicero refers to his youthful *De Inventione* as an "inchoate and rough *commentariolum,*" which is a brief commentary or
treatise.

‡Quintilian 10.7.30.

§Quintilian 10.7.31.

**Quintilian 10.7.30.

††Quintilian 4.3.17, 4.2.25.

‡‡Quintilian 12.10.49–55.

argue that *lumina*—literally lights or bright points—are vital to a delivered speech but should be excluded from the circulated text. In the third book-roll of his *Rhetoric*, Aristotle differentiated an agonistic *lexis* from a graphic *lexis*, emphasizing that certain configurations pack an aural punch but seem silly on a page (for example, *anaphora*) and that polished precision sounds cold in heated moments. For Aristotle, the divide crisscrossed the civic genres, with dikanic being the most agonistic, epideictic the most written, and demegoric somewhere in between. Aristotle did not address the differences between orally delivered and textually published versions of a speech. The debate in Quintilian's time pertained to how to keep a speech in-genre, as it were, when the pulsing environment of delivery seems to require one thing and the mellow papyrus another.

Quintilian characterizes one camp—whose members he calls derisively *subtiles* (delicate), a qualifier often applied to neo-Atticists—as eager to posit a relationship between an orator's famous oral/aural abilities and his lack of textual traces: Pericles left nothing behind, whereas Isocrates left plenty. Their view is that a speech must unleash an orator's energy and oratory's devices of pleasure, since it is those unskilled in rhetoric it is trying to move; the written speech that is "published [*edatur*]," however, must be "scrubbed and filed [*tersum ac limatum*]" and brought under "the law and rules" of composition, since "it will come into the hands of the learned and its artistry will be judged by artists."* The two items thus have vastly different intentions and publics: the orally delivered speech to overwhelm the uneducated, the textually published speech to impress the educated. Quintilian's own opinion is that "it is one and the same to write well and speak well, nor is a written speech [*oratio scripta*] anything other than a record [*monumentum*] of what has actually been delivered."† Quintilian knows readers will wonder how they differ. While willing to grant that Cicero and even the less profuse Demosthenes would have "cut back" their abundance had they been addressing bodies of wise men, he is not willing to imagine that they delivered one speech and published another entirely. "Did they speak better or worse than they wrote? For if it was worse, then they ought to have spoken as they wrote; if better, then they should ought to have written as they spoke."‡ Quintilian seems flustered by contemporary critics who want to go beyond the extant evidence available to them.

Quintilian points to the material limits of such discussions: "is our knowledge of either of those two outstanding orators based on anything other than

*Quintilian 12.10.50.
†Quintilian 12.10.51.
‡Quintilian 12.10.54.

their writings?"* It is impossible to know how much the speech-texts of Demosthenes and Cicero resemble what they actually said, because the only accessible testimonies are written accounts, either the speech-texts themselves or what others have written about them. At a far distance from oral delivery, continuity between what is spoken and what is written is no longer an attainable measure of an orator's quality and qualities. Quintilian thinks continuity between spoken and written is important for living orators because it attests to their integrity: their art is integrated with their practice, and they disdain duplicity. The attitude of the neo-Atticists seems to be that orality is tainted and textuality is pure. They make the rhetorical art a bag of tricks useful for sneaking around judgment rather than a curated tradition of affordances an orator learns so as to carefully enhance or ennoble judgment (their own and that of others). They also focus on one oratorical duty: moving. In essence, they will slum with the plebs orally but snub them textually by removing and refining what learned people will take for lowly, popular language. Quintilian refers to this editorial work as done with the file (*lima*), yet it not the file of which he disapproves but the attitude that it is necessary only *after* delivery.

In the previous book-roll, on memory and delivery, Quintilian had recognized the power of the voice. Even the most worthless orators can be given a reception "on stage [*theatris*]" that they would never receive "in a library [*bibliothecis*]." That is, they use their vocal and gestural talents to great effect but are not worth reading.† Here, too, Aristotle is a touch-point, since he wrote in *Poetics* that a well-constructed drama would affect even those who were not beholding a complete performance. Only one of six parts of tragedy pertains to theatrical-level performance exclusively: *opsis* (spectacle).‡ Plot structure, character, style, thought, and rhythm are all available during readings, whether aloud or silent. Cicero and Quintilian think a speech should function in a similar way. A speech comes into form from rhythms worked out by the *stilus* or by writing exercises internalized and transformed into cognitive habits, it vibrates during delivery because of its patterns (pleasingly irregular, though, so as not to fall into a regular poetic meter), and it pulses even on the page, long after its creation and delivery. A speech-text offers an acoustic representation; the energy of the original delivery has long dissipated, but whatever rhythm made the speech come alive in the first place will be sealed in the text, awaiting activation by a reader. If orators craft speeches respecting and reflecting what instructs, delights,

*Quintilian 12.10.54.
†Quintilian 11.3.4.
‡Aristotle, *Poetics*, 1462aff.

and moves people—*the* people (*populus*)—then they will "hold fast to everything, extending to whatever we believe will help; and these must not merely be produced when we speak but exhibited when we write as well, if, when we write, we aim to give instruction on how it ought to be spoken."* Those who have corrupted eloquence have done so because of a lowly opinion of the capacities of the people, thinking the pleasure that Quintilian believes everyone naturally derives from eloquence to be unique to the less educated and that pleasure increases in proportion to the thickness or elaborateness of style.† Accordingly, they offer speech that is puerile, turgid, inane, delicately blossomed, or raving.‡ And people will respond favorably to that sort of language—that is, until they hear proper eloquence. The orator capable of delivering upon eloquence's true promise "will speak gravely, severely, sharply, vehemently, excitedly, copiously, bitterly, or courteously, openly, delicately, flatteringly, gently, sweetly, briefly, or urbanely, and he will not always be like himself, but he will always be equal to himself. In that way, the use for which speech was above all devised will be secured; that is to say, he will speak with utility and efficiency to effect what he intends, and all the while win the praise not only of the learned, but also of the common folk [*tum laudem quoque nec doctorum modo sed etiam vulgi consequatur*]."§ Within a few weeks of delivery, however, no one will recall exactly what an orator said and how. Within a few years of their deaths, orators who wrote nothing will slip into oblivion. Ultimately, then, the experienced orator must put into his speech-texts all that will guide the younger generation and shape his posthumous reputation. The only inclusions Quintilian permits are items an orator had to cut from delivery for time reasons. The only exclusions are "things said to suit the nature of the judges, which ought not to be handed out to posterity for precisely that reason, since they ought to see what was proposed, not what came of the moment."** Given Quintilian's instructions about how much an orator ought to account for his audience when designing a speech, it seems unlikely that such cuts could be extensive without damaging either the delicate tissue or tough muscle that makes a speech function like a cohesive body in the first place. He must mean, then, the extemporaneous asides that lose their value out of context.

*Quintilian 12.10.53.
†Quintilian 12.10.74.
‡Quintilian 12.10.73.
§Quintilian 12.10.71.
**Quintilian 12.10.55.

Cycling

The rhetorical art an orator practices at the end of his career is that of gracious withdrawal from the places of public speaking. It is not one an orator does well, being more accustomed to stepping in in the nick of time rather than out. Taking leave of those places that have brought him name recognition and acclaim will be difficult, but the acclaim is precisely what he will preserve if he leaves before anyone has a chance to notice a diminishment in his powers. It is not, Quintilian affirms, that he will speak in a way that is "bad [*mala*]," just "less [*minora*]."* The cruelty of aging is that, while knowledge and wisdom stack up, voices, lungs, and bodies wear down. Orators are among the most keen to be good and dutiful citizens, and they continue to serve, but in advisory and instructional capacities.† Mature orators cycle out, new ones cycle in; new orators enter rosters of the to-be-emulated and older ones are replaced, perhaps to come back into vogue. All that churn and shuffle should give a young orator heart, though definitely not swagger. There would be no progress in any art if what was deemed *optimum* was *ultimum*—best was earliest.‡

Quintilian here seems to break from the tyranny of teleology. Ascension and decline, decorum and corruption are co-present along rhetoric's winding path, both within a particular historical period—such as his own—and over the long haul. What distinguishes oratory from most other arts is that being useful is nearly as good as being perfect.§ The *orator perfectus* offers utility, *plus ultra*. The *Institutio* is Quintilian's own offering to that effect: he hopes to have given something likely to be, "if not of great utility to the young, then certainly something I seek more eagerly: the will to be good [*bonam voluntatem*]."** And thus Quintilian closes his truly *magnum opus* by appealing to one part of his *vir bonus* emphasis, ending not on a great note but a good one.

---

*Quintilian 12.11.4. Compare Cicero's evaluations of Hortensius at the end of *Brutus*.
†Quintilian 12.10.80.
‡Quintilian 12.11.28
§Quintilian 12.11.29.
**Quintilian 12.11.31.

CHAPTER SEVEN

PAST, PRESENT, AND FUTURE
PERFECT ELOQUENCE

Long-standing pressures within both rhetoric and poetics pit prompt intervention against formal perfection and the temporal against the eternal. From Alcidamas in the early fourth century B.C.E. to Quintilian in the late first century C.E.,
however, orators have placed their ilk in time-pinched situations to differentiate
themselves from poets.* Moreover, as Cicero lamented in *Brutus*, the significant
energy at play in an urgent oratorical exchange may not enter the rhetorical
record or may not pass its power to the page once it is there, growing dull with
increasing distance. Historically, very few orators have managed to fit their
speeches tightly to a moment, to transfer that kairotic rush into a written form,
to edit it carefully, and to publish a speech-text whose beauty and intensity time
does not diminish. Those who have managed to do so tease and torment their
successors, who wonder what set of circumstances—a given orator's temper-
ament, education, method, political opportunities—conspired to produce such
enduring excellence. That curiosity can be spiked with envy and escapism when
critics feel they are living through a fallow, flat, or fallen period for eloquence.

As I discussed in the previous chapter in the context of declamation, several
works from the first century C.E. contain so-called decline narratives of rhetoric,
oratory, and orators, and scholars have often taken such works at their word.
Poetics, poetry, and poets are occasionally included in the scholarly scope of
decline.† The central issue is the changed fortune of Rome: in a political community that is sleek, expansive, no longer so internally unstable, and directed at the
highest level by an emperor, is eloquence necessary? Possible? Within the larger
history of rhetoric, these decline narratives are but a subset of what Jeffrey
Walker has called, "'the rise and fall' topos," the common contention that

---

*Alcidamas, *On Those Who Write*, §4, §11; Quintilian 10.4.4.
†Given that much more imperial-age poetry survives than oratory, the critical tendency has been—in the past, at least, but less so presently—to name poets after Horace
"silver age" poets, indicating a decline in worth and worthiness.

rhetoric rises and thrives with popular rule and falls and decays with autocratic rule.* In the ancient world, then, rhetoric's high points are democratic Athens between the Greco-Persian Wars and the suicide of Demosthenes and republican Rome between the so-called Social War and the murder of Cicero. This *topos* is problematic because it vastly simplifies rhetoric, poetics, and politics in the ancient world. Walker undermines the *topos* by emphasizing the unceasing civic significance of epideictic rhetoric and by arguing that epideictic rhetoric was rhetoric's first and original form, having been born from poetry. Pernot has done similarly, charting "the unstoppable rise" of epideictic rhetoric across eras and centuries.†

In the mode of Walker and Pernot, I think "decline narratives" may more aptly be called "adjustment narratives." The foremost reason is that speakers and writers of these "problem" periods did not agree they were living through a decline, though they did acknowledge that some of their contemporaries held that view. This chapter brackets a few decades of the imperial period, specifically, the late first century C.E. Across genres, speakers and writers of that time struggled under a weighty archive, organized largely in the Hellenistic period but that for them now included potentially dozens of Romans as well. They continued to accommodate themselves to a (mostly) stable internal order very different from the chaos unleashed during the protracted civil wars of the previous century. Though there was enough sustained high-level political intrigue to keep a sense of anticlimax from settling upon Rome throughout the first century C.E., there seems to have been a pervasive but not total dissatisfaction with the present and the limited oratorical opportunities it afforded. It was not that oratory had been swept from community life—far from it. There was, however, a feeling, even if it was not shared by all the historical actors, that oratorical productions were either lackluster or all luster. In the last extant section of *Peri Hupsous*, likely written in the previous century, Longinus had argued that "it is easy ... and it is particular to humans always to disparage the present [*paronta*]."‡ Very similarly, an orator in the *Dialogus de Oratoribus* of Tacitus remarks that "it is the fault of envious humans that the old [*vetera*] is always held in high regard, the present [*praesentia*] in contempt."§ Since we do not have a secure date for *Peri Hupsous* or the *Dialogus*, arguments for influence in either direction cannot be firmly determined. The shared opinion alone, however, suggests not only that

*Walker, Review of Lamp, 167.

†Walker, *Rhetoric and Poetics in Antiquity*, 3–41; Pernot, *Epideictic Rhetoric*, 1. For a study of official, popular, and vernacular material rhetoric during the Principate, see Lamp, *A City of Marble*.

‡Longinus, *Peri Hupsous*, 44.6.

§Aper in Tacitus, *Dialogus de Oratoribus*, 18.3–4.

some writers in the first century of Rome's imperial period were not despondent about their particular present but also that dissatisfaction was viewed as chronic: displeasure with one's place is an ontological human constant. Rome was on top of the world, but where oratory and poetry and orators and poets were situated by comparison was largely a matter of whether one felt one was standing on the shoulders of giants or in their shadows.

I turn here to Cornelius Tacitus and Pliny the Younger, two orators contemporary with Quintilian but who did not enjoy his level of careful and perhaps involuntary intimacy with Domitian.* Tacitus and Pliny were senators when they survived what is sometimes called Domitian's "reign of terror."† Tacitus would quit public life and take up history, while Pliny remained and advanced, delivering speeches both in Rome and beyond. Tacitus and Pliny were on friendly enough terms to co-plead a case, talk about *eloquentia,* and even exchange their works-in-progress. The work Tacitus shared was likely his *Dialogus de Oratoribus,* upon which I focus first. Set in the mid-70s and written probably in the late 90s, the dialogue exclusively features trained orators, as its title indicates. One of them seems poised to leave the *oratorum vita* for poetry (namely tragedy), and his likely exit is the impetus for the discussion of modern *eloquentia.*‡ The dialogue opens and closes on striking editorial notes, from the emendation of a risky tragedy on the cusp of its publication to the emendation of imperial Rome itself. In the middle, the body-rich Atticism debate appears yet again, as the interlocutors discuss past and present forms of eloquence and mutable preferences for those forms. Pliny and his collection of epistles close out this chapter and rival Isocrates's *Panathenaicus* for the closest look at the editorial method of a public man.§ His details demonstrate that a speech was never *a* speech but rather a series of speeches enjoyed and examined with varying degrees of

---

*For other pairings of Tacitus and Pliny, see Johnson, *Readers and Reading Culture in the High Roman Empire,* 63–73, and Dominik, "Tacitus and Pliny on Oratory."

†The year 93 C.E. seems to have been a particularly bloody year. "Reign of terror" comes from Radice, "Introduction," xi; "tyranny" comes from Kennedy, *The Art of Rhetoric in the Roman World,* 527. Pliny reveals a few grisly details in one of his letters, expressing his certainty that he would suffer the same fate as seven friends of his who were relegated or killed (Pliny, *Epistulae,* 3.11.3). After his assassination, Domitian was subjected to a *damnatio memoriae* (Suetonius, *Domitian,* §23).

‡Maternus at Tacitus, *Dialogus de Oratoribus,* 13.

§Pliny's only surviving speech is his *Panegyricus* to Trajan, delivered in 100 C.E. Pliny's edited *Panegyricus* is the first complete post-Ciceronian oration we possess. Tacitus seems never to have published any of his speeches. He and Pliny co-prosecuted Marius Priscus for extortion (*Epistulae* 2.11), but Pliny seems not to have widely published his part of the proceedings, despite a request from a T. Ceriatis to do so (*Epistulae* 2.19).

intensity by various persons and publics.* Pliny did not subject every speech to iterative reconsiderations or receptions, but only those whose stretch to posterity and into history he was trying to make more likely. The *Dialogus de Oratoribus* of Tacitus and the *Epistulae* of Pliny preserve how extensively nearly every poet and orator treated in this book shaped their thinking, their vocabulary, and their preferences about how eloquence may be perfected and why it should be.

Orators Looking over Their Shoulders

Tacitus opens the dialogue in narrator mode, preparing to transport its dedicatee, Fabius Justus, and other readers into a conversation about the state of eloquence that occurred several decades in the past and at which he was present but in which he did not participate. His justification for this set-up is a self-effacing preference for relying upon his memory rather than his ability. Displacing the discussion from the present may be a safety measure, but it seems to perform the view of one of the interlocutors that every generation frets about what it perceives to be the smallness of its time. The displacement may have been a contrivance to avoid having to address Quintilian's investigations into corrupted eloquence.† Tacitus worries that the very word *orator* has slipped from "our times"—except in reference to prior times—having been replaced by "lawyers, advocates, and patrons."‡ Pouring over this earlier conversation undertaken by "superior men [*praestantissimi viri*]" allows Tacitus and Justus to avoid the burden of working through these heavy matters on their own.§ Their abundant modesty flirts with immodesty.

The conversation commences the day after Curiatius Maternus gives a public *recitatio* (recitation) of *Cato*, a tragedy about Cato the Younger that was not warmly received by all assembled, the powerful in particular, and that was becoming the talk of the town. His friends Marcus Aper and Julius Secundus come to him, worried. They enter his bedroom, where he is seated with that very book-roll (*liber*) in his hands. Secundus hopes Maternus has "taken up the *liber* so you can retouch it [*retractares*] more conscientiously, and, having removed [*sublatis*] material if it has received a perverse interpretation, will you send out [*emitteres*] if not a better [*meliorem*] than at least a safer [*securiorem*]

---

*For a study of genetic and general publics in Pliny's letters, see Gurd, *Work in Progress,* 105–126.

†Kennedy argues that Tacitus's "hatred for the Flavians" would have tainted Quintilian by association (*The Art of Rhetoric in the Roman World,* 523).

‡Tacitus, *Dialogus de Oratoribus,* 1.1.

§Tacitus, *Dialogus de Oratoribus,* 1.3, 1.2.

Cato?"* Right away, Tacitus shows that poetry is not necessarily "safer" or less public than oratory. Even the choice of subject matter can be dangerously provocative, let alone its handling. What danger Maternus courts is never specified; it could be a steep decline in his reputation, but it could be a threat more dire. Maternus, though, refuses to make changes: "You will read what Maternus owed to himself, and all that you heard you will recognize again."† He adds that anything he does omit from *Cato* will go into his next tragedy, already "ordered and formed" in his head. Eager to get to his next project, he discloses that he "hurries to hasten the publication [*editio*] of this book-roll." No Horatian poetic delay here.

Aper contends that Maternus's tragedies have overstepped the boundaries of their designation as side projects. All of this "new work [*novum negotium*]" has made Maternus too busy to respond to his clients. His intense dedication to writing verses has perverted *otium* (leisure) into its opposite, *negotium*. Maternus responds in adversarial language, calling Aper an *iudex*, the Latin word for "judge" that is applied to those who preside over court cases and to those who make judgments in general, particularly of poems. Ovid, for example, punned on its double meaning throughout his exilic poetry, as I showed previously. Maternus purports to be happy that this trial of poetry in which he and Aper frequently engage may be coming to a close at last. As the judge, Aper may decide on a sentence: either forbid Maternus from making verses in the future or compel him to give up narrow (*angustus*) forensic cases so as to cultivate a more sacred and august (*augustus*) eloquence.‡ The reason Aper cannot surrender his friend to the Muses is that Maternus was "born for manly eloquence and speech [*natus ad eloquentiam virilem et oratoriam*] by which he might make and keep friendships, establish connections, and reach out to the provinces," making a name for himself not only in the city but also across the whole empire.§ Aper does not find poetry itself objectionable. Indeed, he and Maternus consider *eloquentia* to be a capacious supercategory that includes both poetry and oratory.** Still, they have different hierarchies of value.

Aper emphasizes the *utilitas* and *voluptas* of oratory, both of which register in the now.†† An orator immediately sees his effect, and the utilities and pleasures

*Tacitus, *Dialogus de Oratoribus*, 3.2. The sense of "better" is that the play cannot be improved upon aesthetically.

†Tacitus, *Dialogus de Oratoribus*, 3.3.

‡Tacitus, *Dialogus de Oratoribus*, 4.2.

§Tacitus, *Dialogus de Oratoribus*, 5.3. Compare Ovid's autobiography in *Tristia* 4.10.

**Tacitus, *Dialogus de Oratoribus*, 10.4, 12.2.

††Tacitus, *Dialogus de Oratoribus*, 5.3 (*utilitas* and *voluptas*). As I have shown previously, immediate usefulness or advantageousness as a criterion of significance was a matter of lively debate in the ancient world. In the final section of *Peri Hupsous* (44.6), Longinus and an unnamed philosopher discuss the decline question. Though neither is

of the oratorical life renew with every speaking occasion. They include the
potent self-confidence that comes from helping troubled others and magnetiz-
ing gathered crowds and the satisfaction that arises from delivering an oration
long cared for and thought out or offering one of new and recent care, not without some trepidation.* All the time, the orator derives from himself. He does not
have patrons to please—he is the patron. His art is freer, his self-reliance unques-
tionable, his place in the city and imperial culture ensured. Aper turns to poetry
and poets with a very lawyerly question: *cui bono?*† Who benefits or is saved
from danger if "Agamemnon or Jason speaks eloquently"? Aper elaborates upon
the situation of a poet they know named Bassus, who has recently been sponsored by Vespasian: "for verses come naturally to Bassus in his home, and pretty
and charming ones indeed, but the result of them, however, is that when, after
a whole year, through entire days, and the best part of the nights, he has hammered out and eked out from the oil [*excudit et elucubravit*], a solitary book, he
ultimately must beg and canvas for people, so that they will deign to listen, and
not even that *gratis*."‡ Orators, in contrast, ready their words quickly, though not
sloppily, for public venues thronged with the curious, the envious, and the
word-delirious. The excitement builds because there is something—someone, and
perhaps more than one—at stake. Those saved from danger remain in the orator's debt. Those who hear the orator remained enthralled.

On the other hand, even a wildly successful poetic *recitatio*—and such an
event is rare, in Aper's estimation—forges no deep and lasting bonds of affection
or allegiance upon which the poet can depend. Exacerbating the poet's social
detachment are the traditional haunts of poetic productivity: empty woods and
groves outside the city. These publicity gaps hurt a poet's chances of securing
fama: "no one knows the mediocre poets, few know the good ones [*mediocris*

---

convinced that democracy is the only nursemaid of *hupsos*, both are convinced that the
verbal productions of what they call "the now [*to nun*]" are not hitting high notes. Longinus blames not the current political constitution but the individual constitutions of
people at present. He contends that the most prominent motivators have become money,
praise, and pleasure, such that people "no longer look upwards or take any further
thought for their good name." They are engrossed in the here and now, generating only
that which will get them immediate recognition (see also Tacitus, *Dialogus de Oratoribus*,
7). Speakers and writers need room and space to try for the heights. For that, two things
are required: first, that they be willing to fail, or at least to flail, in the attempt, which no
one will do if one is always seeking praise, and, second, that they do not have to worry
about their work being useful in the present, whether in making them money or helping
others who need immediate aid.

*Tacitus, *Dialogus de Oratoribus*, 6.5.
†Tacitus, *Dialogus de Oratoribus*, 9.
‡Tacitus, *Dialogus de Oratoribus*, 9.5 (Vespasian sponsorship); 9.3 (Bassus's compo-
sition).

poetas nemo novit, bonos pauci]."* Aper judges Maternus to be a hybrid poet-orator whose noble effervescence has mixed the risks of oratory with the rewards of poetry: the worst of both worlds. With his newest tragedy, Maternus "offends not for the sake of a friend, but, what is more dangerous, for the sake of Cato. Nor is this offense excused by the necessity of duty, nor by the fidelity of an advocate, nor by the impulse of a chance and sudden speech."† Because a poet can choose any subject matter at any time, he does not have those excuses.

Maternus thinks Aper's strategy of degrading poetry relies upon the hasty advancement of a faulty premise: that only those who cannot make cases make verses, since poetry is but a secondary way to attempt to gain acclaim, and a secondary acclaim at that.‡ To the contrary, Maternus estimates that any *fama* he does enjoy originated from his poems and not his speeches; he was a trage-dian before he was a pleader.§ Name recognition alone attracts crowds of clients to his side. A poet may compose verses in solitude if he chooses, but an orator always composes in the middle of battle or with a client peering over his shoulder or crying with wretchedness. The oratorical life is noisy, bustling, exhausting, and ultimately not very rewarding.** Maternus speaks of a "golden age" before oratory and criminality, when poetry was the first and foremost verbal art and poets "sang of good deeds, not defended bad crimes."†† Poetry is the primordial eloquence. In his view, oratory is fallen from its very start; it is born of and reliant upon the urgent and unpleasant. Its current form is worse of all: "this money-grubbing and blood-splashed eloquence is of recent use, and sprang from bad tendencies, and, as you say yourself, Aper, in our time and place, it is treated as a weapon."‡‡ It seems absurd to extol something so base. Throughout time, one can easily find poets whose eloquence is acknowledged to exceed that of ora-tors; some say Vergil bests Cicero, some say Ovid bests orators with whom he was contemporary, Sophocles and Euripides have no less fame than Lysias and Hyperides, and no one supersedes Homer.§§ Poets are not any more necessarily consigned to oblivion than orators. Maternus, though, simply wants a release from the daily grind that requires him to do something *contra animum,* against

---

*Tacitus, *Dialogus de Oratoribus*, 10.1. Recall Horace, *Ars Poetica*, 369–373.

†Tacitus, *Dialogus de Oratoribus*, 10.6.

‡From chapter 5, compare Ovid's account of his rhetorical education and the Muses always dragging him into verse (*Tristia* 4.10).

§Tacitus, *Dialogus de Oratoribus*, 11.2. He speaks of *recitationes* of his earlier tragedies.

**Tacitus, *Dialogus de Oratoribus*, 13.

††Tacitus, *Dialogus de Oratoribus*, 12.3.

‡‡Tacitus, *Dialogus de Oratoribus*, 12.2.

§§Tacitus, *Dialogus de Oratoribus*, 12.5–6.

his being.* It is not an alternative avenue to fame that he seeks but a respite from the never-ending crawl.

In his response, Aper shimmies to adjust to Maternus's backward-looking, bardic preferences. Aper fixates on the word *antiquus*, which literally means "located before," making the *stasis* of definition the grounds of debate.† His thinking seems to be that Maternus needs to update and enlarge his sense of what counts as ancient/located before: is that not simply a matter of perspective? And is it not also true that verbal styles cycle in and out, changing with the times?‡ By way of example, Aper points to successive debates about Atticism.§ Orators who emerge victorious from those debates may seem to be unsurpassable models of excellence. Yet, in Cicero's case, at least, traces of the competition yet remain. Of the speeches of Calvus, for instance, Aper's time possesses twenty-one book-rolls' worth. Aper also mentions letters exchanged among Calvus, Brutus, and Cicero, in which all three launch accusations of fault: Cicero thinks Calvus "bloodless and dry" and Brutus "lazy and loose," while Calvus finds Cicero "loose and nerveless" and Brutus finds Cicero "cracked and enervated."** Remaining within this corporeal frame, Aper pronounces that "*oratio*, just like the human body, is, then, pretty not only when the veins are not prominent, and the bones cannot be counted, but also when a moderate and good [*bonus*] blood fills the limbs [*membra*], and surges through the muscles [*toris*], a ruddiness suffuses the very sinews, and a certain elegance [*decor*] recommends it."†† Though Aper does not go into the minute anatomical detail that Cicero, for instance, goes into in his discussion of rhythm, words such as "limbs [*membra*]" recall the part-by-part construction of a speech.

Sounding very much as Cicero in *Brutus*, Aper details how and why the form of eloquence changes. The current expectations for eloquence demand oratory that is more epigrammatic and poetic than any previous kind: even Horace and Vergil are welcome.‡‡ Aper stresses that "even the throng of bystanders, and the winding and wandering listener who regularly swings by, now demand

---

*Tacitus, *Dialogus de Oratoribus*, 13.5.

†Tacitus, *Dialogus de Oratboribus*, 16.4–5.

‡Tacitus, *Dialogus de Oratoribus*, 16; 18.2

§Tacitus, *Dialogus de Oratoribus*, 18.5–6. As G. O. Hutchinson points out in reference to Quintilian 12.10.16, "the *antiqua* division between *Attici* and *Asiani* could be seen as Greek or Roman," since by the end of the first century C.E. the Cicero-Calvus debate could be considered *antiquus* in its literal meaning of "located before." Hutchinson, *Greek to Latin*, 25.

**Tacitus, *Dialogus de Oratoribus*, 18.5–6.

††Tacitus, *Dialogus de Oratoribus*, 21.8.

‡‡Tacitus, *Dialogus de Oratoribus*, 20.5.

joyfulness and prettiness of speech," and they have no patience for the "harsh and uncombed manner of antiquity [*tristem et impexam antiquitatem*]."* Today, no one has any patience for the quantity of Cicero's "book-rolls [*libri*]" of speeches or for their dominant quality: prolixity. Cicero was the first to truly cultivate *oratio*, but "nothing can be extracted [*nihil excerpere*]" from his bulk; his speeches are sturdy but have "not enough thorough polish and sparkle [*non satis expolitus et splendens*]."† The speeches he gave before his death have more epigrammatic punch, however, but it took him a long time to arrive there.‡ Maternus, then, can be poetic without leaving oratory. Gesturing to the embarrassingly bad poems written by Cicero, Caesar, and Brutus and conveyed by them to a *bibliotheca* (library; which one is not specified), Aper suggests that writing actual poetry rather than allowing a poetic line in one's oratory now and then is never a good thing for a noted orator.§ Aper altogether ignores Maternus's objections to the unstinting demands of clients, the hollowing ceaselessness of the work, and his original identification (by himself and by others) as a tragedian.

A third orator, Vipstanus Messala, arrives when the discussion is well under way, and his views occupy the last two-thirds of the *Dialogus*. He dismisses Aper's attempts to make this a fight about vocabulary; whether we call those who preceded us "ancients" or "elders," Cicero and his generation practiced an eloquence superior to that of the present.** Messala does not think present-day oratory is particularly scrappy *or* lofty. In his opinion, it is flat. It has plateaued because the political situation has stabilized. Oratorical work still needs to be done, but it is carried out in a restrained and business-like manner. Court reforms, he says, are partly responsible, with the result that the courts "are more favorable to truth now but [were] better for eloquence then."†† Here, he uses a language of constriction, saying orators are as if confined to tight garb and small spaces. Courtrooms are no longer thronged with vocal and animated citizens who feel an investment in the outcome, because such grand appeals are not suffered by judges who want pleaders to get to the legal point; the language of prosecution and defense has become managed, compartmentalized, squeezed.‡‡

---

*Tacitus, *Dialogus de Oratoribus*, 20.3. This assessment of public tastes resembles what the chorus said about Athenians before and during the poetic contest in *Frogs*, only the ostensibly antiquated Aeschylus won that competition.

†Tacitus, *Dialogus de Oratoribus*, 22.3

‡Tacitus, *Dialogus de Oratoribus*, 22.2

§Tacitus, *Dialogus de Oratoribus*, 21.6.

**Tacitus, *Dialogus de Oratoribus*, 25.2. For a comparative study of *antiquus* and *vetus*, see Mamoojee, "*Antiquus* and *Vetus*."

††Tacitus, *Dialogus de Oratoribus*, 38.

‡‡Tacitus, *Dialogus de Oratoribus*, 39.

As Michael Winterbottom points out, Maternus does not lack a flair for hyperbole: "he makes it sound as though the past had a monopoly of grand cases with large audiences and high public attention."* Of course, not all cases during Rome's various republican periods were of that quality; moreover, the imperial period saw the occasional major case, such as trials of Verres-like governors.

Spreading, soaring eloquence needs considerable scope, but that is not sufficient. Messala submits that lofty oratory needs and feeds on chaos, a kind not to be found in the current "well put together and quiet and happy [*composita et quieta et beata*]" state of affairs. Indeed, if one could find a community where everyone and everything were perfect, the orator would be totally superfluous.† Maternus had argued as much earlier about oratory's essential and original fallenness, but that observation is not unique to this dialogue. More than one hundred years before, Cicero had observed that if polities and communities were perfect, then laws would be unnecessary, and if the laws were perfect, then eloquence would be unnecessary.‡ Laws and eloquence have a corrective function. Oratory, then, needs tinctures of imperfection and disorder to function, and it needs large amounts to reach the levels of energy and elevation reached by Demosthenes and Cicero. A Cicero will not appear "in a well constituted *civitas*."§

Messala's speech closes with attention to the forum, "which is all of antiquity that remains for our speakers, as a sign of a *civitas* not as emended [*emendatae*] or well-put together [*compositae*] as may be wished."** By whom, he does not say. *Compositio* and *emendatio* are, of course, rhetorical, textual words: like a draft hastily released, Rome remains unfinished. Horace had used *emendatio* to refer to Augustus's improvements to Italy and its laws, making Augustus's changes homologous to the correction and enhancement of poems.†† The word also could be a veiled reference to Domitian. The historian Suetonius, a contemporary of Tacitus and Pliny, explains how Domitian took upon himself "the *correctio*" of common practices he deemed errant.‡‡ Despite the attempts of several emperors to bring the forum (or forensic rhetoric) into formation, it retains a bit of its ancient unruliness. When Messala concludes that "no one can enjoy great fame and great quiet at the same time [*nemo eodem tempore adsequi potest magnam famam et magnam quietam*]," does Tacitus suppose that a great orator

---

*Winterbottom, "Returning to Tacitus' *Dialogus*," 150.
†Tacitus, *Dialogus de Oratoribus*, 41.3
‡Cicero, *De Legibus*.
§Tacitus, *Dialogus de Oratoribus*, 40.
**Tacitus, *Dialogus de Oratoribus*, 41.1.
††Horace, *Epistles*, 2.1.
‡‡Suetonius, *Domitian*, 8.3.

may rise from times that *have* been unquiet, such as the mid-90s were?"* There were, as it happens, many orators active then, but only one name has retained its *fama*.

Lettered Pliny

After dodging Domitian's thunderbolts, the younger Pliny seems to have flourished, oratorically and financially. This much one can glean from his curated collection of letters he had written "carefully [*curatius*]" between 96 (the year Domitian was assassinated) and 108.[†] Unfolding across ten ancient volumes, Pliny's epistolary cache is precious for its observations and reflections about this time span, no part of it more so for the history of rhetoric than the many letters that pertain to his speeches. Repeatedly, he details their production, controlled circulation among critical friends, and prospects for a broad publication. Sometimes friends of Pliny are eager to receive a speech they know Pliny has delivered but not yet published textually; sometimes Pliny is eager to receive critical judgment from friends before he even delivers the speech. Usually, mutual eagerness is in evidence, and sometimes hints of reciprocation and obligation.

Pliny was close to and initiated into rhetorical-public culture by several bookish older men: his uncle and adopted father, Pliny the Elder, who published seven works, amounting to more than one hundred book-rolls, including the famous *Naturalis Historia;* his teacher, Quintilian, who assigned writing and emending essential roles in rhetorical training and practice; and his guardian, Verginius Rufus, who slipped and broke his hip, never to recover, while trying to gather up a heavy book-roll he had been consulting while writing an encomium for the emperor Nerva.[‡] Pliny was also friendly with Tacitus, who delivered Rufus's funeral oration.[§] Tacitus certainly sought out Pliny for editorial guidance, and it is likely to the *Dialogus* that Pliny here refers: "I have read your book-roll [*librum*], and as diligently as I could, noted that which I reckon can be changed, that which can be removed [*quae commutanda, quae eximenda*]."** They have exchanged texts, Pliny reports, and Pliny awaits Tacitus's mark-ups on the book-roll Pliny sent him. This exchange for the purpose of change represents, for Pliny, the merest hint of their mutual regard: "How much it delights me that, if posterity has any care [*cura*] for us, it will be told everywhere that we coexisted

---

*Tacitus, *Dialogus de Oratoribus,* 41.5

[†]Pliny, *Epistulae,* 1.1.2.

[‡]Pliny, *Epistulae,* 3.5 (his uncle's work habits); 2.14, 6.6 (Quintilian); 2.1.5 (Verginius Rufus).

[§]Pliny, *Epistulae,* 2.1.6.

**Pliny *Epistulae,* 7.20.1.

in harmony, simplicity, and fidelity!"* They are not competitors, but their rough contact with each other makes them both better.

In a much longer letter from an earlier book-roll, Pliny engages Tacitus on a topic Pliny frequently discusses with an unnamed friend of learning and skill: the respective merits of amputated *oratio* and that with amplitude. Pliny is setting the terms, and it is clear he does not lean toward the lean. For one, reiteration serves the rhetorical purpose of lending "strength [*vis*]" and "weight [*pondus*]," and it naturally extends the length of a speech. His friend counts among his authorities in brevity Lysias and Cato, while Pliny calls forth Demosthenes, Aeschines, Caesar, and, "in first position [*in primis*]," Cicero to testify for length. Pliny's witness list is strange, since, as I have shown, Demosthenes and Aeschines, like Caesar and Cicero, are generally thought to be at stylistic odds.† Pliny's point, however, is that all of them write long speeches. And good ones; the Latin is that tricky *bonus* previously seen in Quintilian's *vir bonus* formulation. "As with all good things, a good book-roll is all the better when it is bigger. . . . Magnitude in book-rolls lends them a certain authority and beauty."‡ His friend argues that published speeches are always much longer than their orally delivered versions. His point seems to be that a speech must be short and direct to do its persuasive work within the various constraints with which an orator contends, from restrictions issued by judges to lazy listeners. Published speech-texts, then, are artifacts of an orator's inability not to let material he prepared go unused, unrecognized, uncelebrated.

To dispute that claim, Pliny turns to two orations of Cicero, the *Pro Murena* and *Pro Vareno,* in which the subsections about the charges are "short and as if bare [*brevis et nuda quasi*]," indicated by mere titles: "from this, it is apparent that very much he had said was omitted from what he published [*ederet*]."§ Cicero himself discloses that he delivered the entirety of his longest speech, *Pro Cluentio,* himself, and over four days. Despite the odiousness of his client, Cicero won. To squeeze such a speech into "*unum librum,* albeit a large one," would have required Cicero to "cut back and purge [*recisa ac repurgata*] afterward."** Pliny's friend also insists that what makes a delivered speech good differs from that which makes a published speech good. Pliny's response to that point sounds like the views of Cicero and Quintilian, and he acknowledges he does not lack company: "I know it seems this way not only to me, but—though perhaps I am deceived—I am persuaded that just as it is possible that a good delivery [*actio*

*Pliny, *Epistulae,* 7.20.2.
†Pliny himself acknowledges as much at *Epistulae* 9.26.10–11.
‡Pliny, *Epistulae,* 1.20.5.
§Pliny, *Epistulae,* 1.20.7.
**Pliny, *Epistulae,* 1.20.8.

bona] does not guarantee a good speech [*bona oratio*], it is not possible that a bad delivery [*non bonam actionem*] makes for a good speech [*bona oratio*]."* Here, again, the Latin adjective *bonus* acts on several registers. The effective oral delivery of a speech alone will not secure its status as a good speech, but a speech also will not succeed if it reads well but cannot be orally delivered effectively. Pliny's view seems to be that a good speech will outlive its original purpose, but it will have that chance only if it makes a good first impression. (That is obviously a general rule that does not always obtain.) Pliny closes by issuing a clever challenge to Tacitus: "Surely I do not corrupt you to impose upon you the necessity of a short letter if you assent, and a long one if you dissent?"† As was not unique to Pliny and Tacitus, friends and associates mobilize the vocabulary of their respective stylistic leanings to tease each other.

In all, Pliny mentions nearly twenty speeches and seems to have proceeded with plans to textually publish about half of those.‡ He describes his ideal composition conditions, so quiet that he can talk to his book-rolls in peace.§ He mentions a speech that received praise for resembling Demosthenes's prosecution of Meidias, which Pliny admits to trying to imitate, since to emulate it was beyond his powers.** He gushes that his beloved third wife, Calpurnia, sets his speeches to music, issuing him across media.†† Pliny mentions the editorial *lima* in the second letter of the whole collection, the first if one does not count the opening dedication letter. Addressed to one Maturnus Arrianus, Pliny delivers on a promise to exhibit his work to Arrianus to read and emend. To give Arrianus a sense of what he is going for stylistically, Pliny names Demosthenes and a more recent orator, Calvus, as his inspiration and aspiration, adding that he has not foregone Cicero's "unguents."‡‡ Given that Cicero fancied himself the Demosthenes to Calvus's Lysias, it is a strange mash-up of influences. Pliny asks his friend to apply the file assiduously, since Pliny's under encouraging pressure to publish. Pliny himself wants to, "but mostly because the little book-rolls I have already sent out [*libelli quos emisimus*] are to said to be in hands, although by now they have lost the charm of novelty; unless, of course, the booksellers [*bibliopolae*] send only flattery toward my ears."§§ If Pliny's old stuff continues to be

---

*Pliny, *Epistulae*, 1.20.9.

†Pliny, *Epistulae*, 1.20.25.

‡See, e.g., Pliny, *Epistulae*, 1.2, 1.8, 2.5, 4.26, 4.14, 5.12, 5.20, 7.17.

§Pliny, *Epistulae*, 1.9.5.

**Pliny, *Epistulae*, 7.30. As I explained near the end of chapter 1, Demosthenes may not have delivered that speech.

††Pliny, *Epistulae*, 4.19.3–4. 7.4.9–10, where he mentions his poetry being read, sung, and set to the cithara and lyre.

‡‡Pliny, *Epistulae*, 1.2.4. He uses the Greek, *lēkuthos* (oil, oil pot).

§§Pliny, *Epistulae*, 1.2.6.

taken up and read, then new work should bring interested buyers and catch the eye of passers-by. That projection may be wishful thinking on the part of book-sellers, but it speaks either to the production influence booksellers may have had on élite Roman writers or to the habit of those writers to maintain the appearance of bashfulness about publishing their work by displacing zealous-ness onto those who stand to profit most directly from its sale. The preface to Quintilian's *Institutio Oratorio* shows the same dynamics between writer and bookseller.

To honor the various libraries that have come in and out of the picture in every chapter of this book and because it is the earliest letter in the collection to mention the editorial *lima* in the context of a named speech, I focus on an oration Pliny delivered to mark the occasion of his generous sponsorship of a library (*bibliotheca*) opening that day in his hometown, Comum (now Como), in northern Italy, in 96 C.E. His munificence also included support for the welfare of Comum's free-born children.* The letter responds to a request from Pompeius Saturninus that Pliny send him "something from his writings."† Pliny is happy to oblige, since he has been wanting and yet hesitating to ask Saturninus to review a speech Saturninus had already seen. "I am very mindful that you have marked up [*adnotasse*] this one already, but generally; therefore, now I ask not only that you attend to the whole, but also to pursue the particulars with the file [*lima*], as you are accustomed to do."‡ The speech is, in large part, an auto-encomium, and Pliny purports to feel awkward about the *materia* that pertains to his largesse. Yet he speaks of himself out of generic necessity, since a person who gives a substantial gift to a community ought to account for his gift. To lavish gifts without good reason is to risk being considered thoughtless, impul-sive, and crass; good deeds, however, are less twisted out of shape and carped at "when kept in obscurity and silence."§ Pliny, then, finds himself in a "slippery spot [*lubricus locus*]."**

The challenges of this speech, then, include these: it is difficult to praise oneself without turning off others; if one must offer self-praise, then one should use a praise language that is "compressed and lowdown [*pressus demissusque*],"

---

*Pliny, *Epistulae*, 1.8, 1.8.10. For more details about his gifts to Comum, see 4.13.5, 5.72–74, and 7.18.2. Kennedy focuses on 1.8 in *The Art of Rhetoric in the Roman World*, 531–533, where he presumes "the choice of this letter for publication can probably be taken as evidence that Pliny eventually found the speech worthy of publication" (533) and wanted to publish it so that "other philanthropists would imitate his program" (532). Both assump-tions seem a stretch.

†Pliny, *Epistulae*, 1.8.1.

‡Pliny, *Epistulae*, 1.8.3.

§Pliny, *Epistulae*, 1.8.6.

**Pliny, *Epistulae*, 1.8.6.

as if every good word had been squeezed out with effort, and such a style may not read well; it is hard enough to praise oneself for an act benefiting a particular community in a speech delivered to representatives of that community, let alone to sing one's praises in publication for readers disconnected from that place, and not have the praise smack of self-aggrandizement. A unique challenge of this speech is that Pliny delivered it to the council of Comum in its Senate house, intentionally putting "a threshold" between himself and the people of the city so as not to seem inappropriately eager for their affection and appreciation.* The resultant speech is subdued—not what he wants in an *editio* meant to showcase his oratorical powers. Ultimately, Pliny enlists Saturninus to facilitate the editorial process. After Saturninus applies his customary file, Pliny can decide "whether to publish it or hold back [*vel publicare vel continere*]. Perhaps, actually, a view about emendation will be driven out through this very delay in settling on an opinion, and frequent rehandling will either show it is not worthy [*indignum*] of publication, or that process itself will render it worthy [*dignum*]."† Re-reading and reconsideration require time, and delay has pushed each subsequent iteration of those editorial processes further from the creation conditions of the speech. That push is in Pliny's interest, because he feels keenly how different the Comum speech would need to be to be worth circulating around areas other than Comum. Distance—temporal and geographical—must factor into an orator's decision to publish. But, as his own teacher urged, when it comes to emendation, an orator must make up his mind within a non-Isocratean time frame. Saturninus and his trusty *lima* are meant to expedite matters.

This letter demonstrates that an orator—if Pliny may be considered representative, and I believe he may, if only of a certain small subset of preeminent orators—might seek the criticism of a friend (the same friend, even) before orally delivering a speech *and* before textually publishing a speech-text. It also shows that orators did not think a speech-text had to be a faithful transcript of what they said at what occasioned it. A speech-text could be considered a separate rhetorical event, and the degree to which it could and should diverge from what was said was subject to contemplation and conversation. Pliny's letter also tells of the particular anxieties that attend publishing a speech of self-praise; genres pose problems unique to themselves. If Pliny did publish this library dedication speech, it did not survive. Some later editor may have deemed it subpar. If Pliny did not publish this speech, then he executed his editorial duties as he, and perhaps, too, Saturninus, saw fit. When the correction of speech is not enough to merit its publication, an orator must choose protective suppression.

---

*Pliny, *Epistulae*, 1.8.17.
†Pliny, *Epistulae*, 1.8.3–4.

Pliny justifies his elaborate editorial process in a letter addressed to Celer, Latin for "quick," which Pliny is not. In previous correspondence, Celer has told Pliny that some people do not understand why he arranges recitations for his speeches, especially for speeches that have already been delivered. Pliny professes amazement that anyone should think speeches never need emendation—and more than one round. Writers across genres hold readings and have done so since ancient Greece. Pliny does not desire praise at a recitation, and "truly I omit no type of emendation [*emendandi genus*]."* Pliny itemizes his method: first he emends the speech, then he reads it to two or three friends, and soon he hands it over to a few others for them to mark up. If he continues to nurse doubts, then he organizes a *recitatio,* and it is then that "I emend most intensively [*acerrime emendo*]." The purpose of a recitation is to fix concentrated critical energy on a speech to make it the best it can be should the orator decide to publish it more broadly, and Pliny invites only people he trusts. The most important qualities for an orator who wants to be appreciated in his own time and beyond are *pudor, metus,* and *timor,* a sense of shame, fear, and dread. The *stilus* is the best organizer of those hesitating energies.† His own experience confirms the superlative utility of his method. "Nothing is enough for my care [*curae meae*]. I think to give something into the hands of people, and it is not possible to persuade me that it must not be treated by many and often [*et cum multis et saepe*], you must want to please both always and everyone [*et semper et omnibus*]."‡ This near chiasmus of number (many)-frequency (often) to duration (always)-number (everyone) shows that Pliny believes a full editorial period improves a work's chances of an extensive reception. That there are no take-backs means that an orator will not be spared degrading embarrassment in his own time if he releases a speech without full consideration. Avoiding oblivion, however, seems to be a more motivating impetus for Pliny.

For that reason, he is tempted to heed the advice of his friend Titinius Capito to take up history. History appeals to Pliny primarily because it grants immortality to names that ought to live forever and "extends the *fama* of others along with one's own." Historians have a decided advantage over orators and poets. "Small prestige [*gratia*] comes to orations and poems, unless they reach the summit of eloquence, but history delights however it is written [*modo scripta*]. Humans are curious by nature, such that even bare matters [*nuda rerum*] capture the mind, and draw in those who like chit-chat and little stories [*sermunculis* ...

---

*Pliny, *Epistulae,* 7.17.7.
†Pliny, *Epistulae,* 7.17.8 and 7.17.13.
‡Pliny, *Epistulae,* 7.17.15.

fabellisque]."* In other words, history has a low barrier of entry, appreciation-wise. My narrative about the editorial bodies of ancient rhetoric and poetics began with Herodotus, the so-called father of history, who invoked in the very first line of his *Histories* the power of writing to preserve a memory of deeds and doers too monumental to be forgotten.† Poets and orators began to claim that promise for their own arts, but their words were occasional, fitted to moments, and not meant to be universally applicable or admirable. Poets can historicize their art by writing about what and whom they think will be the material of future historians. Orators can historicize their art by ridding their speeches of details that excessively particularize. As Pliny's teacher counseled, an orator should remove from a speech headed toward textual publication any items included in the first place only to persuade very particular people in a very particular moment. Such omissions, however, are not easily done and do not guarantee a compelling speech, which is why Pliny takes the editorial process so seriously. He takes it so seriously, in fact, that he uses that very process as an excuse in this letter: "I have acted in great and substantial cases. Now, even if the hope this affords me is thin [*tenuis*], I dedicate myself to their rehandling, so that no great part of my labor, except that which I would have added out of zeal to what remains, dies along with me. For, if you consider it from the perspective of posterity, whatever is not carried through might as well not have been begun."‡ To publish a speech-text is to complete the circuit of labor. A speech not finished in the manifold manner Pliny details several times throughout his epistolary *corpus* may as well have dissipated into the air into which it was spoken. Editing speech-texts and writing histories are too demanding to do simultaneously.

Furthermore, commonalities between oratory and history ought not give an orator false confidence. Both operate in a narrative mode, but "the one largely seeks out the humble and the sordid and what comes from the middle of things, the other is concerned with the recondite, splendid, eminent; to this one, bones, muscles, sinews [*ossa musculi nervi*] are proper; to that one, a fleshiness [*tori*] and a flowiness; the one pleases with maximum power, bitterness, vehemence, the other with drawing out and suavity and also sweetness; finally, they differ in diction, sound, and structure. For it is reckoned that much separates, as Thucydides maintained, a 'lasting possession' [*ktēma*] and an 'agonistic speech' [*agōnisma*]; the one is oratory, the other history."§ Here Pliny departs from Quintilian, who taught the orator that history supplies oratory with a "rich and

*Pliny, *Epistulae,* 5.8.4.
†Herodotus, *Histories,* 1.1.
‡Pliny, *Epistulae,* 5.8.6–7.
§Pliny, *Epistulae,* 5.8.9–11.

pleasant juice [*succus*]." Quintilian places succulent history between poetry and oratory, though closer to the former, since historians need the odd poetic splash to prevent narrative tedium. Taking a Thucydidean stance, Quintilian opines that "the whole work [of a history] is composed not for present action or agonism, but for the memory of posterity and the fame of its designer."* In his own periodic sentence, Pliny switches the order of oratory and history back and forth, requiring one to read the points of contrast carefully to figure out whether Pliny refers to history or oratory. That chiasmatic composition is too artful to be accidental.† Perhaps Pliny thinks oratory and history are not so very different after all—when a speech can rise above the immediate circumstances of its delivery, that is. Pliny closes by seeking Capito's guidance on whose "*tempora* [times]" to write about, since past and present have their respective liabilities. To treat matters old entails "onerous collection [*onerosa collatio*]," whereas to treat matters "untouched and new" risks "grave offense and light praise."‡ Every Roman poet and orator featured in this book mixed old and new, archival plentitude and contemporary attitude. It is not otherwise that good book-rolls are made. Pliny recognizes as much.

From their perspectives as orators with historical inclinations, Tacitus and Pliny afford several vantages on eloquence and textual culture in the late first century C.E. The interlocutors in Tacitus's *Dialogus de Oratoribus* hold different opinions as to whether the changes Roman eloquence and public life have undergone are to the benefit of an orator. All agree that there is a narrowness to the rhetorical life as it is lived in their era: for Maternus, it takes the form of the suffocating and unrelenting demand of clients, which is why he (re)turns to poetry; for Aper, it takes the form of squeezed, sententious prose, which he much prefers to Ciceronian copiousness; for Messala, it takes the form of ever tighter restrictions on what kinds and lengths of rhetorical and legal appeals are permitted in the courts, which makes the forum the last frontier of potentially unruly oratory. The pinches specified by Aper and Messala make for an eloquence more tight and tidy than that manifested in messier times. In his letters, Pliny showcases myriad local and some national occasions for his rhetorical talents. Both kinds of discourses have communal purpose, but Pliny struggles during his lengthy editorial process to make local speeches of interest to readers beyond a given locality. To help him secure a lasting reputation, he enlists all manner of friends and associates to show him where he errs and to offer alternatives. In that way, Pliny's method is not altogether different from that of Isocrates.

---

*Quintilian 10.1.31.
†Pliny also deploys *asyndeton* and *polysyndeton* to great effect.
‡Pliny, *Epistulae,* 5.8.12–13.

CONCLUSION
Kissing Tiro; or, Appreciating Editing

When reading the book-rolls of Gallus, where to his father
he dared to give the palm-wreath over Cicero,
I discovered some luscious lines of Cicero,
demonstrating his genius, with which he used to spice up serious things, and he
    showed
the minds of even great men to delight in
humane wit and much and varied charm [*humanis salibus multo varioque*
    lepore].
The poem complains, because Tiro, through a naughty fraud, frustrated the one
    who loved him:
a few kisses that came to be owed during dinner
were denied at night time. Reading this, I wonder:
"Why, given that [*haec*], should I hide my loves
and fear to give to the public [*in medium ... damus*] and also to acknowledge
Tiro's trickery, how fleeting Tiro's
favors are, and how his denial of them stirs up new flames?"

Pliny, Epistulae, 7.4.6

Pliny's reference to this queer little poem about Cicero and his beloved
scribe, Tiro, has unsettled some of the recent readers who have even dared to
take it on. William McDermott details that critical "perturbation," and, frankly,
adds to it when he speculates tortuously that the language of love in the poem
is the appropriate affection master Cicero had for his slave when the latter was
a tyke too shy to give him a goodnight kiss.* Betty Radice demurs, though she
does envision an adult and freed Tiro: "the implied relationship between Cicero
and his freedman Tiro is not certain."† Ignoring how much of Cicero's writing

---

*McDermott, "M. Cicero and M. Tiro," 272–275, 272.
†Radice, "Notes," 492 n. 1.

has not survived, Jacqueline Carlon asserts that the verses certainly did not come from anything Cicero ever wrote.* But, in fact, Quintilian references an "amusing little book-roll [*ioculari libello*]" of Cicero's, and Tacitus's Aper chides Cicero for sending book-rolls of poetry to a library.† Unquestioned fragments of only a few verses of Cicero's poetry remain, but they pertain explicitly to his consulship. As for Cicero's affection for Tiro, Cicero's letters contain evidence of fondness and loyalty that does not confirm there was a sexual dimension to their relationship but does not disconfirm it, either. In one letter from the fall of 50 B.C.E., which Cicero dispatched to Tiro while the latter was at a distance, recovering from a serious illness, Cicero writes: "Your favors to me—domestically, forensically, in the city, in the provinces, in matters private, in matters public, in my studies, in my written work—are innumerable: you will overcome them all if, as I hope, I will see you, robust."‡ They did unite, for a time. After Cicero's murder, Tiro dedicated himself to the collection, organization, and publication of Cicero's writings, likely working with a set of instructions or at least a judicious sense of what should circulate and in what form.

The work of Asinius Gallus in which Pliny purports to have found Cicero's love poem is no longer extant, making the citational context unavailable as well. In his reading of Pliny's poem, John Dugan attempts some genealogical guesswork. Asinius Pollio was Gallus's father and not only a contemporary of Cicero but also a neo-Attic competitor.§ "It is plausible," Dugan ventures, "that Gallus sought to use the epigram as confirmation of Cicero's effeminate, aestheticized private existence, evidence of the sort of personal *mollitia* [softness] that his critics found expressed in his prose style. Tiro's involvement in this epigram may have made it particularly suitable to Gallus' purposes since Tiro sought to preserve Cicero's *post mortem* reputation as much as the Asinii wanted to demolish it. . . . Gallus may have presented Cicero's and Tiro's love affair as confirmation of the Atticists' and his father's insinuations about what Cicero's style may reveal about his character."** Starting with my discussion of Aristophanes's version of Agathon in *Thesmophoriazusae* in chapter 1, I have emphasized the common ancient belief in the cross-indexical quality of the way one writes and the way one lives, or, to put it more corporeally, one's body of words and one's actual body. Aristophanes links and likens Agathon's laborious compositional methods and their smooth results to Agathon's beautiful appearance. Both involve

---

*Carlon, *Pliny's Women,* 179 n. 49.

†Quintilian 8.6.73; Tacitus, *Dialogus de Oratoribus,* 21.6.

‡Cicero, *Epistulae Ad Familiares* (Letters to Friends), 16.4.3.

§At 12.10.11–13, Quintilian mentions Pollio and Cicero, including accusations hurled at Cicero by contemporaries such as Pollio.

**Dugan, *Making a New Man,* 348. Brackets mine.

razors. For the Asinii, Cicero's verses about Tiro confirm what Cicero's other writing and speaking had indicated already: insufficient manliness.*

For his part, Pliny seems utterly untroubled by the homoerotic cast of what Gallus puts forth as genuine Ciceronian verses; indeed, Pliny finds it liberating. Pliny offers Cicero's poem as an example of the type of frisky meters he ought to permit himself to write precisely because Cicero had allowed himself to do so. Cicero's example licenses Pliny to publish—the idiom he uses is to put them out in the middle of things (*in medium*)—poems about his own endearingly tricky Tiro. Cicero's publicity on this seemingly private point permits the revelations of those of others. The Ciceronian citation by both Gallus and Pliny speaks to another major theme of this book: whether polemically or invitationally, established names recur. The strength of their example authorizes those who follow them to write in a particular way, or not to do so. I have treated several writers deemed "canonical," but the word "canon," in the sense of a roster of writers or their works deemed first-rate, is foreign to antiquity, outside the development of the Christian canon of texts, of course. The ancient Greek word *kanōn* (measuring rod, standard, model) was by the first century B.C.E. used to name a particular writer as a model "of a genre or of writing in a particular dialect" of Greek.† As Pat Easterling has shown, the ancient vocabulary closest to our sense of "canonical," which itself originated in the eighteenth century, is "the included [*hoi egkrithentes*]" and "the handled [*hoi prattomenoi*]."‡ Writers deemed unworthy were simply ignored. As I discussed in chapter 2, Callimachus called his massive bibliographic work *Pinakes* (*Lists*), and he was trying to maximize inclusion rather than minimize it. He aimed to collect and catch all rather than to canonize a few.

In the Roman portions of this book, I have drawn attention to the terms *vetus* ("old") and *antiquus* ("antecedent" or perhaps "ancient"; literally "that which came before"), *vetus* having the connotation of harshness or hoariness and *antiquus* that of coming first in terms of both chronology and quality. To those concepts, it is time to add another: *classicus*. *Classicus* has been traced to the *magnum opus* of the second-century C.E. bibliophile Aulus Gellius. In his large miscellany, *Noctes Atticae* (*Attic Nights*), Gellius first reports that *classicus* means "first class."§ The whole "class" system was a five-part division based on

---

*Under the most prominent ancient Roman understanding of masculinity, it is the kissing and excessive desire that diminish Cicero's manliness (not necessarily their recipient).

†Easterling, "A Taste for the Classics," 22.

‡Easterling, "A Taste for the Classics," 25. See also Pfeiffer, *History of Classical Scholarship*, 206–208.

§Gellius, *Noctes Atticae*, 6.13.1.

property holdings and mobilized for military purposes. *Classicus* came to apply to texts through metaphoric extension, and that stretch is evident in Gellius's own work. In a later book-roll, amid an argument put forth by the sophist Fronto about the ongoing relevance of the standards of correct Latin in Caesar's *De Analogia,* Gellius is urged by Fronto to read around to confirm Caesar's judgment, checking out only orators and poets "from that earlier cohort [*cohorte . . . antiquiore*] . . . that is, any first-class or upper-class writer, not a lowly one [*classicus adsiduusque aliquis scriptor, non proletarius*]."* This baldly socioeconomic language may reinforce modern notions about the pursuit and patronage of the classical—languages, literatures, architecture, music—by cultural élites. Such a view may be an anachronistic one to impose on Gellius and his circle, but, as James Porter puts it, "classicism and criticism are mutually implicated from the first."† Critics of writing frequently use the language of the vertical (high, low) and ordinal (first, second) as value concepts. For example, all of the writers deemed most "high" by Longinus in his first-century B.C.E. work *Peri Hupsous* (*On Height*) preceded him by centuries.

Gellius, likely with lots of assistance, strove to secure authenticated versions of old book-rolls. He seems to have possessed Tiro's copies or editions of Cicero's speeches.‡ Gellius refers to a copy he has seen of the fifth Verrine oration, "the book-roll tested in its fidelity, since it is the product of Tiro's care and learning [*cura atque disciplina*]," in which Cicero uses a grammatical form that strikes modern readers as incorrect.§ Surely it must be a usage or transmission error in need of emendation, they think. Gellius rises to Cicero's (and Tiro's) defense. He also brings into the discussion another line of Cicero's oratory regarded as a "solecism" by "the vulgar semi-learned."** In his wide-ranging reading, Gellius has found the same grammatical forms in Cicero's well-regarded contemporaries, but he credits Cicero alone with taking advantage of the flex within even right and correct Latin in the service of his singular "care for style and rhythm [*epimeleiai tōn lexeōn modulamentisque*]."†† As Gellius sees it or, more precisely, hears it, the choices Cicero made in grammatical endings are "more pleasant and more complete to the ear, the other option lacking in sweetness and perfection—if a man has an ear perceptive of such things, and not one

---

*Gellius, *Noctes Atticae,* 19.8.15. I treated Caesar's *De Analogia* in chapter 3.

†Porter, "Feeling Classical," 305.

‡For a more philological study of the Tiro passages, see Zetzel, "*Emendavi ad Tironem.*"

§Gellius, *Noctes Atticae,* 1.7.1, 1.7.3.

**Gellius, *Noctes Atticae,* 1.7.17.

††Gellius, *Noctes Atticae,* 1.7.19. Gellius mixes Greek and Latin here.

that is deaf and cannot be bothered."* Cicero's written compositions appeal to the ear.

In a later discussion of euphony, Gellius returns to the fifth Verrine, again casting Cicero's grammatical choices in terms of the greater flexibility of Latin at his time and Cicero's prioritization of the ear: Cicero found it "more soft and more smooth [*mollius teretiusque*] to write" as he did.† Isolating passages in the second Verrine, too, Gellius judges Cicero's choices to be "more fine-tuned and more soft to the ear [*subtilius ad aurem molliusque*]."‡ Cicero's is a sonic rhetoric and a graphic one. All three of those comparatives—more soft, more smooth, more fine—are used by Roman writers featured in earlier chapters of this book to describe the results of editorial processes. When one works words, one rids them of harshness or thickness. As I showed in chapter 3, some of Cicero's own contemporaries deemed his aural inclinations improper precisely because those inclinations played to a love of how words sounded in a sentence, that is, situationally, rather than held to an absolute standard from which one cannot deviate without being wrong. Clearly, those approaches to speaking "rightly" are very different. By the second-century c.e., however, Latin grammar had a foothold (or chokehold) it did not have in Cicero's time. Some second-century readers of Cicero saw embarrassing errors and seemed to blame his famous scribe, copyist, and publisher, Tiro. Gellius would not stand for that. He did all manner of research to prove that Cicero did not deviate from the generous grammar of his time but rather made it work for his eloquence by selecting the best-sounding variant from among those options one could choose. Gellius even cites what Cicero wrote in *Orator* about a responsiveness to rhythm: "as for those who do not feel this, whether they have ears or what in them resembles a human, I do not know."§ To Romans such as Calvus (and maybe Brutus, too), Aper, and the Asinii, however, Cicero would always be wrong.

Whether in verse or prose, one put oneself out in public at great risk, and when the medium of presentation was ink soaked into a fibrous sheet that could circulate far and wide, one was wise to seek critical, trustworthy eyes and ears as well as *exempla* upon whom to model oneself before release. The reliance of writers upon their trusted aids and critics produced or increased intimacy—perhaps even kisses. Ancient writers, especially but not exclusively the ones featured in this book, were keenly aware of their vulnerabilities: futility or mockery in the present and irrelevance or absence in the future. The students, friends,

---

*Gellius, *Noctes Atticae*, 1.7.20.
†Gellius, *Noctes Atticae*, 13.21.15.
‡Gellius, *Noctes Atticae*, 13.21.20.
§Gellius, *Noctes Atticae*, 13.21.24; Cicero, *Orator*, §168.

and family members from whom they sought advice were consulted not because they possessed a flair for a formal perfection that closed a work in on itself but because they were attuned to communal understandings of what qualities and functions made a written speech or poem worth seeking out and keeping around. The vocabulary used to describe those qualities and functions was often derived from or inspired by published works that had passed through many cycles of transmission, their public value deemed unexhausted or inexhaustible. The very longevity of such works suggested they possessed an enduring appeal. New writings that resembled the old could potentially share in that endurance. The intriguing intersection between public understandings and the historical under-pinnings of enduring qualities suggests either that communities knew old book-rolls or that certain compositional constants marked a work as having or doing something valuable. The preceding chapters have demonstrated that ancient writers of both verse and prose thought certain elements of written works rec-ommended themselves to both those who were familiar with the archive of textual culture and those who were not. Cicero, for instance, credited rhythm with being a great unifier, appealing to the learned and the unlearned and to those present at a speech's delivery and those reading it later. In antiquity, one could come across a Ciceronian *Philippic* and appreciate its civic-oriented pulses without knowing anything about Demosthenes's *Philippics.* The same is true now.

The primary argument of this book has been that editing—which, from the ancient perspective I have adopted, refers to a writer-initiated process of pre-paring written words for strangers—was a matter of explicit care for many of the major ancient poets and orators whose works have come through many hands to reach us. Editing was a practice not only undertaken on private, pro-visional texts before their release but also discussed or represented in public, published texts. Besides referring to finishing touches a writer put on his words right before they crossed the threshold, editing became absorbed both into tax-onomies of speaking/writing and into the norms of practice demonstrated by those who had been educated in rhetoric. That is, an editorial mindset trained on eliminating the ugly or unnecessary could and often did inform the earliest compositional forms of a given written work or extemporaneous speech.

Rather than being indicators of political decline or decadence, polished and published prose and verse point to contestation over what sort of words best sustain communal life. Writing is no less democratic or republican than speak-ing: the two verbal forms live parallel lives. My preference for "textual culture" as an alternative to "literary culture" puts emphasis on writing tools as material objects that permitted poets and orators to read works written by others, to experiment with sound and sense while they composed, and to preserve a ver-sion of some set of arguments or appeals for others to read. Explicit attention to editing was a reaction to the pressures of participating in a textual culture whose participants perceived plentitude (of other book-rolls and of rhetorical and poetic options), strove toward a useful formal perfection, and obsessed about preservation. Being the elimination of the extraneous and the compression of the necessary, polish responds to all three of those pressures.

Editorially minded poets and orators sought to start from a place of abundance, variety, and exuberance and then reduce and modify so as to contour to the shape of a genre or the size of a rhetorical situation. Scaling up from a place of paltriness results in language stretched beyond its narrow limits and thus ill-fitting. Abundance means choice, and having choices usually makes for better-adjusted language. The paradox of polished words is that they are constructions that both moved with the moments they were designed to fit and continued to venture forth into new moments. A fascination with the moving and staying power of an ancient work can obscure its histories, though, if one does not consider the vagaries of all those comings and goings. Mark Possanza offers the useful distinction between "the immortal work," which is singular, and "the material text," which is serial. That latter designation is a crucial reminder that ancient writings have histories not only of origination but also of all manner of scribal and scholarly interventions and transmissions. As Possanza observes, "the immortal work may outlast the wrack and havoc of the ages but it is undeniably embodied in a material text, an artifact exposed to the thousand natural shocks the text is heir to, and the most harmful shock, apart from physical destruction, is the debasement of the text, both deliberate and accidental, as it passes through the various stages of reproduction by hand or machine."* That is not the kind of editing upon which I have focused, but, as a type, an editorial approach to ancient texts necessitates consideration of the many contributors to a work beyond "the author."

Robert Gaines proposes that rhetoricians think about the rhetorical tradition not in terms of canon but in terms of corpus, turning attention to material matters—be they spatial, architectural, or textual—contained within or constituted by various ancient media lucky enough to have survived and caught our notice.† His proposed "corpus conception" promotes an understanding of ancient rhetoric as "that body of information that contains all known texts, artifacts, and discourse venues that represent the theory, pedagogy, practice, criticism, and cultural apprehension of rhetoric in the ancient European discourse community."‡ This book's body-based attention to the materiality and sociality of

---

*Possanza, "Editing Ovid: Immortal Works and Material Texts," 311.
†Gaines, "De-Canonizing Ancient Rhetoric," 67, 68.
‡Gaines, "De Canonizing Ancient Rhetoric," 65.

writing and editing shifts the "canonical" frame by placing traditional names in untraditional scenes, namely surrounded by heaps of book-rolls and helpers of various sorts. Recall Isocrates with his friends and students; Cicero with Atticus, Brutus, or Tiro; Horace with his Stoic friend Damasippus and his trusted critic-friend Quintilius; Ovid with the many verse-exchanging poets he names in his letters; Quintilian with Marcellus Vitorius and Trypho; Tacitus and Pliny with each other and Pliny with others besides. Unnamed and uncredited are the scribes (enslaved, freed, or free), copyists, and executors whose labors kept written works from the greedy clutches of oblivion.

We know Tiro's name. It receives marquee treatment in the Cicero trilogy of the historical-fiction writer Robert Harris, which purports to pulls from Tiro's lost biography of Cicero and Tiro's own diary (also lost, if it ever existed at all) to tell a story about the late Republic from Tiro's perspective.* Lost forever, however, are the identities of Isocrates's scribal slave, Cato Maior's thorough eraser of wax tablets, Lucilius's quick-scribbling scribe, and the *amanuenses* Quintilian said were so in style and demand in his time.† All manner of other helpers went completely unmentioned, even in general terms. Kim Haines-Eitzen has compiled scant but compelling evidence that girls and women did scribal and copying work in antiquity.‡ Ann Blair is writing a history of the contributions of *amanuenses* to knowledge projects of the early modern period, across manuscript and print cultures, but those assistants active in yet earlier periods one can but acknowledge in their vast anonymity, be their services friendly, voluntary, or involuntary.§ The energies and talents of unnamed contributors to editorial processes enabled the initial arrival and subsequent survivals of the works treated throughout this book. Behind all bodies of work are bodies of workers.

---

*Harris, *Imperium;* Harris, *Conspirata;* Harris, *Dictator.* There are at least two articles about Tiro from Rhetoric and Communication journals. See Di Renzo, "His Master's Voice," and Bankston, "Administrative Slavery in the Ancient Roman Republic."

†Isocrates, *Panathenaicus,* §231; Horace, *Sermones,* 1.4.9–13; Quintilian 10.3.

‡Haines-Eitzen, "'Girls Trained in Beautiful Writing.'"

§Blair, "Hidden Hands: Amanuenses and Authorship in Early Modern Europe."

Bibliography

I have cited ancient works here only when they were not available in the Loeb series or when I have quoted from the remarks of an editor or translator of a Loeb edition.

Acosta-Hughes, Benjamin, and Susan A. Stephens. *Callimachus in Context: From Plato to the Augustan Poets*. New York: Cambridge University Press, 2012.

Alcidamas. "On Those Who Write Written Speeches or On Sophists." In *Alcidamas: The Works and Fragments*, edited and translated by J. V. Muir, 3–21. London: Bristol Classical Press, 2001.

Allen, Danielle S. *Why Plato Wrote*. Malden, Mass.: Wiley-Blackwell, 2010.

Bagnall, Roger S. "Alexandria: Library of Dreams." *Proceedings of the American Philological Society* 146.4 (Dec. 2002): 348–362.

Bankston, Zach. "Administrative Slavery in the Ancient Roman Republic: The Value of Marcus Tullius Tiro in Ciceronian Rhetoric." *Rhetoric Review* 31.3 (2012): 203–218.

Barchiesi, Alessandro. "Roman Callimachus." In *Brill's Companion to Callimachus*, edited by Benjamin Acosta-Hughes, Luigi Lehnus, and Susan A. Stephens, 511–533. Boston: Brill, 2011.

Batstone, William. "Dry Pumice and the Programmatic Language of Catullus 1." *Classical Philology* 93.2 (April 1998).

Bayliss, Andrew J. *After Demosthenes: The Politics of Early Hellenistic Athens*. New York: Continuum, 2011.

Blair, Ann. "Hidden Hands: Amanuenses and Authorship in Early Modern Europe." A. S. W. Rosenbach Lectures in Bibliography, March 2014. http://repository.upenn.edu/rosenbach/8/.

Bloomer, W. Martin. *Latinity and Literacy Society at Rome*. Philadelphia: University of Pennsylvania Press, 1997.

Bloomer, W. Martin. "Schooling in Persona: Imagination and Subordination in Roman Education." *Classical Antiquity* 16.1 (April 1997): 57–78.

Blum, Rudolf. *Kallimachos: The Alexandrian Library and the Origins of Bibliography*. Translated by Hans H. Wellisch. Madison: University of Wisconsin Press, 1991.

Boatwright, Mary T., Daniel J. Gargola, and Richard J. A. Talbert. *The Romans: From Village to Empire*. New York: Oxford University Press, 2004.

Boyle, Casey. "Low Fidelity in High Definition: Speculations on Rhetorical Editions." In *Rhetoric and the Digital Humanities,* edited by Jim Rodolfo and William Hart-Davidson, 127–139. Chicago: University of Chicago Press, 2015.

Bradley, Mark. *Colour and Meaning in Ancient Rome.* New York: Cambridge University Press, 2009.

Brink, C. O. "Quintilian's *De Causis Corruptae Eloquentiae* and Tacitus' *Dialogus de Oratoribus.*" *The Classical Quarterly* 39.2 (1989): 472–503.

Butler, Shane. *The Ancient Phonograph.* New York: Zone Books, 2015.

Butler, Shane. *The Hand of Cicero.* New York: Routledge, 2002.

Butler, Shane. *The Matter of the Page: Essays in Search of Ancient and Medieval Authors.* Madison: University of Wisconsin Press, 2011.

Cameron, Alan. *Callimachus and His Critics.* Princeton: Princeton University Press, 1995.

Capella, Martianus. *De Nuptiis Philologiae et Mercurii.* Edited by James Willis. Leipzig: Teubner Verlagsgellschaft, 1983.

Carlon, Jacqueline M. *Pliny's Women: Constructing Virtue and Creating Identity in the Roman World.* New York: Cambridge University Press, 2009.

Carlsson, Susanne. *Hellenistic Democracies: Freedom, Independence and Political Procedure in Some East Greek City-States.* Stuttgart: Franz Steiner Verlag, 2010.

Carson, Anne. *If Not, Winter. Fragments of Sappho.* New York: Vintage Books, 2003.

Cartledge, Paul. *Democracy: A Life.* New York: Oxford University Press, 2016.

Cha, Theresa Hak Kyung. *Dictée.* Berkeley: University of California Press, 2001.

Chiron, Pierre. "Relative Dating of the *Rhetoric to Alexander* and Aristotle's *Rhetoric*: A Methodology and Hypothesis." *Rhetorica* 29.3 (Summer 2011): 236–262.

Chiron, Pierre, ed. Special Issue on *Rhetorica ad Alexandrum. Rhetorica* 29.3 (Summer 2011): 233–367.

Citroni, Mario. "The Memory of Philippi in Horace and the Interpretation of *Epistles* 1.20." *The Classical Journal* 96.1 (Oct.–Nov. 2000): 27–56.

Claassen, Jo-Marie. *Displaced Persons: The Literature of Exile from Cicero to Boethius.* Madison: University of Wisconsin Press, 1999.

Cole, Thomas. *The Origins of Rhetoric in Ancient Greece.* Baltimore: Johns Hopkins University Press, 1995.

Connolly, Joy. "Virile Tongues: Rhetoric and Masculinity." In *A Companion to Roman Rhetoric,* edited by William Dominik and Jon Hall, 83–97. Malden, Mass.: Blackwell, 2010.

Cope, Edward Meredith. *An Introduction to Aristotle's Rhetoric with Analysis, Notes, and Appendices.* London: MacMillan, 1867.

Crane, Mary Thomas. "*Intret Cato:* Authority and the Epigram in Sixteenth-Century England." In *Renaissance Genres: Essays on Theory, History, and Interpretation,* edited by Barbara Kiefer Lewalski, 158–188. Cambridge, Mass.: Harvard University Press, 1986.

Crawford, Jane W. *M. Tullius Cicero: The Lost and Unpublished Orations.* Göttingen: Vandenhoeck & Ruprecht, 1984.

D'Angour, Armand. "*Ad Unguem.*" *American Journal of Philology* 120.3 (Autumn 1999): 411–427.

Davis, P. J. *Ovid and Augustus: A Political Reading of Ovid's Erotic Poems.* London: Duckworth, 2006.

Davisson, Mary. "Parents and Children in Ovid's Poems from Exile." *The Classical World* 78.2 (Nov.–Dec. 1984): 111–114.

Derrida, Jacques. *Archive Fever: A Freudian Impression.* Translated by Eric Prenowitz. Chicago: University of Chicago Press, 1998.

Di Renzo, Anthony. "His Master's Voice: Tiro and the Rise of the Roman Secretarial Class." *Journal of Technical Writing and Communication* 30.2 (April 2000): 155–168.

Dickison, Sheila K., and Judith P. Hallett, eds. *A Roman Women Reader: Selections from the Second Century B.C.E. through Second Century C.E.* Mundelein, Ill.: Bolchazy-Carducci, 2015.

Dominik, William. "Tacitus and Pliny on Oratory." In *Blackwell Companion to Roman Rhetoric,* edited by William Dominik and Jon Hall, 323–338. Malden, Mass.: Blackwell, 2007.

Droysen, Johann Gustav. *Geschichte des Hellenismus, Vol. 1.* New York: Cambridge University Press, 2011.

duBois, Page. *Sappho Is Burning.* Chicago: University of Chicago Press, 1995.

Dugan, John. *Making a New Man: Ciceronian Self-Fashioning in the Rhetorical Works.* New York: Oxford University Press, 2005.

Dugan, John. "Preventing Ciceronism: C. Licinius Calvus' Regimes for Sexual and Oratorical Self-Mastery." *Classical Philology* 96.4 (Oct. 2001): 400–428.

Duncan, Anne. *Performance and Identity in the Classical World.* New York: Cambridge University Press, 2006.

Easterling, Pat. "A Taste for the Classics." In *Classics in Progress: Essays on Ancient Greece and Rome,* edited by T. P. Wiseman, 21–37. New York: Oxford University Press, 2002.

Edwards, Catherine. *The Politics of Immorality in Ancient Rome.* New York: Cambridge University Press, 1993.

Edwards, Michael. "Dionysius and Isaeus." In *Hellenistic Oratory: Continuity and Change,* edited by Christos Kremmydas and Kathryn Tempest, 43–49. New York: Oxford University Press, 2013.

Eidson, Diana. "The Celsus Library at Ephesus: Spatial Rhetoric, Literacy, and Hegemony in the Eastern Roman Empire." *Advances in the History of Rhetoric* 16.2 (2013): 189–217.

Enos, Richard Leo. *The Literate Mode of Cicero's Legal Rhetoric.* Carbondale, Ill.: Southern Illinois University Press, 1988.

Enos, Richard Leo. "Writing without Paper: A Study of Functional Rhetoric in Ancient Athens." In *On the Blunt Edge: Technology in Composition's History and Pedagogy,* edited by Shane Borrowman, 3–13. Anderson, S.C.: Parlor Press, 2012.

Fantham, Elaine. "Ovid, Germanicus, and the Composition of the *Fasti.*" In *Oxford Readings in Classical Studies: Ovid,* edited by Peter E. Knox, 373–414. New York: Oxford University Press, 2006.

Fantham, Elaine. *Roman Literary Culture: From Plautus to Macrobius.* Second edition. Baltimore: Johns Hopkins University Press, 2013.

Fantuzzi, Marco, and Richard Hunter. *Tradition and Innovation in Hellenistic Poetry.* New York: Cambridge University Press, 2012.

Farmer, Matthew C. "Rivers and Rivalry in Petronius, Horace, Callimachus, and Aristophanes." *American Journal of Philology* 134.3 (Fall 2013): 481–506.

Farrell, Joseph. "Horace's Body, Horace's Books." In *Classical Constructions,* edited by S. J. Heyworth, P. G. Fowler, and S. J. Harrison, 174–193. New York: Oxford University Press, 2007.

Farrell, Joseph. "The Ovidian *Corpus:* Poetic Body and Poetic Text." In *Ovidian Transformations,* edited by Philip Hardie, Andrea Barchiesi, and Stephen Hinds, 127–141. Cambridge: Cambridge Philological Society Supplement 23, 1999.

Farrell, Thomas F. *Norms of Rhetorical Culture.* New Haven: Yale University Press, 1993.

Fitzgerald, William. *Variety: The Life of a Roman Concept.* Chicago: University of Chicago Press, 2016.

Fleming, David. "Quintilian, *Progymnasmata,* and Rhetorical Education Today." *Advances in the History of Rhetoric* 19.2 (2016): 124–141.

Flower, Harriet. *Roman Republics.* Princeton: Princeton University Press, 2009.

Ford, Andrew. *The Origins of Criticism: Literary Culture and Poetic Theory in Classical Greece.* Princeton: Princeton University Press, 2002.

Fortenbaugh, William W. "Cicero as a Reporter of Aristotelian and Theophrastean Rhetorical Doctrine." *Rhetorica* 23.1 (Winter 2005): 37–64.

Fortenbaugh, William W., ed. *Theophrastus of Eresus: Sources for his Life, Writings, Thought, and Influence.* Commentary Vol. 8. Boston: Brill, 2005.

Fortenbaugh, William W., and Eckart Schütrumpf, eds. *Demetrius of Phalerum: Text, Translation and Discussion.* New Brunswick, N.J.: Transaction, 1999.

Freudenburg, Kirk. "Horace's Satiric Program and the Language of Contemporary Theory in *Satires* 2.1." *American Journal of Philology* 111.2 (Summer 1990): 187–203.

Freudenburg, Kirk. "Introduction." In *The Cambridge Companion to Roman Satire,* edited by Kirk Freudenburg, 1–32. New York: Cambridge University Press, 2005.

Freudenburg, Kirk. *The Walking Muse: Horace on the Theory of Satire.* Princeton: Princeton University Press, 1993.

Frye, Northrop. *Anatomy of Criticism: Four Essays.* Princeton: Princeton University Press, 1957.

Funaioli, G. *Grammaticae Romanae Fragmenta.* Leipzig: B. G. Teubneri, 1907.

Gaines, Robert. "De-Canonizing Ancient Rhetoric." In *The Viability of the Rhetorical Tradition,* edited by Richard Graff, Arthur E. Walzer, and Janet M. Atwill, 61–73. Albany: State University of New York Press, 2005.

Galasso, Luigi. "*Epistulae Ex Ponto.*" In *Blackwell Companion to Ovid,* edited by Peter E. Knox, 194–206. Malden, Mass.: Blackwell, 2012.

Garcea, Alessandro. *Caesar's De Analogia. Edition, Translation, and Commentary.* New York: Oxford University Press, 2012.

Goldhill, Simon. "The Great Dionysia and Civic Ideology." In *Nothing to Do with Dionysos?,* edited by John J. Winkler and Froma I. Zeitlin, 97–129. Princeton: Princeton University Press, 1990.

Goldhill, Simon and Robin Osborne, eds. *Performance Culture and Athenian Democracy.* New York: Cambridge University Press, 1999.

Gottschalk, Hans B. "Demetrius of Phalerum: A Politician among Philosophers and a Philosopher among Politicians." In *Demetrius of Phalerum: Text, Translation and Discussion,* edited by William W. Fortenbaugh and Eckart Schütrumpf, 367–380. New Brunswick, N.J.: Transaction, 1999.

Gowers, Emily. "The Restless Companion: Horace, *Satires* 1 and 2." In *Roman Satire,* edited by Kirk Freudenburg, 48–61. New York: Cambridge University Press, 2005.

Graff, Richard. "Reading and the 'Written' Style in Aristotle's *Rhetoric.*" *Rhetoric Society Quarterly* 31.4 (Autumn 2001): 19–44.

Green, Peter. *The Poems of Exile:* Tristia *and* The Black Sea Letters. Berkeley: University of California Press, 2005.

Grieb, V. *Hellenistische Demokratie: politische Organisation und Struktur in freien griechischen Poleis nach Alexander dem Großen.* Stuttgart: Franz Steiner Verlag, 2008.

Groningen, B. A. van. "ΕΚΔΟΣΙΣ." *Mnemosyne* 16.1 (1963): 1–17.

Grube, G. M. A. "The Date of Demetrius 'On Style.'" *Phoenix* 18.4 (Winter 1964): 294–302.

Gruen, Eric. *Culture and National Identity in Republican Rome.* Ithaca, N.Y.: Cornell University Press, 1992.

Gruen, Eric. "The Polis in the Hellenistic World." In *Nomodeiktes,* edited by Ralph M. Rosen and Joseph Farrell, 339–354. Ann Arbor: University of Michigan Press, 1993.

Gruen, Eric. *Studies in Greek Culture and Roman Policy.* Boston: Brill, 1990.

Gunderson, Erik. *Declamation, Paternity, and Roman Identity.* New York: Cambridge University Press, 2003.

Gunderson, Erik. "Discovering the Body in Roman Oratory." In *Parchments of Gender: Deciphering the Bodies of Antiquity,* edited by Maria Wyke, 169–189. New York: Cambridge University Press, 1998.

Gunderson, Erik. "The Rhetoric of Rhetorical Theory." In *The Cambridge Companion to Ancient Rhetoric,* edited by Erik Gunderson, 109–125. New York: Cambridge University Press, 2009.

Gurd, Sean. "Cicero and Editorial Revision." *Classical Antiquity* 26.1 (April 2007): 49–80.

Gurd, Sean Alexander. "Revision in Greek Papyri." In *Probabilities, Hypotheticals, and Counterfactuals in Ancient Greek Thought,* edited by Victoria Wohl, 160–184. New York: Cambridge University Press, 2014.

Gurd, Sean Alexander. *Work in Progress: Literary Revision as Social Performance in Ancient Rome.* New York: Oxford University Press, 2012.

Habinek, Thomas. *The Politics of Latin Literature.* Princeton: Princeton University Press, 1998.

Habinek, Thomas. *The Roman World of Song.* Baltimore: Johns Hopkins University Press, 2005.

Habinek, Thomas. "Singing, Speaking, Making, Writing: Classical Alternatives to Literature and Literary Studies." *Stanford Humanities Review* 6.1 (1998): 65–75.

Habinek, Thomas, and Alessandro Schiesaro, eds. *The Roman Cultural Revolution.* New York: Cambridge University Press, 1997.

Haines-Eitzen, Kim. "'Girls Trained in Beautiful Writing': Female Scribes in Roman Antiquity and Early Christianity." *Journal of Early Christian Studies* 6.4 (Winter 1998): 629–646.

Harris, Edward M. "Demosthenes' Speech against Meidias." *Harvard Studies in Classical Philology* 92 (1989): 117–136.

Harris, Robert. *Conspirata.* New York: Simon & Schuster, 2010.

Harris, Robert. *Dictator.* New York: Simon & Schuster, 2016.

Harris, Robert. *Imperium.* New York: Simon & Schuster, 2006.

Harrison, Stephen. "Ovid and Genre: Evolutions of an Elegist." In *The Cambridge Companion to Ovid,* edited by Philip Hardie, 79–94. New York: Cambridge University Press, 2007.

Havelock, Eric A. *The Literate Revolution in Greece and Its Cultural Consequences.* Princeton: Princeton University Press, 1982.

Havelock, Eric A. *The Muse Learns to Write: Reflections on Orality and Literacy from Antiquity to the Present.* New Haven: Yale University Press, 1986.

Hawhee, Debra. *Bodily Arts: Rhetoric and Athletics in Ancient Greece.* Austin: University of Texas Press, 2005.

Hawhee, Debra. "The Colors of Rhetoric: A Vibrant Return." Paper presented at the annual meeting of the National Communication Association, Philadelphia, Pennsylvania, November 10, 2016.

Hawhee, Debra, and Cory Holding, "Case Studies in Material Rhetoric: Joseph Priestley and Gilbert Austin." *Rhetorica* 28.3 (Summer 2010): 261–289.

Hawkins, Tom. *Iambic Poetics in the Roman Empire.* New York: Cambridge University Press, 2014.

Hendrickson, G. L., ed. Cicero. *Brutus. Orator.* Cambridge, Mass.: Harvard University Press, 1971.

Hendrickson, G. L. "Cicero De Optimo Genere Oratorum." *American Journal of Philology* 47.2 (1926): 109–123.

Hendrickson, G. L. "The *De Analogia* of Julius Caesar: Its Occasion, Nature, and Date, with Additional Fragments." *Classical Philology* 1.2 (Apr. 1906): 97–120.

Hendrickson, Thomas. "The Invention of the Greek Library." *Transactions of the American Philological Association* 144.2 (Autumn 2014): 371–413.

Hinds, Stephen. "Booking the Return Trip: Ovid and *Tristia* 1." In *Oxford Readings in Classical Studies: Ovid,* edited by Peter E. Knox, 415–440. New York: Oxford University Press, 2006.

Holding, Cory. "The Rhetoric of the Open Fist." *Rhetoric Society Quarterly* 45.5 (Winter 2015): 399–419.

Hook, Larue van. *The Metaphorical Terminology of Greek Rhetoric and Literary Criticism.* Chicago: University of Chicago Press, 1905.

Horsfall, Nicholas. "Empty Shelves on the Palatine." *Greece & Rome* 40.1 (Apr. 1993): 58–67.

Hughes, Joseph J. "Piso's Eyebrows." *Mnemosyne* 45.2 (1992): 234–237.

Hutchinson, D. S., and Monte Ransome Johnson, eds. and trans. Aristotle. *Protrepticus, or Exhortation to Philosophy.* Unpublished Manuscript. 2016.

Hutchinson, G. O. *Greek to Latin: Frameworks and Contexts for Intertextuality.* New York: Oxford University Press, 2013.

Immerwahr, Henry R. "Book Rolls on Attic Vases." In *Classical, Mediaeval, and Renaissance Studies in Honor of Berthold Louis Ullman,* edited by C. Henderson, Jr., 17–48. Rome: Edizioni di storia e letteratura, 1964.

Innes, Doreen C. "Aristotle: The Written and Performative Styles." In *Influences on Peripatetic Rhetoric: Essays in Honor of William W. Fortenbaugh,* edited by David Mirhady, 149–168. Boston: Brill, 2007.

Innes, Doreen C. "Theophrastus and the Theory of Style." In *Theophrastus of Eresus: On His Life and Work,* edited by W. Fortenbaugh, P. Huby, and A. Long, 251–267. New Brunswick, N.J.: Rutgers University Press, 1985.

Irvine, Martin. *The Making of Textual Culture: 'Grammatica' and Literary Theory, 350–1100.* New York: Cambridge University Press, 1994.

Johnson, William A. *Readers and Reading Culture in the High Roman Empire: A Study of Elite Communities.* New York: Oxford University Press, 2010.

Jones, Steve L. "*Ut Architectura Poesis:* Horace, *Odes* 4, and the Mausoleum of Augustus." Ph.D. diss., University of Texas, 2008.

Jonge, Casper C. de. *Between Grammar and Rhetoric: Dionysius of Halicarnassus on Language, Linguistics, and Literature.* Boston: Brill, 2008.

Jonge, Casper C. de. "Dionysius and Longinus on the Sublime: Rhetoric and Religious Language." *American Journal of Philology* 133.2 (Summer 2012): 271–300.

Jonge, Casper C. de. Review of Nicoletta Marini (ed.), *Demetrio, Lo Stile. Pleiadi 4.* Roma: Edizioni di storia e letteratura, 2007. *Bryn Mawr Classical Review* 2009.08.12. http://bmcr.brynmawr.edu/2009/2009-08-12.html.

Kahane, Ahuvia. "Callimachus, Apollonius, and the Poetics of Mud." *Transactions of the American Philological Association* 124 (1994): 121–133.

Kassel, Rudolph, and Colin Austin. *Poetae Comici Graeci, Vol 1.* Berlin: de Gruyter, 1983.

Keith, A. M. "Slender Verse: Roman Elegy and Ancient Rhetorical Theory." Mnemosyne 52 (1999): 41–62.

Keith, Alison, and Jonathan Edmondson, eds. *Roman Literary Cultures: Domestic Politics, Revolutionary Politics, Civic Spectacle.* Buffalo: University of Toronto Press, 2016.

Kennedy, Duncan. "'Augustan' and 'Anti-Augustan': Reflection on Terms of Reference." In *Roman Poetry and Propaganda in the Age of Augustus,* edited by Anton Powell, 26–58. New York: Bloomsbury, 1998.

Kennedy, George A. *The Art of Rhetoric in the Roman World.* Princeton: Princeton University Press, 1972.

Kennedy, George A. *A New History of Classical Rhetoric.* Princeton: Princeton University Press, 1994.

Kennedy, George A. *Quintilian: A Roman Educator and His Quest for the Perfect Orator.* Revised edition. Sophron Editor, 2013.

Kennedy, George A. "Theophrastus and Stylistic Distinctions." *Harvard Studies in Classical Philology* 62 (1957): 93–104.

Kennerly, Michele. "The Mock Rock *Topos*." *Rhetoric Society Quarterly* 43.1 (Winter 2013): 46–70.

Kennerly, Michele. "*Sermo* and Stoic Sociality in Cicero's *De Officiis*." *Rhetorica* 28.2 (Spring 2010): 119–137.

Kenyon, Frederic C. *Books and Readers in Ancient Greece and Rome*. New York: Oxford University Press, 1932.

Ker, James. "Nocturnal Writers in Imperial Rome: The Culture of *Lucubratio*." *Classical Philology* 99.3 (July 2004): 209–242.

Kirby, John T. "Aristotle's *Poetics*: The Rhetorical Principle." *Arethusa* 24.2 (1991): 197–217.

Kirby, John T. "Toward a Rhetoric of Poetics: Rhetor as Author and Narrator." *Journal of Narrative Technique* 22.1 (Winter 1992): 1–22.

König, Jason, Katerina Oikonomopoulou, and Greg Woolf, eds. *Ancient Libraries*. New York: Cambridge University Press, 2013.

Knox, Peter E. "A Poet's Life." In *A Companion to Ovid*, edited by Peter E. Knox, 3–7. Malden, Mass.: Blackwell, 2009.

Kremmydas, Christos, and Kathryn Tempest, eds. *Hellenistic Oratory: Continuity and Change*. New York: Oxford University Press, 2013.

Krevans, Nita. "Bookburning and the Poetic Deathbed: The Legacy of Virgil." In *Classical Literary Careers and Their Reception*, edited by Philip Hardie and Helen Moore, 197–208. New York: Cambridge University Press, 2010.

Krevans, Nita. "Callimachus and the Pedestrian Muse." In *Hellenistica Groningana 7: Callimachus II*, edited by M. A. Harder, R. F. Regtuit, and G. C. Wakker, 173–184. Leuven, Belgium: Peeters, 2004.

Krevans, Nita. "Callimachus' Philology." In *Brill's Companion to Callimachus*, edited by Benjamin Acosta-Hughes, Luigi Lehnus, and Susan Stephens, 118–133. Boston: Brill, 2011.

Krevans, Nita. "Fighting against Antimachus: The *Lyde* and the *Aetia* Reconsidered." In *Callimachus, Hellenistica Groningana I*, edited by M. A. Harder, R. F. Regtuit, and G. C. Wakker, 167–185. Groningen: Egbert Forsten, 1993.

Krostenko, Brian A. *Cicero, Catullus, and the Language of Social Performance*. New York: Oxford University Press, 2006.

Lamp, Kathleen S. *A City of Marble: The Rhetoric of Augustan Rome*. Columbia: University of South Carolina Press, 2013.

Lanham, Richard. A. *The Electronic Word: Democracy, Technology, and the Arts*. Chicago: University of Chicago Press, 1993.

Lanham, Richard. *The Motives of Eloquence: Literary Rhetoric in the Renaissance*. New Haven: Yale University Press, 1976.

Lattimore, Richard. "The Composition of the *History* of Herodotus." *Classical Philology* 53.1 (Jan. 1958): 9–21.

Leeman, A. D. "Julius Caesar, the Orator of Paradox." In *The Orator in Action & Theory in Greece & Rome*, edited by Cecil W. Wooten, 97–110. New York: Brill, 2001.

Leen, Ann. "Cicero and the Rhetoric of Art." *American Journal of Philology* 112.2 (Summer 1991): 229–245.

Long, Christopher P. *Socratic and Platonic Political Philosophy: Practicing a Politics of Reading.* New York: Cambridge University Press, 2014.

Longo, Oddone. "The Theater of the *Polis.*" In *Nothing to Do with Dionysos?*, edited by John J. Winkler and Froma I. Zeitlin, 12–19. Princeton: Princeton University Press, 1990.

Lowrie, Michèle. Review of Thomas Habinek, *The Roman World of Song. Bryn Mawr Classical Review.* 2006.04.34. http://bmcr.brynmawr.edu/2006/2006-04-34.html.

Maehler, Herwig. "books, Greek and Roman." In *Oxford Classical Dictionary,* third edition, edited by Simon Hornblower and Anthony Spawforth, 249–252. New York: Oxford University Press, 2003.

Malcovati, Henry, ed. *Oratorum Romanorum Fragmenta, Liberae Rei Publicae, I. Textus.* Third edition. Torino: Paravia, 1953.

Mamoojee, A. H. "*Antiquus* and *Vetus:* A Study in Latin Synonymy." *Phoenix* 57.1/2 (Spring-Summer 2003): 67–82.

Marshall, Anthony J. "Library Resources and Creative Writing at Rome." *Phoenix* 30.3 (Autumn 1976): 252–264.

Marshall, C. W. "Literary Awareness in Euripides and His Audience." In *Voice into Text: Orality and Literacy in Ancient Greece,* edited by Ian Worthington, 81–98. New York: Brill, 1996.

Martelli, Frances K. A. *Ovid's Revisions: The Editor as Author.* New York: Cambridge University Press, 2013.

Marvin, Carolyn. "The Body of the Text: Literacy's Corporeal Constant." *Quarterly Journal of Speech* 80.2 (1994): 129–149.

McDermott, William C. "M. Cicero and M. Tiro." *Historia: Zeitschrift für Alte Geschicte* 21.2 (1972): 259–286.

McDonnell, Myles. "Writing, Copy, and Autograph Manuscripts in Ancient Rome." *The Classical Quarterly* 46.2 (1996): 469–491.

McGowan, Matthew. *Ovid in Exile: Power and Poetic Redress in the* Tristia *and* Epistulae Ex Ponto. New York: Brill, 2009.

McLuhan, Marshall. *The Gutenberg Galaxy: The Making of Typographic Man.* Toronto: University of Toronto Press, 2010.

Montanari, Franco. "From Book to Edition: Philology in Ancient Greece." In *World Philology,* edited by Sheldon Pollock, Benjamin A. Elman, and Ku-ming Kevin Chang, 25–44. Cambridge, Mass.: Harvard University Press, 2015.

Mossé, Claude. *Athens in Decline, 404–86 B.C.E.* New York: Routledge, 1973.

Murphy, James J. "A Quintilian Anniversary and Its Meaning." *Advances in the History of Rhetoric* 19.2 (2016): 107–110.

Murphy, T. "Cicero's First Readers: Epistolary Evidence for the Dissemination of His Works." *The Classical Quarterly* 48.2 (1998): 492–505.

Nieddu, Gian Franco. "A Poet at Work: The Parody of *Helen* in the *Thesmophoriazusae.*" *Greek, Roman, and Byzantine Studies* 44 (2004): 331–360.

Ober, Josiah. *The Rise and Fall of Classical Greece.* Princeton: Princeton University Press, 2015.

Oliensis, Ellen. *Horace and the Rhetoric of Authority.* New York: Cambridge University Press, 1998.

Oliensis, Ellen. "*Ut arte emendaturus fortunam:* Horace, Nasidienus and the Art of Satire." In *The Roman Cultural Revolution,* edited by Thomas Habinek and Alessandro Schiesaro, 90–104. New York: Cambridge University Press, 1998.

Ong, Walter. *Orality and Literacy: The Technologizing of the Word.* New York: Routledge, 2002.

O'Sullivan, Lara. *The Regime of Demetrius of Phalerum in Athens, 317–307 B.C.E.* Boston: Brill, 2009.

O'Sullivan, Neil. *Alcidamas, Aristophanes, and the Beginnings of Greek Stylistic Theory.* Stuttgart: Franz Steiner Verlag, 1992.

O'Sullivan, Neil. "Caecilius, the 'Canons' of Writers, and the Origins of Atticism." In *Roman Eloquence: Rhetoric in Society and Literature,* edited by William J. Dominik, 32–49. New York: Routledge, 1997.

O'Sullivan, Neil. "'Rhetorical' vs 'Linguistic' Atticism: A False Dichotomy?" *Rhetorica* 33.2 (Spring 2015): 134–146.

Parker, Holt N. "Books and Reading Latin Poetry." In *Ancient Literacies: The Culture of Reading in Greece and Rome,* edited by William A. Johnson and Holt N. Parker, 186–232. New York: Oxford University Press, 2009.

Pearcy, Lee T. "The Personification of the Text and Augustan Poetics in *Epistles* 1.20." *The Classical World* 87.5 (May–June 1994): 457–464.

Pernot, Laurent. *Epideictic Rhetoric: Questioning the Stakes of Ancient Praise.* Austin: University of Texas Press, 2015.

Pernot, Laurent. *Rhetoric in Antiquity.* Translated by W. E. Higgins. Washington, D.C.: The Catholic University of America Press, 2005.

Pfeiffer, Rudolph. *History of Classical Scholarship: From the Beginnings to the End of the Hellenistic Age.* New York: Oxford University Press, 1968.

Pfeiffer, Rudolph, ed. *Callimachus, Vol. 1, Fragmenta.* London: Oxford University Press, 1949.

Pfeiffer, Rudolph, ed. *Callimachus, Vol. 2, Hymni et Epigrammata.* London: Oxford University Press, 1949.

Phillips, John J. "Atticus and the Publication of Cicero's Works." *The Classical World* 79.4 (Mar.–Apr. 1986): 227–237.

Pollitt, Jerome Jordan. *The Ancient View of Greek Art: Criticism, History, and Terminology.* New Haven: Yale University Press, 1974.

Porter, James I. "Feeling Classical: Classicism and Ancient Literary Criticism." In *Classical Pasts: The Classical Traditions of Greece and Rome,* edited by James I. Porter, 301–352. Princeton: Princeton University Press, 2006.

Porter, James I. *The Sublime in Antiquity.* New York: Cambridge University Press, 2016.

Porter, Stanley E., ed. *Handbook of Classical Rhetoric in the Hellenistic Period 330 B.C.–A.D. 400.* New York: Brill, 1997.

Possanza, Mark. "Editing Ovid: Immortal Works and Material Texts." In *A Companion to Ovid*, edited by Peter E. Knox, 311–326. Malden, Mass.: Blackwell, 2008.

Poulakos, John. "*Kairos* in Gorgias' Rhetorical Compositions." In *Rhetoric and Kairos*, edited by Phillip Sipiora and James S. Baumlin, 89–96. Albany: State University of New York Press, 2002.

Powell, Anton, ed. *Roman Poetry and Propaganda in the Age of Augustus*. New York: Bloomsbury, 1998.

Radice, Betty. "Introduction." Pliny. *Letters and Panegyricus*, Vol. I. Cambridge, Mass.: Harvard University Press, 1989.

Radice, Betty. "Notes." Pliny. *Letters and Panegyricus*, Vol. I. Cambridge, Mass.: Harvard University Press, 1989.

Ramsey, John T. "Introduction." *Cicero Philippics I–II*. New York: Cambridge University Press, 2003: 1–28.

Richlin, Amy. "Cicero's Head." In *Constructions of the Classical Body*, edited by James I. Porter, 190–211. Ann Arbor: University of Michigan Press, 1999.

Roman, Luke. *Poetic Autonomy in Ancient Rome*. New York: Oxford University Press, 2014.

Schenkeveld, Dirk M. "Prose Usages of Ἀκούειν 'To Read.'" *The Classical Quarterly* 42.1 (1992): 129–141.

Sciarrino, Enrica. *Cato the Censor and the Beginnings of Latin Prose: From Poetic Translation to Elite Transcription*. Columbus: Ohio State University Press, 2011.

Scodel, Ruth. "Self-Correction, Spontaneity, and Orality and Archaic Poetry." In *Voice into Text: Orality and Literacy in Ancient Greece*, edited by Ian Worthington, 59–79. Boston: Brill, 1996.

Seo, J. Mira. "Plagiarism and Poetic Identity in Martial." *American Journal of Philology* 130 (2009): 567–593.

Small, Jocelyn Penny. *Wax Tablets of the Mind: Cognitive Studies of Memory and Literacy in Classical Antiquity*. New York: Routledge, 1997.

Starr, Raymond J. "The Circulation of Literary Texts in the Roman World." *The Classical Quarterly* 37.1 (1987): 213–223.

Stroup, Sarah Culpepper. *Catullus, Cicero, and a Society of Patrons: The Generation of the Text*. New York: Cambridge University Press, 2010.

Sutton, E. W., and H. Rackam, trans. Cicero. *On the Orator*, Books I–II. Cambridge, Mass.: Harvard University Press, 2001.

Thomas, Rosalind. *Herodotus in Context: Ethnography, Science, and the Art of Persuasion*. New York: Cambridge University Press, 2000.

Thomas, Rosalind. "Introduction." In *The Landmark Herodotus*, edited by Robert B. Strassler, ix–xxxvi. New York: Anchor Books, 2009.

Thomas, Rosalind. "Prose Performance Texts: Epideixis and Written Publication in the Late Fifth and Early Fourth Centuries." In *Written Texts and the Rise of Literate Culture in Ancient Greece*, edited by Harvey Yunis, 162–188. New York: Cambridge University Press, 2003.

Timmerman, David M., and Edward Schiappa. *Classical Greek Rhetorical Theory and the Disciplining of Discourse*. New York: Cambridge University Press, 2010.

Too, Yun Lee. *The Idea of Ancient Literary Criticism.* New York: Oxford University Press, 1999.

Too, Yun Lee. *The Idea of the Library in the Ancient World.* New York: Oxford University Press, 2010.

Too, Yun Lee. *The Rhetoric of Identity in Isocrates: Text, Power, Pedagogy.* New York: Cambridge University Press, 2009.

Trypanis, C., ed. "Note." In Callimachus. *Aetia, Iambi, Hecale, and Other Fragments.* Cambridge, Mass.: Harvard University Press, 1973.

Usher, Stephen. "*Sententiae* in Cicero *Orator* 137–9 and Demosthenes *De corona.*" *Rhetorica* 26.2 (Spring 2008): 99–111.

Valiavitcharska, Vessela. *Rhetoric and Rhythm in Byzantium: The Sound of Persuasion.* New York: Oxford University Press, 2013.

Van der Valk, H. L. M. "On the Edition of Books in Antiquity." *Vigiliae Christianae* 11.1 (Mar. 1957): 1–10.

Vico, Giambattista, and Max Harold Fisch, trans. *The New Science of Giambattista Vico.* Ithaca, N.Y.: Cornell University Press, 1994.

Walker, Jeffrey. Review of *A City of Marble: The Rhetoric of Augustan Rome* by Kathleen S. Lamp. *Rhetoric & Public Affairs* 19.1 (2016): 166–169.

Walker, Jeffrey. *Rhetoric and Poetics in Antiquity.* New York: Oxford University Press, 2000.

Walzer, Arthur. "Quintilian's 'Vir Bonus' and the Stoic Wise Man." *Rhetoric Society Quarterly* 33.4 (Autumn 2003): 25–41.

White, Peter. "Bookshops in the Literary Culture of Rome." In *Ancient Literacies: The Culture of Reading in Greece and Rome,* edited by William A. Johnson and Holt N. Parker, 268–287. New York: Oxford University Press, 2009.

Whitmarsh, Tim. *Ancient Greek Literature.* Malden, Mass.: Polity Press, 2004.

Wilamowitz-Möellendorff, Ulrich von. "Asianismus und Atticismus." *Hermes* 35 (1899): 1–52.

Williams, Gareth D. *Banished Voices: Readings in Ovid's Exile Poetry.* New York: Cambridge University Press, 1994.

Williams, Gareth D. "Ovid's Exile Poetry: Worlds Apart." In *Brill's Companion to Ovid,* edited by Barbara Weiden Boyd, 337–381. Boston: Brill, 2002.

Williams, Gareth D. "Representations of the Book-Roll in Latin Poetry: Ovid, *Tr.* 1,1, 3–14 and Related Texts." *Mnemosyne* 45.2 (1992): 178–189.

Wilner, Ortha L. "Roman Beauty Culture." *The Classical Journal* 27.1 (Oct. 1931): 26–38.

Winkler, John J. and Froma I. Zeitlin. "Introduction." In *Nothing to Do with Dionysos?,* edited by John J. Winkler and Froma I. Zeitlin, 3–11. Princeton: Princeton University Press, 1990.

Winterbottom, Michael. "Returning to Tacitus' *Dialogus.*" In *The Orator in Action & Theory in Greece & Rome,* edited by Cecil W. Wooten, 137–155. Boston: Brill, 2001.

Wise, Jennifer. *Dionysus Writes: The Invention of Theatre in Ancient Greece.* Ithaca, N.Y.: Cornell University Press, 1999.

Wisse, Jakob. "Greeks, Romans, and the Rise of Atticism." In *Greek Literary Theory after Aristotle,* edited by D. M. Schenkeveld, J. G. J. Abbenes, S. R. Slings, and I. Sluiter, 65–82. Amsterdam: VU University Press, 1995.

Worman, Nancy. *Abusive Mouths in Classical Athens.* New York: Cambridge University Press, 2008.

Yunis, Harvey. "Introduction: Why Written Texts?" In *Written Texts and the Rise of Literate Culture in Ancient Greece,* edited by Harvey Yunis, 1–14. New York: Cambridge University Press, 2003.

Yunis, Harvey, ed. *Written Texts and the Rise of Literate Culture in Ancient Greece.* New York: Cambridge University Press, 2003.

Zetzel, James E. G. "The Bride of Mercury: Confessions of a 'Pataphilologist." In *World Philology,* edited by Sheldon Pollock, Benjamin A. Elman, and Ku-ming Kevin Chang, 45–62. Cambridge, Mass.: Harvard University Press, 2015.

Zetzel, James E. G. "*Emendavi ad Tironem:* Some Notes on Scholarship in the Second Century A.D." *Harvard Studies in Classical Philology* 77 (1973): 225–243.

Zetzel, James E. G. *Latin Textual Criticism in Antiquity.* Salem, N.H.: The Ayer Company, 1981.

Ziogas, Ioannis. "The Poet as Prince: Author and Authority under Augustus." In *The Art of Veiled Speech: Self-Censorship from Aristophanes to Hobbes,* edited by Han Baltussen and Peter J. Davis, 115–136. Philadelphia: University of Pennsylvania Press, 2015.

Index